ME AND THAD

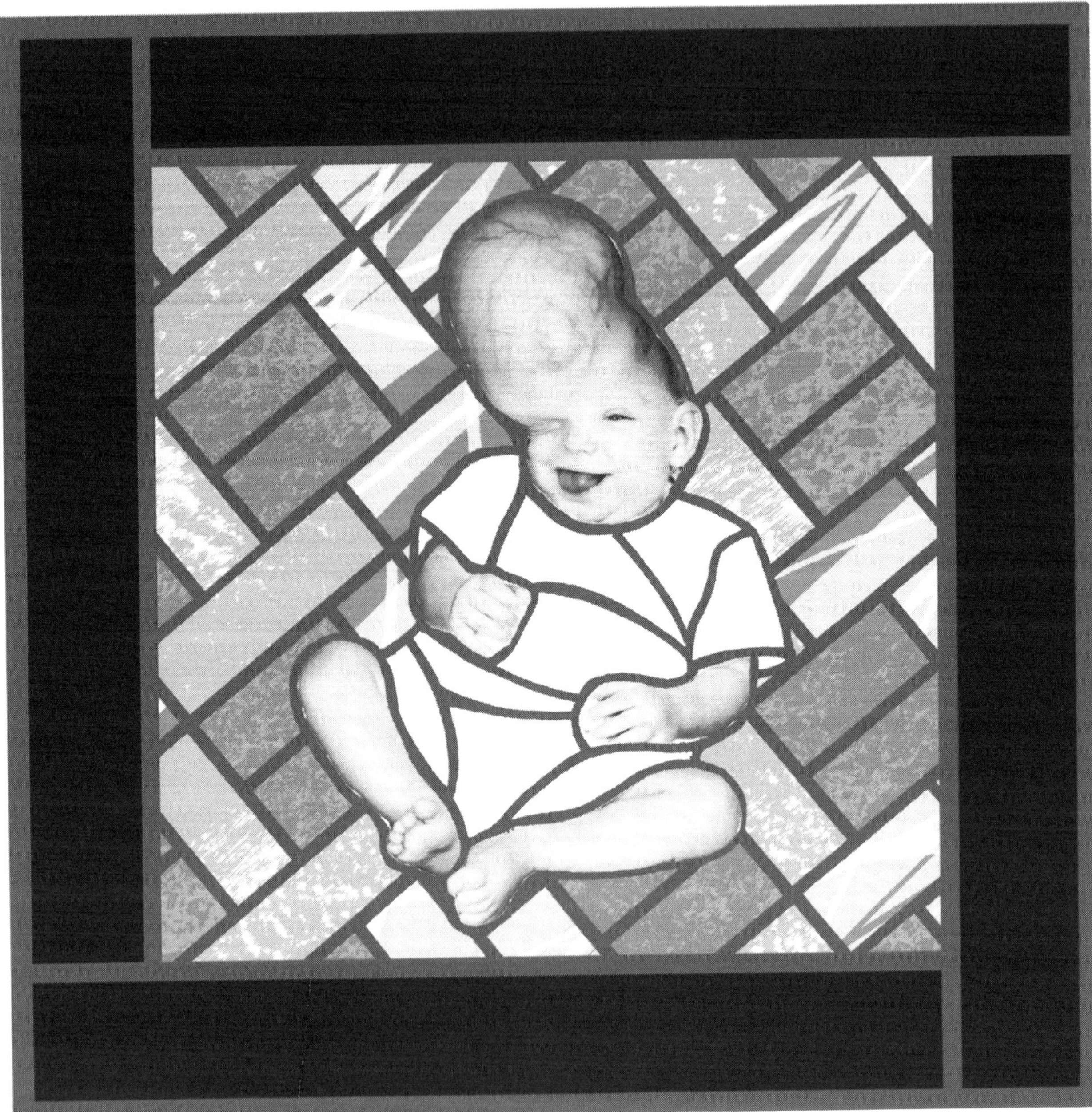

ME AND THAD

TIM SUTTON

MORMON ARTISTS GROUP

Published by Mormon Artists Group
457 West 57th Street, Suite 601
New York, NY 10019
mormonartistsgroup@me.com

THAD AARON SUTTON

There was a time in my life when family seemed more of a burden than a blessing. If it had been up to me, I might have walked away—I was nine.

My father was a pilot in the Air Force. He flew C-130's, four-propeller mid-sized cargo planes that were useful in practically every military situation because they didn't require a long runway. We lived on the very last street in a housing development on Dyess Air Force Base on the outskirts of a mid-sized West Texas town called Abilene. If you stood on the far end of our fenceless backyard facing away from our pale green, three-bedroom cinderblock house, you could see a "meadow" of tall, dry grass leading to a stand of low, scraggly, mesquite trees draped in mistletoe in front of a rough, unpaved perimeter road and a barbed wire fence marking the edge of federal property. Beyond that was a dirt-laden forever with an occasional farmhouse and a lot of sky. Abilene, Texas, was the seventh place I had lived during my nine years on earth.

That year was 1976, the United States Bicentennial. As a fourth grader with a love for words (I won my second grade spelling bee), I was thrilled. Two hundred years wrapped up in 12 letters, B-I-C-E-N-T-E-N-N-I-A-L. I practiced it until I could spell it, a word for this year only. I mean, how many times in my life would I have the opportunity to use this word to describe anything? It was a year of patriotic fervor, and being an enthusiastic, flag-waving Mormon, a military kid, and a Cub Scout, I was immersed in the word. It was a monumental year, and one that I would never forget, but not for patriotic reasons. 1976 carved a significant place in my history because that was the year my brother Thad was born.

At the time, my family consisted of my dad (Tom), my mom (Laraine), six boys—Tony, age 13, Todd, 11, me (Tim), 9, Thomas, 6, and twins Troy and Trent, 2—and our dog Kipper, a feisty, fluffy American Eskimo ball of long white fur and nervous energy. My parents say they didn't start out with the intention of giving all their boys names that started with the letter T. Tony (which was officially Anthony, but that name was only used when Mom was angry or if she needed to get Tony's attention), Todd, and Timothy seemed like the right names for each of us as we were born. Thomas was supposed to be their last child. He looked like a Thomas to them, so they gave him my dad's first name. A few years later, when they decided to try for more children, they realized they had created a pattern that would need to be continued in order to make any new arrivals feel like part of the family. When the twins were born, Troy and Trent seemed to fit their personalities like a glove.

With six children under the age of 13, pregnancy was not an unfamiliar experience in the Sutton household. Mom's pregnancies always included debilitating morning sickness, which was an incredible misnomer in her case since she tended to be sick and throwing up around the clock through the whole first trimester. If I had been in her shoes, I would have quit after the first child. Mom felt it was worth it though, and she persevered through many first trimesters.

Late in 1974, Mom was three months into a pregnancy when she started bleeding heavily. Dad took her to the hospital, and she returned home the next day, having lost the baby. Mom had never had a miscarriage before. It was a devastating experience that only women who have had a miscarriage can fully understand. Whatever hope she held onto in order to get through those difficult initial months, whatever future she envisioned, whatever connection and love she felt towards that developing baby were dashed, and it was back to the day-to-day grind without so much as a day off.

In a household like ours, there wasn't much time to rest and recover, or even to grieve. Dad traveled often and for extended periods of time. At that stage in his career, he was gone more than he was home. There were music lessons, scouts, school, sports, and church activities, which not only required transportation, but often enlisted participation of at least one parent. In addition to that, Mom was the Primary President in the Abilene Ward of The Church of Jesus Christ of Latter-day Saints. This meant that she was in charge of organizing and facilitating all of the congregation's children's classes which met on Thursday afternoons—teachers, children, activities, all of it. Somehow, she was able to make it work smoothly and more often than not, enthusiastically; though she admits there were many tearful nights in the master bedroom once the rest of the house was asleep.

Mom called us a family of "jocks and musicians." My parents wanted us to be well-rounded children who experienced positive reinforcement through activities as diverse as Little League Baseball, Boy Scouts, singing and private piano instruction, which included public recitals a few times a year. We enjoyed performing. I'm afraid we were one of those families who opened the curtains and turned on the spotlights whenever anyone visited. Occasionally, we'd even sing in church until that fateful Sunday in Sacrament meeting when Tony, Todd, Thomas, and I were singing the children's favorite, "I Hope They Call Me on a Mission," and devolved into a giggle-fest about halfway through. I don't remember who started it, but I do remember that there was very little singing toward the end of the performance.

Little League Baseball was difficult for me. Tony and Todd were both good at sports. Tony was a pitcher on his team and Todd was a catcher. I was an uncoordinated, late bloomer. For someone who couldn't throw well or catch a ball, Little League was torture. When I wasn't warming the bench, I played right field where no one ever hit the ball. I would get bored and wrap my legs around each other, balancing with my glove arm draped over my head. Or, I'd sit down and pick dandelions. If a ball ever did come my way, I'd run after it or I'd hold my glove up in the air while it sailed past me, then I'd run after it.

Once, I was holding my glove up to catch a fly ball. I could see it coming. I could see my glove. I could see it coming. I could see my glove. I could see it coming as the ball missed my glove and hit me squarely in the right eye. My coach made it very clear that I was a liability if our team wanted to win games. I was the weak link. It didn't matter that I was successful in other activities, or that I was energetic and well-liked by my teachers in school. This label, this feeling of worthlessness affected how I perceived every other part of my life, including my connection to my family.

My low self-esteem didn't start in Little League, though. Dad tells a story of when he and I were working together in the carport when we lived in Colorado Springs. I was four years old, and I was trying to build a boat, which included hammering a nail into a board. Dad came from a family of carpenters, and I think he was pleased to see me taking the initiative on a creative project of my own. I was having trouble getting the nail to stay still, hitting my fingers more often than the nail. Dad showed me several times how to do it. He was an instructor by nature and loved helping anyone do anything the right way. Dad recalls it this way, "After several tries...you threw the hammer across the floor and exclaimed in exasperation to yourself, 'I can't do anything right!' You can't know how that hurt me because I had done that to myself so many times before, and I knew what you were feeling, yet I couldn't really help you feel any more confident. The evidence was there, at least from your perspective."

Knowing that I was struggling in Little League, Dad would ask me to play catch with him in the front yard. Sports had not come as naturally to him as to his brother Bob, but he worked really hard and practiced a lot, and eventually became a proficient ball player. As an adult, I know that these efforts to help me came from a place of support and love, but as a self-conscious nine-year old, I resented him for singling me out and confirming that I was useless at baseball. I would never be as good as Tony or Todd for whom throwing a ball seemed to be second nature.

I also couldn't compete with my younger brother Thomas, whose six-year old enthusiasm, infectious smile and fearless social interaction made him irresistible. I was a skinny kid with strawberry blonde hair and freckles. I didn't think I was particularly cute, and from my perspective, I certainly didn't get the same kind of attention that Thomas got from the outside world. The sad thing was that all Thomas wanted was to be my friend, to play with me, to go where I was going, and to be where I was. There were many times in this era that I wasn't very nice to him.

The twins were magnets for attention, as all twins are. Since they were only two years old, they were essentially still babies, so I wasn't threatened by them, nor did I compare myself to them. They were just fun, little, tow-headed firecrackers.

I don't want to give the impression that I was a broody, mopey kid. I wasn't. I was basically happy, and I loved to help out with anything at home, at school, and at church. I was successful in school, even a leader. But that didn't change the fact that I often felt awkward, incapable, separate, disgruntled, and out of place. At my core, I felt profoundly different from the rest of my family. Sometimes, my temper would flare out of nowhere. I would lash out with inexplicable intensity, throwing every book off of a wall-sized shelf unit, yelling, stomping or slamming doors. I even pulled Thomas off the couch once by his arm, and he split his head open on the coffee table requiring a trip to the emergency room and several stitches. I was always as surprised as anyone else by the magnitude of these outbursts. I would be mortified, but I couldn't explain where the frustration came from that drove my rage. I had no idea why I did the things I did.

During the Summer before Thad was born, we took a long trip from West Texas to Palmyra, New York, the birthplace of Mormonism, to see early Church history sites and the annual Hill Cumorah pageant. We traveled with our Grandpa Sutton and met up with Grandpa and Grandma Clouse who were finishing Mormon missionary service in Pennsylvania.

My father's parents were not members of the Church. Dad was baptized into the Church when he was at the Air Force Academy. Grandpa Sutton was a contractor in Marion, Indiana, where my father grew up the oldest of five kids. Grandpa Charlie was a gifted carpenter. The furniture and cabinetry he made were gorgeous. One of my favorite things to do whenever we visited them was to spend time in his workshop, which was in the garage behind the house that he and his sons built by hand. I'd stand in the midst of piles of sawdust and breathe in the smell of wood mixed with the lingering, sweetly acrid aroma of pipe smoke. In the workshop I could see furniture in all of its stages from rough-hewn wood planks to a beautifully sanded and stained table or hutch. I marveled that someone could create such beauty. It also inspired me to think that maybe I could be good with my hands, too. Perhaps I could create something beautiful out of something as normal as a plank of wood.

That Summer of '75, it was Grandma Sutton who influenced me most directly. She was kindness incarnate, and she believed in me as only grandmothers can. Like Grandpa Charlie, Grandma Ginny was gifted with her hands. She could knit a beautiful sweater in a day, if not a few hours. She owned a small craft store and she encouraged me to try my hand at many things. We started out with latch-hook rugs, needlepoint, and macramé. Tony and Todd were avid Boy Scouts. They tied knots for tents and boats and other practical things while I tied knots to make decorative plant hangers and owls.

Whenever we visited Indiana, I would leave with a box full of projects. For a boy who deep down didn't think he was good at anything, these gifts were a revelation. When I finished one of these projects, I felt a lovely combination of accomplishment and hope. I could look at a framed needlepoint on the wall, a latch hook pillow in the octagonal shape of a GO! sign on my bed, a colorful woven pot holder under a hot casserole dish, or a knotted jute and bead masterpiece suspending a potted plant in a living room window, and say to myself, "I made that!" I had created something pretty and sometimes even practical, and it made a difference to me. Each project was a small reminder to me that I mattered.

My parents encouraged me while I worked on these projects, and they displayed them throughout the house. They weren't shy to point out to anyone visiting, "Tim made this." My parents were proud of each one of us. They derived a lot of pleasure from seeing us try new things, even if we weren't always totally successful. The front of our refrigerator was covered with a constantly-evolving gallery of school projects. They tried to make sure that at least one of them could attend all of our baseball games, choir concerts, and piano recitals. They wanted us to feel strong and confident and successful. They were our biggest fans. I knew that. It was clear. But still, I struggled.

Grandma and Grandpa Sutton weren't Mormons, but Grandma was a devout church-going Christian, and in my eyes, she really took the "Love your neighbor as yourself" philosophy to heart. It was how she led her life. Maybe it came naturally to her—she made people feel welcome and accepted. Grandpa was kind of grumbly and skeptical when it came to religion, while at the same time being sensitive about being judged for being grumbly and skeptical about religion.

My dad sincerely wanted to convey to his parents and siblings the beauty he found in the Mormon faith. He wrote many letters to them through the years, opening his heart and bearing witness to the truths that had become so vital in his life and the life of his growing family. Perhaps that was one of the reasons he invited Grandpa Sutton along on our excursion backwards through early Church history sites through Ohio, Pennsylvania, to upstate New York where it all began at the Sacred Grove, and the Hill Cumorah near Palmyra.

Grandma couldn't come with us because of her store and because she was taking care of her mother, great-grandma Bogue, at the time.

In Pennsylvania we met up with Grandma and Grandpa Clouse, my mom's parents. They were Mormons through and through. Already in their 70s, they were about 10 years older than my father's parents (my dad was the oldest in his family and my mom was the youngest in hers). They were retired and devoting their time in service to the Church and other people. In the Summer of '75 they were finishing up a two-year mission in Pennsylvania which included some proselyting but also a lot of physical work. I know my grandfather helped build at least one chapel and probably more. I remember hearing my mom express concern about how tired he looked when we met them in Pennsylvania. Grandpa wasn't a complainer, though. He'd spent many years building roads in Arizona. He was a big man with big, strong hands who seemed to get a lot of joy out of making breakfast. I especially remember lots of hand-cranked, homemade ice cream, hand-squeezed orange juice (from oranges grown in his own backyard) and hand-pulled molasses taffy when we would visit them in Arizona.

Grandma Clouse was tiny and full of energy. She was funny and affectionate. She loved music. She would play "Lincoln's Funeral March" on the piano by memory all by herself in the afternoon. It was a tune her father taught her, and it was a surprisingly upbeat song—maybe someone from the Confederacy wrote it. My brothers and I loved to sing and play the piano, and we had a captive audience with Grandma Clouse. She would set aside whatever she was doing to see us perform in her living room.

Grandma Clouse was a quilter. She made beautiful patchwork quilts out of old clothes. We spent years wrapping ourselves in Grandma's quilts as we watched TV. They were on our beds. They came with us to drive-in movies and on road trips. We wore them out with so much use. Because my dad was military, we moved about every two years. We never lived close to our grandparents, so both of our grandmothers found ways to embrace us from a distance—Grandma Sutton with her sweaters and Grandma Clouse with her quilts. This trip in 1975 was fun and unique because on our way back, we stayed a few days in Indiana with everyone. All four of our grandparents were together. We were young, so we spent our days running around and playing, but it felt special to have everyone in a single place. I would see the adults lounging on the patio together or standing and sitting around the dining area next to the kitchen playing games or talking. I didn't want that Summer to end.

During this trip, I learned that hay fever was more than just sneezing and a runny nose. We spent a lot of nights camping in campgrounds surrounded by tall grass. One morning, I woke up and I couldn't open my eyes no matter how hard I tried. The goop that my body had produced dried as I slept, gluing my eyes completely shut. It was disgusting and funny at the same time. A faint green light made its way through the goop-laden opening. After a few hot compresses, I was set to go, but I wasn't the only one affected by the elements on this trip. Mom suffered from terrible asthma which meant lots of coughing, labored breathing, inability to sleep, and utter exhaustion during the whole trip.

By the time we got home, she was really sick, and much to her surprise, she discovered that she was expecting another child. She was particularly concerned about being pregnant since she had been taking so much medication to control her asthma on the trip. Her doctor assured her, though, that according to his books there were no dangers of birth defects from the drugs she was taking. He repeatedly told her that all was well.

The timing of the pregnancy was inconvenient. Dad was transitioning into a job that would allow him to be home more often, but it meant that he would be gone for two months attending Safety School in California. True to form, the morning sickness hit Mom like a sledge-hammer, leaving her bedridden. Dad wrote in his journal, "Laraine is still very sick and I am in great pain worrying about the possibility of it continuing on into the months that I have to be in California." He fasted and prayed a lot and gave my mom a few Priesthood blessings in the weeks prior to his departure, but nothing seemed to be working. Then, a respite came a few days before he left. He wrote:

> Laraine is much better today. I am greatly pleased and thankful. I pray that the condition will continue to improve. Miracles don't happen often in my life. Although my wife is sick and my family is suffering, I still have to go to work.

The reprieve lasted long enough to see my dad off, long enough to give my mom some rest, then it was back to the first trimester blues. Each morning, I would get up with my older brothers, and we'd get dressed, clean up our rooms, and feed the twins before we went to school. I don't know how Mom managed the hours until we returned home, though she gave us a hint in one of her entries into our family history collection:

> My memories of this time are of lying on the couch and watching the twins play around the room. When I felt a little better, I would do some laundry, try to straighten up the house, clean the kitchen and change diapers. One of my most vivid memories of that time is when I was so ill and weak from vomiting that I could not walk. Our dog, Kipper, had eaten some leftover hot dogs. She came into the living room where I lay on the couch and threw up in the middle of the floor. I tried to get up, but became very ill and couldn't move very fast. In the meantime, Troy and Trent toddled over to Kipper's mess and began to play with it and eat the hot dog bits. I began crying and pleading with them to get out of the mess. I finally succeeded in crawling over to where they were with some Kleenex and got them to help me clean it up, not eat it up. They were having such fun!

We didn't have hot dogs in the house for a *long* time after that.

From California, Dad contacted Ann Perry, one of the women at church who had a child the same age as the twins. She readily agreed to take the twins every day and bring them back after dinner, bathed and ready to sleep for the night. Colleen Worley, the Relief Society President, organized everything so that most of our meals were taken care of by friends and acquaintances at church. I didn't realize how remarkable that was at the time. I was old enough to be thankful for it and to be excited about how many different kinds of casseroles and salads there were, but I wasn't experienced enough to know that there were many people in the world who didn't have this kind of community to rally around them in times of need.

Eventually, we got back to a normal routine. Dad returned. Mom started to feel better. It was Spring. We were all busy. Mom was on the PTA board, and Dad was on the board of the Little League and a counselor in the ward bishopric. Mom's due date of April 25th was fast approaching. Unlike her earlier pregnancies, this baby rarely moved. The rest of us boys had been kickers and rollers in the womb. My parents were concerned that this child was going to be handicapped in some way.

A few days after the due date, Mom's midwife decided to do an X-ray. It was customary in the military hospitals to have the patient carry the X-rays back to their primary physician. Whenever that happened, Mom would always take a peek at the film as she walked down the hall. This time, though, the X-ray technician decided to deliver the film to the midwife himself. Trying to quell feelings of apprehension, Mom walked slowly back to the obstetrics ward and waited for the results. The midwife explained that the baby was in the right position, which was good news. The image though looked unclear and full of shadows. For that reason, she opted not to show it to my mom. By the time Mom got home and shared the experience with my dad, they were both convinced that something was wrong.

On the following day, April 29, Mom went into labor. After an hour, the baby's head started to crown. It was soft. Thinking the baby had shifted and was coming out breach, the midwife immediately sent for the doctor who was on call for emergencies like this. Within a few minutes he was scrubbed in and assessing the situation. They told my dad to leave the room. He stepped behind a curtain where he could be out of their way but continue to watch the delivery. The staff pushed aside the mirror that had been positioned for Mom to watch the delivery. Disconcerted and anxious from the disruption and chaos in the room, Mom focused her attention on the delivery itself, breathing and pushing. At 6:23 p.m., the 7 lb 13 oz baby boy came fast and easily. Mom caught a glimpse of the baby as they bundled him up and rushed him out the door. He was pinkish-purple and seemed to be a good size. Dad saw the baby too from his hiding place, and he knew why everyone was scrambling—his infant son's head was badly deformed.

Mormons tend to see the world differently than others do. Maybe that's too simplistic a statement to make. But it seems to me that a Mormon approach relies on intuition and feelings while others leans on reason and science; one looks for inspiration as the other seeks tangible precedent. It's not as simple as that, I know, and belief isn't exclusively a Mormon trait, but on the day Thad was born, the divide between these world views became very wide for my family.

While Dad discussed the baby's condition with the doctor in the hallway, Mom was taken from the delivery room and moved into a recovery room. The midwife explained that the baby had a rare deformity—very rare. Essentially, he was born without bones to cover the top of his head. She told my mom that the shadows she had seen on the X-ray hinted at something like this, but that she had been praying all night long for this baby, hoping that somehow the X-rays had just been blurry for another, non-threatening reason. Exhausted and anxious, Mom asked the midwife how soon she would be able to see her new son. She was told the doctor would have more news.

Knowing that they had a small window of time, Dad called Bishop Worley from the Church and asked him to come as fast as he could. If they wanted to give the infant a name and a priesthood blessing, it would have to happen immediately. Once he made that call, Dad went into the recovery room to be with Mom. They embraced as only new parents can. Mom asked him if he had seen the baby. Dad smiled, caressing her hair, and said, "Yes, I did. I think he's pretty cute."

The attending physician joined them and explained emphatically that babies with this birth defect never survive. He felt strongly that my mom should not even see the infant, that holding her son would create a connection, a bond that would make the situation that much more devastating for her. He was certain that it would be best for everyone if the baby simply died. He did not know my mother. Mom sat up in her bed, looked the doctor directly in the eye, and in a low, measured voice demanded that they bring in her newborn son. She wanted to hold him, to know him, to love him before he passed away. No one was going to take that away from her.

Dad brought their son into the room and placed him in my mother's arms. The nurses had gently wrapped the baby in a white hospital blanket, leaving only part of his face exposed. Mom lifted the blanket so that she could see his whole head. In that moment, she felt as if she'd always known him. She whispered, "He's beautiful." Then, she looked up at Dad and said, "I've seen him before!" Mom unwrapped her tiny son, counting his fingers and toes, noticing how strong his body was, how healthy it seemed, and she covered it with kisses. To her, the entire room was filled with a spirit of love and strength that seemed to emanate from her baby. All the apprehension she had been feeling vanished, and she felt enveloped in a nourishing cocoon of calm.

The doctor informed them that if there were any chance for the baby to survive, he would need to be taken by air evacuation to Wilford Hall Medical Center in San Antonio, Texas. The hospital staff made preparations for the evacuation while my dad and Bishop Worley took the baby into their arms. They gave him a name and a priesthood blessing. His name would be Thad Aaron Sutton, and he was promised that he would be able to serve the Lord and to fulfill the measure of his creation, and also that he would be used as God saw fit. Afterward, my parents were left alone in the room with Thad. They held him, and cuddled him. It was a relief to be together in this moment. They suddenly knew that however long it lasted, they had a future with their new son. He was a part of them. He would be a part of their family.

Through all of this, we were at home waiting for our new brother. We were helping a few women from the church to clean up the house and to get everything ready for the baby. When Dad arrived, he told us that Thad would not be coming home. In an instant, the mood of the house changed. He gathered us boys around him and said that our little baby brother was born with a severe defect, that nobody knew what his future might be, and he said that all we could do was to hope for the best and to pray for Thad.

Dad gathered his things and left to go back to the hospital. At 3:45 a.m., Thad was taken onto a C-141 with a Capt. Hassal as his escort, and they took off for San Antonio. Dad would be driving the 250 miles down to San Antonio to meet them at the Wilford Hall Medical Center. After the plane left, an intern told my father that it was good that he was going down to the hospital to be an advocate for the baby; otherwise, Thad might simply be allowed to die.

Officially, Thad's deformity was a severe type of encephalocele, which is a "rare neural tube defect (occurring in 1 out of 5,000 babies worldwide) where brain membranes protrude through openings in the skull." Neural tube birth defects happen very early in the pregnancy, within the first three or four weeks, often before the mother is even aware she is pregnant. The developing tissues start to differentiate in the first couple of weeks, the neural tissues being some of the first in line. The tissues wrap around and join edges forming a sort of capsule. They start to adhere on the lower end rather like a Ziploc bag; then, within a week or so, the part that will develop into the brain seals itself up, and the nervous system is well on its way to becoming actualized. If there are faults in the connections along the neural tube as the fetus grows and develops, membranes (or as in Thad's case, actual brain tissue) can push through to the outside or simply lie on the outside where no bones have formed to enclose them.

For Thad, this opening incorporated much of the front right side of his skull including most of the bones that would have formed his right eye socket. A large portion of his brain (especially compared to his small infant head) extended through that opening covered by a layer of skin. When any brain tissue is involved in an encephalocele, the likelihood that the baby will survive the pregnancy is very low; therefore, the prognosis for a baby like Thad born with over half his brain outside the protection of the skull was not a good one.

It is unknown what causes this type of birth defect, though medical studies have pretty much ruled out asthma medication, which was my mom's big fear when she found out she was pregnant. In the 1970s and 80s, interest in folic acid, a B vitamin, encouraged research and studies that eventually found that having sufficient folic acid in the system when a child is conceived seemed to lower the incidence of neural tube birth defects, especially in women who had already had one child with such a defect. Nevertheless, it wasn't until 1995 (19 years after Thad was born) that women of child-bearing age were encouraged to take 400 micrograms of folic acid every day.

In the beginning, Mom struggled with feelings of guilt that somehow she had caused this to happen. She was traumatized and overwhelmed. Naturally, she lived on the verge of tears which would more often than not break their bounds whenever the subject of the baby came up. Still, Mom had experienced that transcendent moment of recognition in the hospital, and that moment became a touchstone that helped her reclaim, when necessary, a perspective that wasn't skewed by fear or guilt or other mortal variants. Thad's birth codified for our family the relationship between spiritual experiences and everyday life. It would be nice to live in a complete state of spiritual awareness, to continually see life through God's eyes; but the reality was our eyes were mortal, our hearts were mortal, our experience was mortal. The challenge was to live in the world, but to hold onto those moments of spiritual awareness which could tip the balance by adding just the right amount of hope.

As Mom struggled to process her feelings of grief, despair, hope, and determination, friends and acquaintances from both the church and the military reached out to embrace her and to buoy her up. Most notably, during the 24 hours in the hospital after Thad was born, friends came by to express love and concern. It wasn't just one or two, it was many people who came and opened their hearts to her. They shared things like, "I had a child die," or "My brother was disabled." They wrapped Mom in the hope they had gleaned from their own sadness and adversity. It was a communion of shared experience that opened her world up in a way that was profound and humbling. "People have had such sorrow in their lives," she commented later, "and we were bonded immediately. We were all of a sudden brothers and sisters in experience."

When Dad arrived at the Wilford Hall Medical Center on the morning of April 30th, the doctors who received Thad said there was nothing they could do. They reiterated the fact that babies with this severe a condition rarely live more than a few days. Dad wrote in his journal, "I held him for a few minutes. He is cuddly and sweet. Tears flow freely.... It seems that there is no purpose for him to live, but it's heart-rending to think of him dying. I fast and pray. I trust in the Lord."

Grandma and Grandpa Clouse drove non-stop from Arizona as soon as they got the news of Thad's birth. They stayed with us so Mom could be in San Antonio right away. When Mom arrived at Wilford Hall, Thad was doing very well. His vital signs were good. He was eating and sleeping well. In fact, the nurses commented that Thad demanded to be fed. His sucking response was not very strong but he fed well with a preemie nipple the nurses had decided to try.

Mom asked the medical team how long they thought it would be before she and Dad could bring Thad home. The doctors did not think that bringing Thad home was a good idea. He would require a lot of care, which would take attention and nurturing away from the other children. In addition, the response of the outside world to a deformed sibling would also take a toll on the family. Putting all that aside, though, the doctors felt it was irresponsible for my parents to allow their children to become attached to their new brother all the while knowing that they would lose him sooner than later. In any event, that was not going to happen right away. The doctors needed to keep Thad for the time being in order to see if he would continue to eat and gain weight, and to find out how the rest of his body and capabilities were affected by the birth defect.

On our end, it wasn't hard to sense the gravity of the situation. As one of the three older boys, I felt a responsibility to help out as much as I could. Tony, Todd and Thomas did, too. Because of this, I started to feel like I was finally part of the family. We were working as a team because that is what the situation called for. My insecurities and low self-esteem didn't disappear, but they were superseded for the moment by the more pressing needs of the family.

It helped that this upheaval had a face. There was a photo of Thad from the day he was born taped to the refrigerator door. Dad supplied us with many photos, a veritable gallery. We knew what Thad looked like. He was real to us. On May 4th, when my parents got home from my mom's first trip to San Antonio, Dad called us all together for a family meeting, including Grandma and Grandpa Clouse. He and Mom talked about their experience at the hospital. They explained what was happening with Thad. They talked specifically about the concerns expressed by the doctors about bringing Thad home. They sincerely asked us what we thought about it. We were all anxiously awaiting the time when we could actually meet Thad. The idea of him not coming home had never even crossed our minds. Even though Mom and Dad spoke very clearly about the possible sacrifices we would need to make having a special needs child in the home, not having him with us was unfathomable. All I had was a picture taped to a refrigerator door, but I loved Thad. I wanted him home, and so did everyone else. That night my dad wrote in his journal, "We've talked a lot about our son Thad and everyone seems to be peaceful about it."

When my father spoke with the doctors on the phone after the initial test results were in, they were even more convinced that Thad's prognosis was dire. In a nutshell, they determined that if he did live longer than a week, he would not progress much further than breathing and eating. Their opinion was that however long Thad lived, he would be a vegetable. Certainly, in these cases, so as not to give false hope, physicians tend to skew toward the worst-case scenario. My parents were back in San Antonio a couple of days later, one week after Thad was born, and they saw a "fragile, but very hardy" little infant. Dad felt that in spite of the prognosis, Thad had a long life ahead of him, and however long that meant, he would be a part of our family.

On the 12th of May, Mom drove to San Antonio with Grandma and Grandpa Clouse, who were anxious to meet Thad, but nervous at the same time. They came from a generation that considered birth defects or handicaps a shame on the family, something to be kept hidden from view. Though they didn't espouse those ideas themselves, they were certainly aware of them. They were also supremely concerned for their daughter and what lay ahead for her. Their fears were allayed when they arrived in the neo-natal intensive care ward at Wilford Hall. Similar to what happened with my mom when Thad was born, Grandma and Grandpa Clouse felt a deep spiritual connection to Thad from the moment they laid eyes on him. Grandma often said that holding Thad was like holding a little piece of heaven. They spent time holding him and getting to know him before continuing their trip back to Arizona.

A few months later, in September, Grandpa Clouse wrote down some of his thoughts during a church service on the back of a Mesa 5th Ward Sacrament Meeting program:

> We have had sent to our family a very special spirit...We don't know how long our little Thad will be here to bless us, but this much we do know. Due to his handicap, he will never be able to lead the life of a normal boy. He perhaps will have to spend his life on the bed. We know he will need much loving care. The Savior said, "Inasmuch as you have done it unto the least of these you have done it unto me." It would be rejecting the will of the Lord to even hope within our hearts that this boy be called back home. But, only that the Lord's will be done. When this little boy has fulfilled his mission and we, not him, have been properly tested in this matter, then the Lord's will will be done. Why would one be so selfish as to entertain an idea that this child is not entitled to life? He is entitled to live just as much as I am entitled to

> live...May we prove to our Heavenly Father that we accept his will and trust that in his loving care this little fellow will not need to suffer.

There was a remarkable outpouring of love and support during this first month while Thad was in San Antonio. Grandma Sutton wrote this:

> Mom is going back to Dorothy's next weekend to stay awhile, then if you need me, I could fly down anytime. I do not know when and I'm sure you don't know either as long as Thad remains in San Antonio...I have good help at the store and they can manage this time of year very well without me for 2 or 3 weeks. If the opportunity arises and you get to go to Arizona for a rest and recuperation, Laraine, and Tom has used up his leave, you might be glad to take me up on it. Don't miss going if it is just a matter of someone to look after things. It would be a change of scenery for me and I'd be happy to fill in wherever needed. You know that!
>
> We do hope and pray things are going well for the baby. Medical science can do many wonderful things anymore, but whatever comes we know he is God's little one and that He loves him as we do and much more than we are capable of, being love itself!

Grandma and Grandpa Sutton did come down a few months later, and I was thrilled. Any time I could spend with Grandma Sutton was something I looked forward to greatly.

On May 30, 1976, a month after Thad was born, my parents brought him home, and our life together began. He was so small and his head was so big. The brain side of Thad's head was about one and half times larger than the rest of his little infant head. It jutted up and to the right, away from the from the bony side, and held its own. It was firm and soft to the touch, like a head of over-steamed cauliflower. Interestingly, his skull bone at the edge where it met the brain veered upward almost perpendicularly for about an inch creating a ledge of sorts from the front starting smoothly just above the forehead, then moving along the back portion of the brain, gliding smoothly down past the crown where it disappeared. It seemed to provide a degree of support for the brain. His right eye was like a recessed cave between his cheek and the overhanging brain, which were secured together by a piece of white surgical tape.

Never once did I feel a sense of revulsion at the sight of Thad. He was like a little ball of light with a misshapen head. Any awareness of his deformity became less relevant upon seeing his engaging smile or the perpetual twinkle in his left eye. He was present and aware, and from the get-go, he loved to be held. Mom allowed us older boys to help take care of Thad, but we were given specific instructions on how to hold him. We were instructed to always hold his head because his neck was not ready to hold the weight of his head. If we needed to walk while we were holding him, we had to be especially aware of where his head was at all times in order to avoid bumping his brain into anything. I'm awestruck that Mom would trust us the way that she did from the moment Thad came home. I can only imagine the protective anxiety she felt inside as we learned by doing. Perhaps she understood that holding Thad would help us bond with him. Fortunately, although there were certainly mistakes and mishaps along the way, none of them was life-threatening.

About a week after Thad came home, they were back in San Antonio for a check up. Dr. Tomasovic, Thad's attending physician, was encouraged by how well Thad was developing. He told my parents that he knew of a boy in Florida with a similar condition who lived until he was 17 years old. Thad's life was still uncertain, but they would be there to track it and help whenever they could. There was certainly more to explore and more to learn. At this point, Thad was thriving, so Dr. Tomasovic decided it was time to sew Thad's right eye shut since there was essentially no bone structure to support it or to provide a barrier against pathogens. This was something they had put off initially, not wanting to put Thad through any unnecessary procedures if he wasn't going to survive. It didn't happen on that trip, but it took place about a month later. Tests and procedures were done to learn more about the scope of the defect and to determine if there was anything that could be done to improve the quality of his life.

Mom and Dad put Thad's crib in their room so that they could hear him while he slept. Because of the tenuous nature of his existence, Mom became hyper-aware of every little thing. She would make sure he was close to her in whatever she was doing. If that wasn't possible, she would regularly ask us to check in on him. It got to the point where she wouldn't even have to ask us. If we happened to walk by his crib or playpen or blanket on the living room floor, we'd check him. "Thad is breathing, Mom," became a common call, like birds in a treacherous forest. *Everything is ok for now. No need to worry.* Troy and Trent were around all the time, and they were vigilant, even at 2 years old. They would check on Thad, run back to Mom and mimic whatever they had seen, whether he was sleeping, how he was breathing; they even could somehow evoke the back and forth flutter of Thad's left eye.

Mom recalled this time:

> I was paranoid he would die alone and I couldn't bear that thought... One day he had been on my mind a lot. I went and knelt in my bedroom by Thad's bed. I always said my prayers by him because the Spirit was strong there. I poured my heart out. We were grateful to have this child and all the boys who brought happiness in our lives. I expressed my concern that I didn't want Thad to pass away alone. He was like this little stick that stirred things in the family with an undercurrent of love. Was Thad going to live or die? I didn't want the constant worry. I think all new mothers do that anyway, but I was almost to the extreme. I just continued to kneel there and the thought came to my mind, "Not now, but in the coming years." So, I had time for my family and that burden was lifted. We were [still] mindful of him but that worry [that put] my hand on his back and the kids running in and out [was gone]. "Thad, you are going to be here awhile."

In August, during a surgery that included a brain scan, they almost lost Thad twice, but he pulled through. What they learned from this procedure was that his skull was filled with brain matter mixed with scar tissue. There was no way to reduce its size or to really know where any of the brain centers were. This made any sort of brain surgery precarious because they would be going into it completely blind.

My parents quickly learned how expensive Thad's care was becoming. It wasn't just the medical bills, it was the travel, the lodging, the food: it added up. Looking into the future, even with basic medical being covered by the military and incidental medical insurance, having a special needs child was a dauntingly expensive endeavor. Dad's salary as a Major in the Air Force was already being tested by having seven children. So, in September, my dad started a job helping someone collect data on gasoline usage in West Texas by going to gas stations all over the region once a month on a Sunday night from about midnight to 6 a.m. and writing down the numbers on the gas pump meters. This added a little over $300 a month to the family budget.

Dad would do the survey with one of us older boys helping; but, if he was off flying for work, Mom would bundle up all the sleeping little kids into the station wagon with one of us older kids to help. This was before 24-hour gas stations were prevalent, so it was kind of spooky pulling up to these vacant businesses in the middle of the night with a flash light and writing down the usage numbers off of each gas pump. When it was my turn to help, with my active imagination, every shadow was a murderer. I wrote down the numbers as fast as I could and jumped back into the car.

Dr. Tomasovic told my parents that they should consider taking Thad to the Children's Hospital of Boston for further testing. This hospital was at the forefront of care for children with neural tube birth defects. It was possible that due to their expertise, the Children's Hospital of Boston might be able to provide more options for Thad than they could at Wilford Hall. The only problem with that option was that a visit to Boston and any subsequent tests or procedures would not be covered by insurance. As far as my parents were concerned, anything that could possibly improve Thad's condition and his future was worth exploring. There was, however, a deadline associated with the Boston opportunity because intervention like this needed to happen within the first year. In an effort to make this possible, Mom got a job at the State School for the Mentally Handicapped as a night dorm mother. She would be at the school from 10 p.m. to 6 a.m., 4 or 5 nights a week. This made my mom really tired and my father very distressed because he took his role as provider very seriously.

Not much changed in the day-to-day Sutton life after Thad came home. There was a place for him in our family. We adapted to his needs, but we were still incredibly involved in our individual activities. Though we helped as much as we could, the weight of Thad's care fell on my mom. We still had school and music and sports and scouts and church and neighborhood playing. What I can say is that with the frequent trips to San Antonio, we were sort of required by circumstance to take up the slack and care for ourselves and each other.

Many of the trips to San Antonio were one-day ventures, requiring at least 10-12 hours driving, depending on the traffic, plus whatever time was spent at the hospital. Mom would bring one of us along to keep her awake on the road—heaven knows West Texas is not known for it's visual diversity. It was practical for my mom to have company because it made for an exhausting day, and she could have someone there to talk to. It gave each one of us an opportunity to have a one-on-one adventure with Mom and Thad and to feel like we were part of everything that was going on in the family. When there was nothing left to talk about or songs to sing, we'd make up stories and songs or play road trip games like the alphabet game or the license plate game. On more than one occasion, at the end of the day, we'd have to pull off to the side of the road and sleep for a while before continuing on toward home.

Often, when Mom was away, Dad's work and church responsibilities required him to be away as well. He was home, but he wasn't *home*. I was the scaredy-cat in the family. I would call Dad at the church asking when he was coming home. It was unsettling for me not to have parents around, especially at night. The funny thing was that even with his days working and flying and nights counseling people at church or whatever, Dad was around more now than he'd ever been our whole lives. One Friday, he and Mom did the San Antonio trip, getting home in the wee hours of the morning only to wake up a few hours later to take us and some other kids from church on a 20-mile bike hike to the Buffalo Gap State Park. I completed both legs of that adventure and felt a supreme sense of accomplishment. From then on, Todd and I rode our bikes everywhere.

I wonder if God arranged things so that Dad's career responsibilities changed right before Thad arrived, so we'd have at least one parent at home most of the time. The Mormon side of me says, "Absolutely!" The scientific side of me says, "Wow, were we lucky!" There seemed to be so much divine presence in our family at the time of Thad's birth, like we were living with a spiritual force field of some kind. Even as kid, I could feel the hand of God in our lives. I knew that this experience mattered, though I'm not sure I will ever be able to articulate exactly the depth of that sentiment.

Initially, aside from the obvious deformity, Thad appeared to be developing normally, albeit at a somewhat slower pace. He was responsive to his environment. He would coo and smile a lot. His grip was firm when he held onto your finger. He would move his arms and legs at different speeds depending on how excited he was. He particularly liked toys that made noise, moved, or flashed light. If they could do all three things, Thad was in heaven. We had a bevy of rattles and other infant toys. We knew that we could get his attention and play with him just by shaking a rattle close to him. He would smile and kick his legs out. Thad had a particular fondness for one rattle that was bright orange on one side and white on the other. I don't know if it was the particular sound it made, or if it was the color combination, but soon, he would reach out for the rattle and when we gave it to him, he would shake it and smile his full infectious smile and shake it some more.

From the beginning, on one end of Thad's crib hung a colorful mobile. When we placed Thad in his crib, underneath the mobile, he would watch it, but it didn't seem to fascinate him very much. A few months later, Mom put a toy across the other end of his crib that had a clear oblong ball in the middle which contained smaller colored balls that made noise when it was spun. On either side of the clear ball, spaced evenly between the ball and the edge of the toy, there was a three-pronged colorful plastic armature with arms that were about 5 or 6 inches long. They also spun when hit. Thad would lie underneath this toy and laugh and flail his arms and legs when we made it move. Sometime within that first year, he began reaching out and hitting the armatures himself. Initially, he couldn't quite reach the ball with his hands, but he figured out that his feet could be very useful for that purpose. He wasn't propelling himself around, so someone must have put him in the crib with his head toward the mobile, away from the toy, giving his feet the time and space to discover just how much happiness they could create on their own.

In October, 6 months after Thad was born, Mom took him into her room to change his diaper. She set him on her bed perpendicular to the edge, then turned around to get the supplies she needed to get the job done. When she turned back around, Thad was teetering on the edge of the bed. Mom screamed, dropped everything and lunged for the bed, catching Thad just as he started to fall. ("Look, Mom, I can roll!") From then on, we surrounded Thad by pillows whenever he was on a bed that wasn't his crib.

There are several conditions that often accompany encephaloceles including further deformity in bones of the face and skull, visual impairment, partial or total paralysis, uncontrolled movement, developmental delays, inhibited growth, mental retardation, and seizures. Some of these associated conditions can be determined right away while others reveal themselves through the course of a life. One of the first anomalies that became apparent was that Thad seemed to be prone to respiratory infection, leading to frequent sniffles and coughs and even to hospital stays with recurrent pneumonia. His first bout of pneumonia happened in January, 1977, postponing the trip to Boston for a week. In addition to that, somewhere between August and February of his first year, he started to have seizures which affected his lungs. First, he would go quiet; all movement would stop. Then, his eye would flutter more erratically from side to side. Within seconds he would stop breathing and begin to turn blue before his breath started again with a gasp a few moments later. It was scary.

Mom turned 34 on Dec. 1st, and we rolled into the holiday season with bells on. Christmas was a busy and fun time for us. As was our tradition, we spent Christmas Eve Day making cookies, fudge, and divinity, creating gift plates of homemade sweets for the friends that we would carol to that evening. We were exuberant singers. Thomas, Troy, and Trent took turns handing over the plate of sweets to whomever came to the door. Mom wrapped Thad in blankets and held him as we sang our favorite carols, "We Wish You a Merry Christmas" and "Far, Far Away on Judea's Plains," among other songs celebrating the birth of Jesus. When we finished our rounds, we spent time in our living room listening to Dad read the Christmas story from the Bible, then we all went to bed. Tony, Todd, Thomas, and I shared a room. Troy and Trent shared the smaller room, and Thad slept in his crib in my parent's room.

The new year came, and we had a lot to look forward to. Since the trip to Boston was postponed because of Thad's pneumonia, everyone was home for my 10th birthday on January 28th.

When it became clear that no outside insurance would pay for the Boston trip and the care involved, Thad's pediatrician at Dyess petitioned the Air Force powers-that-be to consider covering all of the costs. It was a long shot, but his efforts were successful. Because of this unexpected and humbling generosity on the part of the pediatrician and the military, the money that Mom had saved while working at the State School for the Mentally Handicapped could be used for housing and expenses while they were in Boston.

So, in February of 1977, when Thad was 9 months old, he and Mom left for a two week stay in Boston. Mom rented a room about 6 blocks away from the Children's Hospital of Boston. Mom was really pleased with Dr. John Shillito, one of the top neurosurgeons in the country. He spent several hours examining Thad, and he was impressed with Thad's maturity and activity. That was hopeful.

Over the next couple of weeks of testing and consultation, the picture became more clear. Nothing that they could do would improve Thad's mental attributes or reverse any damage caused by the birth defect. There was a surgery, though, that they could do which involved chipping away most of the cranial bones, settling the brain into a more uniform position, then planting bones around the brain which over many weeks would grow together and form a skull. If they went through with the surgery, and if Thad survived, the end result would be mostly cosmetic—he would have a more normal looking head. Not insignificantly, his brain would be completely surrounded by bone which would be eminently better than his current condition.

My parents struggled to determine what was best for Thad, so they took their quest beyond themselves, and put it squarely in the hands of God. After much fasting and prayer by my parents (and by many friends and family members across the country), in light of the touch-and-go nature of the surgery the previous August, and understanding that Thad would be in a tremendous amount of pain for many weeks without improving his actual condition, my parents decided to forego the surgery. They felt that in light of the uncertainty that marked the quantity of years he could live, that the quality of his life here, in this moment, was most important.

While in Boston, Mom learned once again how generous people can be. When members of the Mormon congregation found out that Mom was there, a family named the Wheelwrights invited her to stay at their home so she could save the money she'd set aside for rent. When it came time for her to leave, a group of her new friends and acquaintances pooled money together and bought her and Thad tickets on a direct commercial flight home to Abilene so that they would not have to bounce across the country for a few days on military flights before arriving back at Dyess Air Force Base.

Boston was the final bastion of medical hope for Thad. My parents were coming to the realization that he wasn't going to be miraculously cured through medicine or prayer or anything. Thad was Thad, and he was going to be with us as long as he wanted to be here because he clearly had a powerful will to live. He was a bundle of paradoxes. He was fragile, but hardy. Dad wrote in his journal, "He makes your heart heavy and yet spiritual simultaneously."

My thoughts about Thad began with the photo that was taped to the refrigerator and continued to mature through our day-to-day relationship. Thad was clearly deformed, but he was beautiful. He was amazing. His deficiencies did not diminish him in my eyes nor in the eyes of my family. I still felt deficient without being able to name why, but Thad gave me hope that as a complete package I was beautiful and lovable and worthwhile.

After Boston, life at home returned to a day-to-day rhythm. Because Mom involved us in Thad's care, we each found our individual ways to connect with him. I liked to read, especially out loud, and it was easy for me to cradle Thad as I sat on the couch reading. I read novels like *Where the Red Fern Grows, The Island of the Blue Dolphins,* and *Oliver Twist.* We also had this large paperback collection of poetry and short stories called *Especially for Mormons,* published by Deseret Book. (I was a Mormon, so this collection was for me!) There were numerous volumes, and each volume was a different bright color. The one we had was orange. The stories were designed to teach a lesson and inspire emotional responses. I loved to read from this book. Sometimes I'd just hold Thad while I read to myself, but most of the time, I read aloud giving the best interpretation I could, changing voices if there were dialogue, being dramatic if the narrative called for it. Often, by the end of a story, I'd be in tears because that's the kind of story that filled this collection. I was a sucker for a tear-jerker. Thad seemed to pay attention while I read. He'd settle in and barely move while he looked up at me and listened. Unlike me, though, he tended to fall asleep by the end of each story—no tears shed.

Thad also paid close attention when there was music in the house, which was often. Our piano was placed on the far wall of the main room in the house by the dining room table, just on the other side of the sofa which separated the "living room" from the "dining room." Mom and Dad wanted us all to be able to play the piano. They paid for us to have piano lessons from the time we were old enough to sit on the piano bench and reach the keys without too much trouble. Their goal was not to make us concert pianists, per se, but rather to give us something we could do well, feel good about, and use to contribute to church meetings if we were ever in a situation that required a pianist but didn't have one, like on our missions.

Our piano teacher, Mrs. Mills, was a middle-aged woman who came to our house once a week. She was an accomplished pianist which was impressive to me because her left hand was paralyzed. All of the fingers on her left hand, including her thumb, pulled in and back. She would use that hand to hit single notes while her right hand flew all over the keyboard. It was impressive! Mom would say to us, "You see, disabilities are only a handicap if you let them hold you back." It didn't matter that Mrs. Mills wasn't playing the music exactly how it was written because it sounded full and rich and musical. If you weren't watching her play, you probably wouldn't know there was anything unusual going on.

We were required to practice at least 30 minutes a day verified by a white kitchen timer which sat on the piano next the metronome. Tony, Todd, and I had been playing piano for a few years. I didn't enjoy playing the piano initially because I didn't have the patience to practice scales and exercises over and over again. When Tony or Todd complained and wanted to quit piano, Mom would say, "If you quit piano, you have to quit sports." They would grudgingly get back to practicing their 30 minutes a day. I think Mom inherently knew that threat wouldn't work with me, but somehow she encouraged me to persevere. Then, one day, what I was playing started to sound like music, and I was hooked. I loved it.

By this time, along with finger exercises and scales, we practiced simplified versions of classical pieces like "Für Elise" and Chopin's "Prelude in C," as well as pedagogic creations with titles like "The March of the Gladiators" or "Bill Grogan's Goat." Thomas was just beginning, so he was playing favorites like "March of the Middle C Twins" and "Twinkle, Twinkle Little Star." You could say that Thad was a captive audience. Because he spent a lot of time in the living room, either on a blanket on the floor or in his playpen, he was surrounded by very deliberate playing with occasional forays into musicality for at least 90 minutes a day. Thomas wasn't required to practice 30 minutes, yet. Fifteen minutes was fine for him.

During Family Home Evening, we spent a lot of time singing—church songs, schools songs, folk songs. We liked to sing, and Thad smiled a lot as he listened to the exuberance that filled our living room on Monday nights. On a more personal note, Mom brought music into Thad's care. She would hum while she held him and make up songs while she fed him. She would sing him to sleep with Burt Bacharach's "Close to You." This became Thad's and Mom's song. It was her way of saying "I love you."

Why do birds suddenly appear every time you are near?
Just like me, they long to be, close to you...
On the day that you were born the angels got together and decided to create a dream come true...

Mom brought music into her motherhood because her mother used music as a way to express her maternal feelings. When words aren't enough, add music. This is probably why I never doubted the authenticity of musical theater. As a way to process and express her feelings toward Thad, Grandma Clouse penned some lyrics and set them to a Christmas song called "Starbright." She ended up writing something like fifteen verses with several versions of the chorus, but it was the first verse and the first chorus that said it all. Those were the words we all sang to him. It became our lullaby, our calming tune, our "We're in this together" song, and our simple "I love you" melody. Thad would smile and snuggle into whoever was singing it.

Our Father in Heaven loves us.
He had a sweet spirit with him
Who wanted to come to this earth
And so he sent you to our home
(Chorus) Thad Aaron, our precious baby,
May God look down on you tenderly
Thad Aaron, we love you, darling
Our home is blessed dear
Because of you.

The power of music to express feelings deeper than words alone resonated through our family, especially with regards to Thad. His reactions to music were keen. He would always listen, whether the music included words or not. It was further evidence to us that there was more going on inside of him than we were capable of understanding.

In addition to the music that we generated ourselves, we listened to music all the time on the stereo. In Abilene, at the time Thad was born, my Dad had a record player as well as a reel-to-reel tape player on the shelves in our living room. He'd recorded many, if not all, of his album collection onto reels of tape. For me, the tapes were much more fun to play because they involved a process that felt more grown up than putting a needle onto a black disc. Since I had to rely on my parent's taste in music in 1976, I was listening to the Osmonds, Carole King, The Carpenters, The Ray Conniff Singers and The Mormon Tabernacle Choir. I would lie on the green shag carpet on the living room floor next to Thad with the sunlight hitting us and listen to The Ray Conniff Singers make scandalous songs like "Gypsies, Tramps, and Thieves" and "Angel of the Morning" sound like cotton candy. I skipped around our house singing every word to "Gypsies, Tramps, and Thieves" without knowing what the song was really about. "I was 16 he was 21-1-1-1-1. Drove him up to Memphis. Papa would have shot him if he knew what he'd do-o-o-one."

The Osmonds were everything to me. They were Mormons, and people liked them. Dad had recorded all of our Osmond albums onto one big reel of tape. I repeatedly listened to songs like "Down by the Lazy River," "Yo-Yo," "One Bad Apple," "We All Fall Down," and "Crazy Horses." To me, though, the most significant Osmond song, was a cover they did of the Hollies' hit, "He Ain't Heavy, He's My Brother." I felt like it was written just for us.

The road is long, with many a winding turn
That leads us to who knows where, who knows where
But I'm strong, strong enough to carry him
He ain't heavy, he's my brother
So on we go, his welfare is my concern
No burden is he to bear, we'll get there
For I know he would not encumber me
He ain't heavy, he's my brother

It wasn't just Thad that came to mind when I heard this song. I was learning that in a family we all relied on each other. Perhaps this experience was maturing me faster, perhaps I would have matured anyway. I still struggled with self-esteem. I still felt profoundly different. The distinction was that when Thad entered our family, I no longer felt like an outsider. We had to work together like a team. In doing so, I think we learned more about each other and that what we each brought to the table was important. Tony was practical and funny. Todd was responsible and grounded. I was creative and enthusiastic. Thomas was sensitive and kindhearted. Troy and Trent were two.

In those moments when we were stepping outside of ourselves to care for Thad, we realized that we each had something valuable to contribute, that our individual talents complemented the talents of everyone else and that being part of a family was a real blessing. I felt a connection to my family that I had not recognized before. I felt gratitude for my family in a way that was new, tangible, and recognizable. Acts of service didn't transform me from night to day into a confident, well-rounded, Mormon, young man, but in the act of service I discovered the nature of love. Something as simple as holding Thad in my lap and reading to him gave me a reprieve from my life. It was one of many tiny things that made Thad less of a burden and more of a refuge.

Close to the end of his first year, we noticed that Thad was beginning to test the weight of his head in space as we held him in an upright position against our body. Periodically, he would lift his head off the shoulder of whoever was holding him, just a little bit, then set it back back down. He would also do this when he was on the floor. If he was on his belly he would lift his head off the floor just about an inch, then relax back to the floor. At the beginning of April, 1977, he did the unthinkable. Thad was lying on his stomach and he lifted his head all the way up to look around. His arms were planted on the ground and his legs kicked out behind him. Then, he slowly set his head back down on the floor. It didn't appear to be very significant to Thad, but it was a huge event in all of our eyes. How did his little neck lift his head and cautiously place it back down? By our reactions, you would have thought he'd won a gold medal at the Olympics. Looking around became a regular thing for him. He would look straight ahead, then shake his head fast, then slow, then fast again.

Soon after that, Thad began to scoot around on his tummy. If he was in his crib or on the floor and a rattle or toy was out of reach, he found a way to get there. His head was still too heavy for his neck to hold up for any length of time, so he would use it as a fifth limb to get him around. Or, if he was on his tummy, he would lift his head and use its weight to help him roll over. He was unstoppable. We could give him a bit of exercise by shaking a rattle just out of his reach causing him to scoot and wriggle his way toward it; then, we would move a little further away so he could wriggle some more. He didn't cover long distances, but it was really fun to see him enthusiastically move around the floor. We'd always give the rattle to him in the end, and he would flip onto his back and shake the rattle with triumphant glee. We found immense satisfaction and joy with each milestone Thad passed in his developmental journey. He wasn't supposed to live through the night he was born, and now he was scooting and wriggling his way toward his first birthday. We often joked, "Thad's pretty active for a vegetable!"

In the Spring of 1977, Mom and Thad were back at Wilford Hall for a check up. By then, everyone on the floor knew them. It was, "Hi Thad! You look great! Hi Mrs. Sutton! How are you doing? How are the kids?" Mom felt very comfortable and welcome there. Dr. Tomasovic always gave my parents clear assessments of Thad and explained everything in a way that they could understand. They never left a consult unsure of Thad's present condition. If there were concerns, my parents were confident that they would be given the right tools to manage them.

On this particular occasion, Dr. Tomasovic asked Mom if he could bring in a group of new residents at the beginning of the consult to introduce Thad and to talk about his condition. Of course, Mom said yes. When the residents entered, Dr. Tomasovic introduced Mom and Thad to them. He explained the nature of Thad's encephalocele, the progress Thad was making, and the challenges that he faced. Still, almost one year later, they did not know what his life expectancy might be, nor did they know specifically how much Thad would be able to develop, but they remained hopeful. At the end of the presentation, Dr. Tomasovic asked if the residents had any questions. The first resident to raise his hand asked, "With so many people in this hospital who have viable futures that depend on our attention and expertise, why should we waste our time on a patient like this?"

YOU'RE BEAUTIFUL AS YOU ARE

No one had ever challenged Thad's value as a human being so directly. As Mom blinked in a "Did I just hear... wait, huh?" kind of way, Dr. Tomasovic abruptly ended the Q & A by escorting the residents out of the room. After several minutes, he returned and apologized for the resident's insensitivity. He made it very clear that there was no doubt in his mind that Thad and every one of his patients was worth every minute of his time and more. Still, he told Mom that he was grateful for the resident's question because it opened the door to a conversation that he needed to have with her. Early on, they had talked about the fact that there were people in the world who would embrace Thad as well as my parent's decision to care for him; and, there would be others who would shun, perhaps even ridicule, them. What just happened illustrated that the medical community was not immune to that divide.

Dr. Tomasovic explained that for the length of Thad's life, however long that ended up being, there would be doctors who would understand and value Thad, and there would be doctors who would be dismissive and condescending. Because of that, one or both my parents would need to be present and proactive in all of Thad's care. If they did not understand something, they would need to insist that someone explain it to them until they were 100% clear. They would need to be present in any check-up or procedure, and they were never to feel intimidated out of voicing their concerns or standing their ground. He explained that no physician should ever do anything to or near the soft, brain side of Thad's head. For example, since there were large veins visible on the surface, just under the skin that surrounded Thad's brain, Dr. Tomasovic explained that without my parent's intervention, doctors, nurses, interns or EMTs might be tempted to insert IV's into those veins. That should never happen, and the responsibility for Thad's safety within the medical community landed on my parent's shoulders. It was a very serious conversation, and by the end, Mom was equally overwhelmed and empowered.

Now that Thad was a constant part of our lives, we, the family, also began to learn many things. The hypotheses we started with were challenged as we stepped outside the harbor of our home and into the world. It's one thing to know in your heart that all would be well, that Thad was really special and cool, and that someone's worth was not determined by what they looked like or how easily they fit into the cultural norm of acceptability. It was a whole other ballgame to walk down the street with a shockingly deformed child in a stroller.

Except for the hospital, the only place we really went with Thad initially was to church. From what I can remember, the people in our congregation were very accepting. Because of their willingness to help out in the initial months of Thad's life, many members of the ward felt like they were part of Thad's experience. He was adopted into the ward family perhaps more completely than most because so many members had stepped out of their lives and into ours during that very difficult time.

Church was a place where people understood the spiritual paradigm that informed our whole perspective on Thad's experience. Mormon theology teaches that we lived as spirits in the presence of God before this life and that our spirits will continue to live after this life where they will be joined in the resurrection with a perfected, immortal body. Mortality, as we know it, is a small but vital part of an eternal timeline—a way for us to put into practice the many things we'd been learning as spirits in the pre-existence. This belief took the randomness out of Thad's birth for me. People could talk about folic acid or drug side-affects or coincidence, but I felt deeply that whatever the mortal cause of the birth defect, Thad's spirit had been given a choice to enter this encumbered body or to wait. Whatever he needed to learn in this life was tailored to this experience somehow, and he chose to follow it through. It wasn't random, but utterly specific to his eternal development. Each member of the family had their own spiritual conviction that grounded us as a family. For me, peace and purpose came from this perspective; and yet, it was a lot of crazy talk to anyone who didn't share our theological underpinnings.

Our life with Thad quickly moved into the outside world, because Mom and Dad continued to provide transportation and support for the many activities we kids were involved in. Whether he was in a car seat, a stroller, or being held by either parent, Thad came along and shared in our experiences. Out in public, Thad was a magnet for attention. Although people in general are accustomed to disabilities like blindness or deafness, overtly physical disabilities are less common and more shocking; so, like it or not, they inspire curiosity. Talking to strangers was not always easy or convenient, but each person who asked about Thad was doing it because he was new to them, and they deserved respect and courtesy for it. Our family needed to learn how to manage this reality. Listening to our parents, we learned how to encapsulate Thad's story in a way that anyone could understand.

Except for random people—like the lady who accosted Mom in the grocery store and reprimanded her for bringing Thad into public—blatantly negative responses were few and far between. Adults tended to avert their gaze, unless they had some connection to a special needs child; then, if the opportunity was right, they would begin a conversation about Thad. Parents handled it in one of two ways: they would silence their curious children and continue walking; or they would ask us to explain to their child what had happened to Thad. Interestingly, when young children approached us on their own, they seemed to be less curious about Thad's head, and more concerned about what happened to his eye. They tended to be very gentle in how they talked to us and to Thad.

Older kids and early teenagers were less gracious. I felt very defensive, but not because I was afraid of what they would think of me. Thad was my brother, and yes, he was different, but that didn't give anyone the right to diminish him. I was proud of Thad. As I would push him in his stroller, I wore an "I dare you to stare" armor. It gave me a sense of strength that I'd never felt before.

My first experience feeling protective of Thad happened at a local choir festival in Abilene. Our elementary choir performed with other school choirs in the city. After the concert, Todd and I were walking around the auditorium together, pushing Thad in a stroller. We noticed a group of boys our age pointing and talking and laughing. When our eyes met, they scattered. We didn't have to do anything, but in that moment I felt like I would have done something if they'd persisted. It wasn't easy for me to defend myself from deriders and bullies; but, no one could mess with Thad, or any of my family for that matter. I had the strength and courage to stand against them. Todd and I told our parents what happened at the choir concert. We were full of righteous indignation. How dare they make fun of Thad! Mom and Dad thanked us for taking care of Thad, and they gently reminded us that those kids didn't know Thad the way we knew him. They encouraged us to be kind to everyone, even in the face of derision. Yeah, well, they still ran away.

By the time Thad's first birthday came around, we were feeling the groove. We pretty much incorporated Thad and his unique needs into our daily life, and as the newness wore off, our normal lives and challenges returned. The frequent trips to San Antonio continued for Mom and Thad (and whomever accompanied them); so, oftentimes, Dad was in single-parent mode juggling work, church, and civic responsibilities as well as six boys who had many activities of their own that required assistance, transportation, and encouragement.

As I look back on it now, it was an interesting turn of events because my parent's roles flipped. For the first time in their married life, Mom was finding out what it was like to be away from home frequently and for extended lengths of time. Up to this point, Dad's Air Force career had required him to be away from home for days, weeks, and months at a time—even a full year when he went to Vietnam when I was one year old. I imagine there were plenty of times in those early years when he may have felt like he was viewing our lives as if they were being captured in time-lapse photography. Mom wrote a letter to her parents from the motor home one evening, parked under a light about 20 feet from the guard station in the hospital parking lot in San Antonio. She wrote, "I hope the family at home is doing well. I really hated to leave the kids this time. It seems they are growing up so fast and time is slipping away so quickly."

At home, Dad was learning what life was like as a "single parent." He was thrown into the deep end with all six of us. Mom had had twelve years to develop systems, routines, and a wide array of chore charts, adding one child at a time every few years (except when the twins were born). Dad wrote in his journal, "I am more determined to make my house a house of order. The only hinderance to order is six little boys and a demanding baby." It's clear though that he loved the time he was now able to spend with us. On March 21, 1977, he wrote, "A very hard day's work and a heart-warming family night made my day very full. The twins led several songs with their usual enthusiasm. Half-way through 'I've Been Working On the Railroad,' Troy called out, 'Everybody clap your hands!' That was surprising to me to have it come from a three year old. I thoroughly enjoy my sons. They each have so much to offer."

About a month later, during another maternal absence, Dad wrote, "The twins gave me the biggest pain today. They just don't respond to logic. Today they destroyed their room, resisted all enticements and directives to do otherwise. They stayed generally obnoxious all day. Laraine comes home tonight about midnight so I'm cleaning house and getting ready for Sunday." That response was so typical of my dad. Although a compassionate man by nature, his interaction with the world for most of his life was principally through logic, reason, and talking. He completed a Master's degree in Counseling/Psychology and that was his approach to child-rearing. He rarely raised his voice at us or anyone, but we knew that if we did anything wrong, we were in for a lengthy conversation with questions about why we chose to behave in a certain way. It was maddening. There were many times I wanted to say, "I don't know why I did it. Please, stop talking and just hit me like every other father in the world!"

Another month passed, and another trip took Mom, Thad, and the twins away to Arizona for a few weeks so Mom could spend some time with her parents and siblings. Dad recorded this experience:

> We had a real drama tonight. Tim got up [this morning] claiming to be sick and wanting to stay home. I learned that he had failed to complete his homework and didn't want to go to school until his homework was done. I told him he must go to school and take the consequences. Then I left for work. He didn't go. I phoned his teacher and learned that he had been in trouble at school for writing notes which were degrading to another boy. We had a counseling session in the evening and discussed the whole situation. We discussed his early life when as a little baby he developed an insecurity feeling about Thomas being his replacement as our baby in the family. I hope he'll be able to understand the motivation for his feelings.

I don't remember this experience, but as I read it for the first time, I felt a pang of emotion. I was 10 and very naive, so I don't know what I could have possibly written to another boy that was degrading, but I do know that whenever Dad spoke to me about my early childhood and the feelings of displacement and abandonment that according to him I must have felt, it was always one of three things that prompted the discussion: my low self-esteem, my occasional displays of uncontrolled rage, or gender-appropriate behavior.

Over time, I was able to manage the self-esteem deficit by recognizing all that I could possibly contribute to the family and to the world and by balancing that against the areas where I believed I fell short. With regards to my temper, Dad made it very clear that losing my temper was completely unacceptable, so I had to learn more acceptable ways to express or manage my emotions that didn't involve nuclear explosions. Although this process took time, the doors in our current and future homes breathed a collective sigh of relief.

Dad believed very strongly in our capacity as human beings to change anything about ourselves. He felt that all behavior was learned and what was learned could also be unlearned. Not only was he an acolyte of Og Mandino, Dale Carnegie, and other motivational gurus, but he had the gospel and the Church on his side. With grit and determination coupled with prayer and righteous living, our potential for growth and change were limitless. He firmly believed that self-esteem was a by-product of successful self-control. I was told by my dad and other leaders in the Church that if I were to behave in the ways they were proposing, even if it didn't come easy at first, these patterns would become a part of who I was. I could be exactly what God wanted me to be: a righteous, upstanding, Mormon man with a beautiful, loving wife and a passel of children.

I didn't see the point of trying to be a guy's guy, or to behave in ways that didn't feel authentic; but, I did see the value in trying to manage my temper as well as learning the fundamental principles of the Gospel and making them a part of my daily life. I knew I had potential, and they were offering me a tried and true roadmap to a successful and fulfilling life.

Thad was exploring his own potential on the trip to Arizona in May of 1977. One afternoon on my grandmother's living room floor, Thad lifted himself up onto his hands and knees. He rocked forward and backward rolling the top of his head on the floor then completed the feat by lifting his head all the way up to a silent drumroll as if to say, "Look what I can do, Grandma!" The cheers and calls to "Come and look!" startled Thad back onto his tummy, but over the course of their stay, he spent a lot of time on his hands and knees looking around. He would rock back onto his heels, then forward into a full crawl stance, then back to his heels. He was growing more and more confident. A week or so later, when they got home, we had a very exciting show-and-tell in our own living room. A few days after that, during a routine check-up in the Dyess Medical Center, Thad got up on his hands and knees on the examination table and lifted his head. The intern was so excited, he ran into the hallway and called to everyone on the floor to come and see what Thad was doing.

Over the next few months, Thad experimented with this new activity. He'd bounce to his heart's content in his crib or on the floor. We encouraged him to advance that movement into forward motion by shaking a rattle in front of him or cheering him on. "C'mon Thad! Come over here! You can do it! Right over here! Woo-hoooo!" Thad loved the attention and the enthusiasm. It would make him bounce faster, but he was happy doing his own thing. With both hands and knees on the floor, he was stable. When he decided to move forward to reach the rattle, he would go down to his belly and scoot.

By August, Thad was mastering control of his head when he was being held in a vertical position. He would often hold his head off the shoulder of whomever was holding him and look around. Initially, we would make sure to have a hand cradling his head whenever he did this, but his balance and control was getting better and better. When it became clear that he knew where to stop before falling backward, we'd just make sure that our hand was securely on his upper back. Soon, placing his head on the shoulder was no longer the norm.

When and how he placed his head on our shoulders when we held him acquired meaning for us. For example, when we first picked him up, or when he was transferred from one holder to another, Thad would wrap his left hand around the neck of whomever was holding him, and get a hold on their hair if he could. Then, he would place his head face down, so that his mouth and teeth were against the shoulder. After that, he would lift his head up and look around or turn his head to the side so his sewn eye rested on the shoulder. Maybe he did that with his teeth to get his bearings, but it seemed to us that it was some kind of greeting. In the movies, people kissed each other on the cheek when they greeted each other. Thad gently bit our shoulder and pulled our hair. The balance he was experiencing when we held him started to influence his other activities, and he started to experiment with sitting up. We had to surround him with pillows at all times because he was top-heavy. His center of gravity landed higher on his body, so the momentum he would use to get into a sitting position would more often than not carry him all the way over onto his back.

In the Summer of 1977, Mom and Thad were at a Little League baseball game watching some of us play. A man came over to Mom and asked her about Thad. They began a friendly conversation, and it turned out this man ran a program for infant early intervention at the West Texas Rehabilitation Center, which was located in downtown Abilene, not far from where we lived. The Center's goal was to help every child reach their maximum level of functional independence and provide support and education to their families. This man suggested that my parents bring Thad in to be evaluated, that perhaps they could help. So, in August, at 16 months old, Thad entered the ThrouTwo Program, which was designed to assist the developing brain and body through early stimulation using exercises and games. We were very fortunate that Thad became involved in outside education programs early on because it gave us many sets of outside eyes which helped him immensely and helped us as well.

The fact that the West Texas Rehabilitation Center was committed to providing support and education to the families was a real gift to my parents. Thad was their seventh child, so much of the terrain was familiar to them, such as caring for Thad's basic needs, protecting him, loving him, encouraging him, and taking joy in whatever sign of progress he made. Still, there was enough that was unfamiliar in this experience that they often felt adrift, even helpless. Feeling powerless to affect change inspired fervent prayer on the part of my parents. In fact, we were all praying as individuals and as a family to bless and take care of Thad, but even more, to help us know how to best help him. The day that man walked over to Mom at the baseball game was, in my mind, a direct answer to 15 months of prayers. Until that moment, aside from the assistance the physicians and medical teams close to Thad's case in Abilene and San Antonio ably provided, my parents were unaware of the resources that were available to them, especially so early in Thad's development.

Mom took Thad to the Center two times a week where the therapists worked with him for an hour or so. Then, one or two other days a week a therapist came to our home to work with him and my mom for another hour. The therapists used exercises and games that they taught my Mom, and she relayed to my Dad and to us. These were tools that we could use to assist in Thad's development. We were no longer helpless bystanders fumbling around and hoping for the best but participants in the process.

One afternoon when Mom was leaving the Center, she strapped Thad in his car seat and walked around to the driver's side. As she got into the car, she saw a man drive up in a pick-up truck. He pulled up to the door, stopped his car, and got out. He was a small man with greying hair, probably in his fifties. He walked around to the passenger side and gently lifted out a teenage boy who was about the size of a ten-year-old. Once the boy was out of the truck, the man adjusted his hold a little to make sure he was secure then carried the boy into the building for therapy. Mom was struck by the tenderness this man exuded as he carried his son, then the thought came, "There go I." It wasn't a sad thought, or an oppressive one, but it felt profound and weighted. At the time, Thad's life expectancy was still up in the air. There wasn't a real sense that he would make it for more than a few years. Still, she took in the moment, watching the doorway through which they'd disappeared, before starting the car and driving home.

In October of that year, when Thad was 18 months old, he successfully sat up on his own for the first time during a visit to Wilford Hall. Just as had happened at Dyess when he got up on his hands and knees, there was great jubilation on the pediatric floor. I don't know what the deal was, but Thad seemed to enjoy revealing his momentous accomplishments when he was away from home. Once again, Mom came home from a trip and said, "You won't guess what Thad did?" So, we had a sitting party to celebrate.

Sitting gave Thad a whole new experience. It changed his visual perspective from that of a reclining position where he always looking up unless someone was holding him in a vertical posture. In a similar way, it lifted his visual experience off the floor. He spent a lot of time sitting with a straight back and looking around. He became so confident that he would throw his head back behind him without falling over and bring it back up. He loved to do this when there was a bright light near him. He would shake his head back and up, catching the light in his eye and laugh.

Sitting also made his crib time more fun. He discovered that while sitting, he could rest his head on the bar that separated the oblong ball from the three-pronged spinning armature of his favorite toy that hung across the crib. This placed his eye pretty close to the clear ball so he could watch the smaller, colorful balls inside bounce around as he spun the clear ball for many minutes at a time. He would laugh, but there were times when he spun and watched and spun and watched like it was the most important thing in the whole world.

It was around this time when we happened upon another toy that rocked Thad's world. It was an elongated, white plastic cube with the top end narrower than the bottom, where a built-in red turntable allowed the toy to be spun. On each side of the cube there was some kind of activity. It had a mirror and a little thing that sprung back and forth behind a clear plastic cover. I don't remember the other two sides. The important thing to Thad, it seemed, was that it made a grinding, rattly sound as it spun, and the mirror would catch and flash light as it spun by. He would spin it on the floor, on the tray of his high chair, and in his bed. It would make him laugh, but again, he also took it very seriously. He concentrated as he watched it spin, and he could keep it spinning for a long time. Sometimes he would lie on his stomach, on a blanket on the floor, with his sewn eye toward the floor and stare with his good eye into the mirrored side of the toy, which he would move back and forth before spinning it some more.

This progress was heartening, but we still had to be aware of the fact that Thad's birth defect meant that his brain was not protected the way everyone else's brain was protected. Thad's medical teams at Dyess and at Wilford Hall were sort of scrambling because they could no longer place arbitrary limits on Thad's potential. If he was becoming mobile, they needed to find a way to protect his head. Soon, they took a mold of Thad's head and created a white, hard plastic helmet with a thin foam cushion layer on the inside. The plastic itself was not super thick, but it added weight to Thad's head which he had to get used to. There were holes drilled around the helmet to create some ventilation, but in the Texas heat, we noticed that it made his head really sweaty. He didn't seem to like it much. Still, we put the helmet on him when we were driving or when we were out and about in situations that were out of our control.

As he developed, Thad began to interact with us verbally. He liked to mimic sounds. If we slid our voice from a low pitch to a high pitch, he would repeat that. We would do that over and over. Eventually, he gained control of the game. He would slide up his voice and someone, whoever was closest, would copy him, and he would laugh. Then, it evolved into a slide up/slide down game. He would slide up and we would slide down or vice versa. He seemed to get a kick out of that game.

He also acquired a series of syllables that he liked to verbalize either singly or repeatedly: *da*, *aeh*, and *nnnn-nnna* were the most common. The exuberance with which he said the syllables was an indication to us about his level of enthusiasm. If he happened to be uncomfortable or unhappy, like when he had his helmet on, a lackluster and sometimes grating *aeh* would be all he could muster; but if he was excited or happy, he'd shoot out a long and loud series of *da* before falling into a fit of laughter.

Right around the time that Thad sat up for the first time, when he was 18 months old, on a bright Monday morning, as Mom picked Thad up out of his crib, he made his first *mama* sound. Mom burst into tears and covered his face with kisses. He kept surprising us. All of this movement forward bolstered our hope that he would persevere and continue to defy the original skepticism about his future. It helped us to feel like Thad's time on this earth was not in vain. In our eyes, each day that passed demonstrated the beauty and power of God's love.

As I culled through boxes of journals and letters and memorabilia in order to fine tune the details of Thad's story, I came across this beautiful letter that Mom wrote to Thad:

> November 11, 1977
>
> My dearest little Thad,
>
> I feel I must write you a letter tonight and express some of my thoughts and feelings that I have. You have been with us for almost 18 1/2

months and what you have taught me is immeasurable. These last few days I have been so filled with love and appreciation for you and I cannot imagine earth life here without your sweet presence in our home. Heavenly Father has allowed you to stay here so much longer than anyone ever expected, and from the beginning you have endeared us to you with the sweetness that you radiate to our family and everyone. My dearest babe, there is not a time that I hold you that I do not thank my Heavenly Father for you. You are beautiful to me and I love your sweet beautiful body and your little crooked head with your sweet wet mouth and sparkly eye. Your blond curls I love to touch and fluff up. Your bed has been in our bedroom close to me and your Daddy from the day I brought you home from the hospital when you were one month old. You are always close. I could wake in the night and hear you sleeping peacefully, or cooing and playing with your toys in the crib, or jump up suddenly to be with you when your seizures hurt and scared you and you would cry out.

This past month you have learned to sit up all by yourself and how beautiful you look sitting up straight and tall in your bed or on the floor, watching all the actions of the family, the pretty lights, or all the interesting things about. You want to communicate and your many *ma mmmmma, Da da da da da, eeeeah* sounds echo sweet sounds of love.

You never cease to amaze me at your ability to be happy constantly and how you find joy and contentment wherever you are. Only when you have been very sick have you been fussy and unhappy. You love to be held and carried around. However, when I must lay you down, you smile, roll over, play with your hands, watch and scratch...the pictures on your bumper pads, try playing with some crib toys, and better yet, chew and kick with your blanket. And you will entertain yourself for longer periods of time, but I love to peek in and pick you up and kiss and love you. Immediately you will bite my shoulder, and then put both hands in my hair and play with my hair.

Your hands are very expressive and I can read some of your feelings by how and what you do with your hands. From birth, you have watched your hands and they have been very expressive to us both. Your hands and fingers are long and slim, good for playing the piano.

Today while I was driving the thought was impressed upon my mind to be humble, meek, submissive, patient, long-suffering, full of love. We must become as a little child with these qualities in order to return to our Heavenly Father. For the last 18 months you have been my example of these qualities, qualities that I truly desire, but in the hustle of living have not been truly sensitive to, but you, dear, have opened my eyes and sensitized my understanding to what it truly means to be perfect in humility, patience, long-suffering, submissive, cheerful, and full of love, for you are all of these things and you have shown me how I must be. Accepting of all things, cheerful constantly and giving love at all times. You have given me understanding. Even though you are very young, you have shown me Christ's way. I thank you for this. I love you as a special blessing in my life. I am grateful that the Lord had allowed us this time together, my heart is eternally bound with love for you, and I pray I may be a worthy mother. I love your Daddy very much, and I love your older brothers each in their own special way and we all love and cherish you. If we could, perhaps we would change your deformity to perfection. However, at this time it isn't in the plan, and besides, you're beautiful as you are.

I have learned to live one day at a time and have faith in the future. I pray that the future will be bright for all of us. You have been doing so well from the beginning of your turn on earth, with just enough problems to keep me realizing how delicate this earth life is. With your suffering my appreciation and love for you and your brothers has grown a hundred-fold. Earth life is a precious gift and must be used wisely and happily, keeping our eyes on the "eternal goal."

I love you dear one. You are sleeping so peacefully now. I would like to pick you up and hug you again before I sleep.

Thank you for being my loving teacher.
Mother

In spite of all the progress Thad was making, his limitations were real. They were pervasive, and we continued to learn about them as he grew. With a birth defect involving the brain, seizures are not an uncommon occurrence since they are the result of abnormal electrical activity in the brain. Like most people, when Thad came into our lives, we were vaguely aware of only one kind of seizure, the Grand Mal, but we soon learned that there are many different kinds of seizures. Sometimes, Thad would just disappear behind his eye for a few moments before resuming whatever he was doing. Other times, his eye would start to quiver and his lips would move randomly but it would seem like he was totally present and involved, almost conversation-like, with whatever was going on in his head. Then, there were the times when Thad would look like he was concentrating really hard before exploding into an uncontrolled profusion of laughter, mixed with a very loud machine-gun delivery of his favorite syllables and sounds. This type of seizure was particularly surprising and funny when it happened in the middle of a church service. It was often accompanied by the shaking of his head to the left side and the quivering of his hands which were often drawn in close to his body.

And, of course, there was the Grand Mal. Thad's whole body would stiffen. His head would turn severely to the upper left. It would be like he was taking in a very long, deep breath, then his body would erupt into erratic shaking and jerking. Sometimes it was more contained, but other times it was like every single muscle in his body came to a dance party hopped up on amphetamines without any sense of rhythm or coordination. They never lasted more than a few minutes, thankfully, and afterwards he would fall into a deep sleep. Grand Mal seizures are like earthquakes because they come out of nowhere; they don't last for more than a few minutes; they are violent; and everyone involved, whether the person having the seizure or the people around them, is powerless and must wait it out. Those witnessing a seizure must do their best to prevent lasting damage or injury.

Because Thad was either strapped into his wheelchair or lying on a bed or floor surrounded by pillows, his seizures rarely posed any imminent harm. Nevertheless, because they came out of nowhere, there were times when he'd start a seizure just as someone put food in his mouth, and it was all we could do to try to get the food out in order to prevent him from choking. The other precarious times were when we were showering him or bathing him. From very early on, Dad took Thad into the shower with him, then handed him off to Mom or whoever was there to get Thad dressed before continuing his own shower. It was so much easier than getting Thad in and out of a bathtub. But, holding a very slippery body with one arm while scrubbing him off with soap, and shampooing his hair with the other hand, it was really scary if he started to shake uncontrollably. Bath seizures were no less scary, just less slippery.

Thad started having seizures very early. On his trip to Boston in January, Dr. Shillito prescribed Phenobarbital and Clonazapan to help mediate Thad's seizures. His first seizures caused him to tense up and then stop breathing. Just as he was turning blue, his breathing would start up again. It's no wonder Mom was terrified that she would come into a room one day and find that he had passed away without anybody around. This is why, "Mom, Thad is breathing!" became a common refrain in our house.

Autumn was not a pretty time in West Texas. What trees there were just dropped their dead leaves onto the brown and yellow grass without any fanfare of color. If an artist chose to paint Abilene in October, the title of the painting could only be "A Study in Brown." One Autumn Sunday that year, we were at church in the chapel attending Sacrament Meeting, the main Sunday meeting. My dad was sitting up on the stand behind the pulpit since he was the first counselor in the bishopric. All of us were sitting in a pew about halfway down the aisle from the front with Mom, who was holding Thad. Six kids and a mom took up most of the pew. I sat next to Mom in the middle of the pew. Thad started to have one of these tense body seizures, so Mom just held him and waited for his breathing to start again as it always had. Then, she leaned over to me and said, "Tim, go get your Father." I stood up and made my way out of the pew to the right, and Mom stood up and made her way out of the pew to the left which was closer to the exit into the foyer. I didn't really know what was going on, but I felt very important walking up to the stand in front of the whole congregation in the middle of the meeting. I told Dad that Mom needed him outside. Dad practically ran out of the chapel without actually running or seeming too distressed. I followed him out. One of the other members of the bishopric came out with us as well. This was serious.

As I walked through the doors into the foyer behind my dad, I saw Mom standing there weeping as she tried to blow air into Thad's lungs. She was distraught. Thad was blue and limp. Dad took Thad into his arms and Mom kept saying, "I can't get him to breathe! I can't get him to breathe!" Mom was never a stoic person, but the depth of her anguish in this moment terrified me. They rushed Thad out the door to take him to a nearby hospital, and I was left alone in the foyer looking through the glass door to the parking lot as my parents drove away, not knowing if I would ever see Thad alive again.

Thad had been with us for over a year and although we talked about the precarious nature of his existence and the possibility that he might not live very long, I didn't know until that very moment the weight of what that all meant. The reality of losing him landed on my soul like a ton of black tar. Equally troubling was the fact that I knew that if Thad passed away, Mom would be devastated in profound and irretrievable ways.

JUST KICK

Thad didn't pass away that October Sunday. Dad called the church from the hospital and let us know that everything was ok. Someone from the ward brought us to their house for dinner after the service, and Mom and Dad picked us up on their way home. Mom recounted that experience to her parents in a letter:

> Thad is doing so well and is so happy. His spasms are still happening though and Sunday at church his breathing stopped again. I rushed out and Tim went up and got Tom so Tom was able to help this time. It is such a helpless situation as he seems to revive on his own and our efforts are secondary. When all the emergency is over, he gives me one of his big grins and sighs as if to say, "It's over and I'm alright, Mom!

Those initial seizures where he stopped breathing didn't happen much after that. He did have similar seizures where he would stiffen and seem like he was holding his breath, but that was a completely different nuance. We'd just talk to him calmly, caress his arm or his head and encourage him to let go and breathe again. Thad started taking Phenobarbital that first year and never stopped taking it. When necessary, there were other anti-convulsive medications prescribed as different types of seizures manifested themselves. He finally seemed to respond best to a cocktail of Phenobarbital, Carbamazepine, and Valproic Acid. The dosage was maintained at a level just shy of too much, and he still had between 4 and 8 seizures of one kind or another, per day.

Given the delicate nature of Thad's birth defect, his propensity toward seizures, and his reliance on full-time care, another reality for my parents was that it was very difficult to find anyone who could babysit Thad. Since our family was large and each of us was involved in many outside activities, that meant Thad could either come along or stay at home with someone who wasn't involved in that specific activity.

Transporting Thad was relatively easy in the beginning. We would just put his helmet on, strap him into a car seat and go. The doctors made adjustments to

Thad's helmet as he grew, since the helmet conformed tightly to his head. He went through three helmets that first year. After that, it became apparent that Thad was impressively self-aware. When he was crawling around or sitting, he was conscientious about how he held and placed his head. His balance was impeccable. Thad's medical team decided that the helmet was superfluous. If, in the future, Thad started to walk and became more active, other protective alternatives could be researched or developed; but, for the time being, Thad was helmet-free.

In going out and about, we never really worried about what people would think or how they would respond to seeing Thad. But we needed to consider where the activity was taking place. Would this be a safe environment for Thad? Would it be easy to get around once we got there? Was there any obvious danger toward his head during the activity? If the activity were outside, what was the temperature going to be like, and would there be shade? Thad was very sensitive to heat, and he would lose energy and get dehydrated very quickly. We would also need to consider if Thad's presence at the event (i.e., his chattering or possible loud seizures) might detract from the ambiance of the event. If so, someone stayed home with Thad or we found a place to sit that was close to an exit.

We had a fold-up stroller that we'd carry in the trunk of the car that was easy to set-up and to push around. When we brought Thad with us to Little League baseball games, church activities, choir or band concerts, birthday parties, or whatever public event we were involved in, his eye would brighten, he'd have a big smile, and he'd use the back of his hand to articulate the air or the sound coming out of his mouth, leading to a chuckle or a laugh. Thad loved being around people and activity, so getting him out into the world of our activities was very important.

Now, after almost two years, we were finally settling into the idea that there were no more predictions about the length of Thad's life. He could live for years, or he could die tomorrow. There was no way to tell. So, when we looked into the future, Thad was a part of it. It was the reality we had been hoping for, because now, we could look into the future without large scale trepidation. This didn't negate the nagging possibility that we could wake up one morning and Thad would be gone, but that likelihood was smaller now, so it became a background voice in our lives rather than a lead singer.

The adjustments we made as a family to accommodate Thad's special needs weren't such a big deal in the grand scheme of things, but Dad's career hung in the balance. The nature of a career in the United States Air Force as a pilot involved going wherever they deemed your services necessary, for however long they deemed them necessary, either with or without your family in tow. At the beginning of his career and marriage, that meant more time in Greenland, then home in Texas or Alaska, a full year in Vietnam, and plenty of three to four month tours all over the world. We moved practically every 18 months to two years. Each assignment brought more experience and more exposure for my father. Certain assignments were clearly stepping stones for promotion to higher ranks, while others were less so.

Dad wanted a successful career. He was in the third graduating class from the Air Force Academy in Colorado Springs, Colorado. He loved flying. He loved the challenge of being an effective leader. The Air Force was a perfect career for him. Nevertheless, he wasn't one to wear blinders. Around 1972, he was given an opportunity to be an assistant gymnastics and wrestling coach at the Air Force Academy. He took it because he thought it would be fun for him and for the family. My first memories are from this time in Colorado. He was right. We had a great time.

Every other assignment was designed to advance his career, moving Dad forward rank by rank, toward a successful military career. The rank of General seemed not only possible, but maybe even likely. Since Dad was at the mercy of where the opportunities arose, the choices that he and Mom had to make were less about which assignment to take, and more about which neighborhoods in the new area that fell within their budget had the best public schools. They made tremendous efforts to create a positive, supportive environment in our home, believing that if we felt safe and secure, we could adapt to wherever we ended up living. Family was the home base.

Once Thad was born, though, other considerations came into play. What were the hospitals like? Were there physicians who understood neurotubular birth defects? Were there appropriate physical therapy departments in the hospital? What was the availability of programs for special needs children either on the base or off? It was a lot to consider. I remember conversations between my parents about certain possible assignments and whether they would be viable options given Thad's needs. Dad's career advancement took second place. That's not to say he wasn't given wonderful opportunities, but his career did slow down, and the likelihood of making General moved further and further away.

We moved to Montgomery, Alabama in the Summer of 1978 so that Dad could attend Air War College. A railroad track lay just beyond the chain link fence at the edge of our backyard. Our house was located three houses down from a road that crossed the railroad track, which meant that the trains sounded their horns as soon as they reached our backyard. Troy and Trent were rambunctious 4-year olds at this time. One day, right after we moved in, they heard a train coming, so they ran out to the chain link fence to watch the train go by—little boys and trains! They climbed up the fence right next to each other and held onto the top bar. When the train reached our yard, the horn bellowed, and I guess it was louder than they'd imagined because they both covered their ears with their hands and fell off the fence backward.

All along the railroad tracks and the cement culverts in our neighborhood grew wild blackberry bushes. I don't know how long blackberry season was, but Todd, Thomas, and I had a great time walking on the big, loosely piled rocks that created the base for the railroad track, climbing up and down the slanted cement walls of the drainage ditches which seemed huge to us, and picking buckets full of large, ripe, fresh blackberries. We brought them home to Mom, who was horrified by our adventure because apparently there were lots of poisonous snakes in the area, and we were traipsing around in their territory sticking our hands into and around bushes without a care in the world. That didn't stop her from making fresh blackberry pie, though. I remember being surprised and delighted that you could make a pie out of blackberries. We'd also cut the berries up and put them on vanilla ice cream or just by themselves in a bowl sprinkled with a little bit of sugar. It's an amazing feeling eating something you've made an effort to procure yourself. But mostly it was the adventure of harvesting the berries along the railroad tracks and up and down the culverts with Todd and Thomas that made the experience memorable especially since there wasn't much else that was memorable about Montgomery, Alabama for a 6th grader in 1978.

Thad was two, and he was crawling and sitting and crawling some more. It was hard to keep him still. He would crawl all the way across the room to get to where his toys were. He loved his toys, and he took them very seriously. He played so much with his favorite spinning toy, that we had already had to replace it twice. Our house had a long living room just to the right of the entrance way with tall windows that faced the front yard. In the afternoon, light would stream into the living room making long sectioned squares of light on the pale beige shag carpeting. Thad loved to be in this room at that time of day. He would crawl over and sit in the shafts of light, swinging his head back and forth behind him so that his eye caught the light as it moved around him.

As Thad's teeth came in, it became apparent that although it wasn't visible from the outside, his facial bones were affected by the birth defect. His jaw was formed in such a way that when his back teeth touched, his front teeth were still far apart. This made closing his mouth and chewing impossible. As a result, he never graduated to eating food that wasn't pureed. He had a very high palate, and he would mash the food against it with his tongue working it back so that he could swallow. He would eat the same food we were eating; we'd just stick it in a blender for him. We fed him a lot of bananas because they were easy to mash up, especially when we needed to give him his Phenobarbital and other anti-seizure medicine that came in pill form. We'd crush the pills and mix them into the banana mash.

Keeping Thad hydrated was not an easy task, and one that we had to be vigilant of because he wasn't able to drink well. His sucking response had never been very strong, then as we started giving him water with a glass, the structure of his jaw prevented him from closing his mouth and made drinking problematic. We'd put a towel around his upper torso, incline his head a bit then gently pour water or juice or whatever into the lower part of his mouth. He'd sort of let it run back down his throat with only a little tongue movement, but much of what we poured into his mouth ended up on the towel because he didn't know how to use his bottom lip to keep the liquid in his mouth. Often, no matter how careful we were being, he would choke and cough because the water went back too fast or there was too much at one time. It was hard to know how much fluid we were actually getting into him. In addition to using cups, we tried using a spray bottle as well as a large needle-less syringe because it allowed us to be more specific about where the water went. Thad did not enjoy the drinking ritual, and he would move his head back and forth and close his mouth tightly as best he could to avoid it, covering what he couldn't close with the back of his hand. So, we'd have to gently hold his head still, talk to him nicely, and coax his jaw to relax by stroking the muscles on the sides. This way we could get as much water into him as possible. Drinking was not something that Thad ever mastered, but it was one of those necessary struggles. We began to notice that his head would go through phases of firmness and, though this is purely anecdotal and non-scientific, we started to use that as a gauge for Thad's level of hydration. In our minds, the firm brain was the healthy brain, and the softer brain needed water.

Because of our previous experience with the West Texas Rehabilitation Center, one of the first things that Mom and Dad researched before moving were physical therapy and developmental programs for disabled children. It was here, in Alabama, that Thad learned to stand for the first time. The therapist working with Thad would help him stand, and when he tried to squat she would pinch his butt which would make him stand up again. "You don't pinch him hard, and he's wearing a diaper" she would tell my mom, "but all you mothers are alike. You just can't do that." And she would laugh.

I remember seeing Thad stand for the first time holding onto Mom's hands. We were in the den by the kitchen where most of our family activities happened: Family Night on Monday evenings, scripture reading before school, TV time, family prayers in the morning and evening. It was the comfortable room. Mom stood in the open doorway that led to the kitchen and dining alcove. The door to the backyard was to her right. Thad sat on the floor in front of her. She said, "Are you ready, Thad?" then held onto his hands and helped him stand. He did it! He was a little wobbly, but he was doing it. He was standing and smiling. We couldn't believe it! We cheered and clapped and jumped up and down. We hugged each other. Knowing my family, we probably got so excited we started running around the house like excited Jack Russell terriers. We got a standing board that

Mom could lean against a bed. She would place toys on the bed, and he would play while he stood. Mom would stay close by to make sure he didn't fall, but he got really good and could stay on the board up to 20 minutes at a time. It was a great exercise for balance and weight-bearing and for developing core muscle strength. Incidentally, my mom wasn't afraid to pinch his butt.

Around this time, my parents started to wonder if they should have any more children. "Seven was plenty!" they'd say, but they couldn't shake the feeling that there were a few more spirits waiting to join our family. Mom was now 36 years old, so if this were going to happen, their timeline was getting short. There are health concerns for mother and child once a woman passes 35 years old, but my parent's biggest concern, and this was echoed by their doctors, was the possibility that any new children could have similar birth defects as Thad. Neural tube defects, the general category of brain and spinal cord deformities which includes encephaloceles, happen in 3,000 pregnancies each year in the U.S. If 6 million pregnancies happen each year in the U.S., the odds of having a child with a neural tube defect is 1 in 2000. However, if a couple already has one child with an neural tube defect, their chances of having another rise to 4 in 100. My parents were not blind to the risks, so they did what they always did in the face of important decisions: they made it a matter of fasting and prayer.

Whether or not my parents had more children was not a matter of discussion in the family. I don't remember having any family councils to discuss the whys and wherefores nor the pros and cons. This was a decision that only my parents could make. We were young, and I think if they had asked us, we would have said, "Yay! Let's have another baby!" I agree with what Thomas said a few years ago, "Being young, I thought God said, 'Bing, you're pregnant! Time for you to have a kid!' If God sent us a handicapped child that's alright. If he wants to send us more, that's fine, too." We didn't know what it meant to financially support a family. Nor did we understand the weight of responsibility a parent feels when considering each individual child and their future. Add onto that the Russian roulette nature of birth defects, to which we were totally oblivious, and it seems pretty clear that our input might not have helped very much.

This part of the story is not mine to tell in any detail because it didn't happen to me directly, and it is deeply personal to my parents. The bare facts are that my parents spent time thinking about it, studying the risks, asking advice from trusted friends, family members and physicians, and, most importantly to them, periodically fasting and constantly praying. Finally, Mom felt secure in her feelings that they should try to get pregnant again. It was in no way a blithe decision. Mom was certain that this was the right decision.

On May 19, 1979, a beautiful, petite, curly, blonde-headed girl came into our family. Mom was concerned that our first, and probably only, sister would feel left out or separate from the family if she didn't have a name that started with T, but Dad had always wanted a daughter named Lara (short for my mom's name) Lee (my dad's middle name). Dad won. Lara Lee filled our house with incredible excitement and life. *We had a sister*! It was fun to hold her and dress her in frilly dresses and stick bows or lacy headbands on her head. Lara had a quiet energy. Her big, blue eyes took everything in. At the same time, she was blessed with a powerful set of lungs. She could certainly make herself known if she needed anything. One day, while I was babysitting, Lara started to cry. I fed her and changed her diaper, but she was still unhappy. I walked around the house holding her, trying to soothe her by singing and dancing, things that had been successful many times before, but not that day. Finally, I thought I might as well finish my chores, so while holding a screaming Lara in my right arm, I started to vacuum the hallway and living room with my left. Before I knew it, Lara calmed down and fell asleep. I often wondered if Mom was ever curious as to why the house was always freshly vacuumed whenever it was my turn to babysit.

Mom smoothly incorporated Lara's routines with Thad's. They were always together, rolling around on the floor together, playing with the same toys. Thad liked the companionship.

We were only in Alabama for a year before moving back to Abilene, Texas. We did not move onto the base where we lived before, but my dad found a house on Meadowbrook Lane in a residential neighborhood about a mile away from our church. I was starting 7th grade at Mann Junior High. I joined the swim team and the concert band, where I started learning to play the trombone because bassoons weren't an option. Some paper routes opened up in our neighborhood, so Tony, Todd, and I were able to earn our own money delivering the *Abilene Reporter News* in the morning and afternoon as well as the weekends. Having our own money was great, but waking up at 5 a.m. to roll and deliver papers regardless of the weather was kind of torturous for me. Actually, it was probably more torturous for Tony, Todd, and Mom since I was neither the happiest nor the most effective person at that time of morning.

Todd was always the first one up. He and Mom would bring in the stacks of papers and start rolling them. Tony was up and rolling papers as soon as they hit the living room floor. I would arrive in time to start carrying stacks of rolled papers out to the car. We had three routes that comprised most of our outlying neighborhood. On Sunday mornings we delivered over 500 newspapers. Initially Mom or Dad (when he was in town) would drive, and we'd stand out the back of our Chrysler station wagon with a stack of papers on the roof listening closely for instructions from the person in charge of the customer list, "Throw, throw, skip, skip, throw...no, not there!"

Some time in November of '79, Mom started to show signs of the first trimester blues. When the pregnancy was confirmed, my parents petitioned the Texas Department of Public Safety for Tony to get his driver's license a year early. Dad's new job meant he was back to being gone for weeks, sometimes months, at a time. Mom was very sick, and was likely to be so for a few months. We had a large paper throwing business. It couldn't be effectively done on foot or on a bike. Fortunately, the Texas Department of Public Safety agreed that the family would benefit from Tony having a driver's license. Tony was stoked, and because of his responsible personality, he was a great paper route/errand/activity driver.

I had a fairly successful elementary school experience. In the one-teacher-all-day format, I was confident, competent, and well-rounded. The familiarity and reliability of the experience made for a safe environment. I got along with my teachers because I was an enthusiastic, outgoing kid who liked to learn and loved to help. Plus, the activities that we did in school, even during recess, fell within my skill set. The fact that I was a late bloomer when it came to hand-eye coordination didn't affect me too much during school hours.

This changed when I entered junior high school. I was excited to change classrooms and teachers every hour because that's what my older brothers had been doing, and it felt very grown up. But I wasn't able to establish a significant connection with any of my teachers, so I didn't have the adult support that I was accustomed to. Plus, I had to do Physical Education class, which meant doing all the sports that intimidated me and made me look incompetent and clumsy in front of my classmates. That was not fun. To top it all off, I was a new kid in school, so I didn't have a history with anyone there. The judgments they made about me were purely based on what they saw—the skinny red-headed kid who liked music but couldn't throw a ball to save his life. In the general population of Mann Junior High, what happened in PE class was more indicative of someone's identity or someone's worth than any other aspect of the school day experience. That was the harsh reality I was up against. That was junior high school.

One afternoon early in the year as I was leaving the band building, I pushed the door with my back and rotated toward the front as the door opened. My arm swung around as I turned, landing my hand squarely on the breast of an eighth grade smoker chick whom I had not seen because I went through the door backwards. I was mortified and befuddled. I profusely apologized for touching her breast before scurrying off to wherever I had been going. Before the day was out, the whole school was talking about the red-headed band kid who was obviously gay, because what pre-teen boy would apologize for touching a girl's breast? All the doubts about my masculinity created in PE class were now certain in the minds of the junior high populace. I didn't really know what "gay" meant, but based on the tone with which it was spoken, it was clearly a deplorable thing, and the label stuck.

At the same time, I was entering puberty. The truth is I wasn't interested in girls in the same way my peers were. I liked them. Most of my friends were girls. But, I wasn't fascinated by them. I wasn't interested in boys either. I was neutral when it came to real live people. But I had a huge crush on Robert Urich, who played the dashing Vietnam vet turned private eye, Dan Tanna, on the ABC series VEGA$. He was attractive and friendly. He had dark hair and he wore his shirts unbuttoned low enough to see a hint of his strong pecs and the hair that covered them. I practically swooned when they showed him walking toward the camera in slow motion. Robert Urich was everything I was not, so I practiced walking like him in slow motion. I also started unbuttoning my shirts one or two buttons further down than before in the hopes that it would reveal something more than a pasty white ribcage. Dad kindly pulled me aside one day when he noticed my new fashion choice. He put his arm around my shoulders and said, "Tim, some men like to wear their shirts like that because they have hair on their chest. You might get there in a few years, and you can do whatever you want; but, for now, can you please button your shirt?" He didn't say anything about the way I was walking, so maybe I was more successful in that department.

Thad was turning four in the Spring of 1980. All of her other children had looked forward to starting kindergarten around that age, so Mom started researching what school options were available to a child with multiple handicaps. Thad's physical therapy at the West Texas Rehabilitation Center was progressing. He was still using the standing board regularly and doing very well, but that was a one-on-one experience. There was something to be said for getting out of the house for a period of time each day and participating in activities with other children. Mom wrote this note down on a piece of paper dated March 9, 1980:

> We went through an interview with the education board to review if Thad can enter the education stimulation program for multiple handicapped children. If Thad is to learn some things, it seems to me that he needs lots of stimulation and direction. I notice at times that he is bored and that is why he swings his head etc. so much.

Thad didn't enter a program in the education system that year but continued to be helped through the efforts of the therapists at the West Texas Rehabilitation Center. In a letter to her mother, Mom wrote, "Every now and then Thad will come out with "bye bye" when I say bye bye and also "ma ma." He does enjoy the interchange of conversation even though I am not sure of what we are talking about at times, but he laughs a lot, so it must be a pretty good joke."

It was evident that developmental stages were taking place, but Thad's ability to speak was not materializing. As he grew, he continued to use the initial percussive syllables and tone games he started early on. Still, it was apparent that he understood certain phrases. We could ask him, "Are you hungry?" and he would laugh if he was hungry or grunt if he wasn't hungry. Although we never knew for certain how much he understood, over the years we became accustomed to his signals, and we were able to assign meaning to them based on their context. He could communicate when he was happy, sad, hungry, uncomfortable, or content. He never used words, but he was very social and liked to interact with people. That was one of his special gifts. He was able to communicate that he was present and aware of the people around him and of his surroundings.

Our affiliation with the West Texas Rehabilitation Center was something that had an impact on me because in the Summer between my 7th and 8th grade years, I did some volunteer work in the therapy pool helping children with Cerebral Palsy. I would hold them up in the water as we went through exercises to stimulate the neural pathways through their whole body in a weightless environment. My job was all about helping them float and encouraging them.

There was one boy in particular whose smile and energy impressed me deeply. I don't remember his name, but I do remember that he would enthusiastically come into the pool area on the kind of crutches that hooked around his forearms. I would hold him so that he was floating on his back in the warm water of the large therapeutic pool. I would say, "Ok, now, whenever you are ready, just kick! Try to push me to the other side of the pool! That's it, kick!" He would kick with all the passion he could muster. "You're doing great! That's fantastic! Keep going!" The smile that filled his face and the light that sparkled in his eyes broke my heart and elevated it at the same time.

Just as Thad's birth created opportunities for my mother to share in the heart-breaking and often inspiring stories of people she had thought she knew well, having Thad in our daily lives opened the doors of our experience to other children with disabilities and their families. We didn't form families of disabled children support groups, but our circles touched, our paths crossed, and we learned and were enriched in the exchange. In the case of this young boy in the pool, I thought a lot about his gusto and whole-hearted commitment to the simple act of kicking his feet in water. He wasn't concerned about how perfect he was at it, but only that he was trying. I wasn't concerned that he was swimming perfectly, but only that he was taking pleasure in being joyfully weightless in the water.

It was a lesson that was difficult for me to internalize, though. I was constantly afraid that I didn't measure up. Could it be that in each moment of my life, kicking *my* legs was all that mattered? Was it possible that listening to the voices of encouragement and believing them was enough to lift the burden of self-doubt and allow me float weightless and free? I could see it in other people. I could desire it for them. But, I was not sure that I qualified for the same consideration.

It was a great Summer for me, and toward the end of it our family welcomed another member. On August 4, 1980, Travis Jared was born with bright red hair, and big, mischievous, blue eyes—more excitement, more life. I was pleased because until that moment, I'd been the only red-head in the family. I was actually a strawberry blonde. Travis was a true red-head. He and Thad became best buds! It was fun to hear them hold long conversations based on the syllable *da* as they shared Thad's spinning toy or rattles and crawled around the living room floor. At the same time, Lara was toddling all over the house, and her maternal instincts were becoming apparent as she insisted on helping to dress and feed Thad and Travis.

That year, a performing group from Brigham Young University called The Young Ambassadors came through Abilene. They performed on a Saturday night in a theatre at one of the colleges in town. It was a wonderful show full of dancing and singing and big smiles you could see from the back row. I was mesmerized. Just like the Osmonds, they were Mormon like me, and they were really cool. I got as many autographs on my program as I could. Because they performed on a Saturday night, they stayed over and came to our church meetings the next day. I glommed onto some of the performers. I sat next to them during Sacrament Meeting. I talked to them as much as I could. We had two of them over for dinner after church, then we went back to the chapel to attend a Fireside that they had prepared. There was more singing, but it was churchy music and some talks about love and other things. I was moved by the whole experience, but what sealed the deal was that they sang a harmony-laden version of "He Ain't Heavy, He's My Brother" to finish off the fireside. I thought to myself, "I want to be one of them!" I became pen pals with two of the female performers, and we traded letters for a few months.

We didn't stay in Abilene for long the second time around, only about a year and a half. We moved to Southern Illinois in the Spring of 1981 for the last three months of my 8th grade year. This was the only time we ever moved during a school year. I was happy to leave Texas, though. The Mann Junior High School experience had not improved. Outwardly, I remained confident and gregarious. I was even awarded the Horace Mann Award at the end of my seventh grade year for being an outstanding student. Still, the prevailing attitude toward me by my classmates was insidious, and I allowed it to chip away at my already tenuous self-esteem.

I breathed a sigh of relief when we left Texas behind. There were challenges to moving frequently, but the opportunity to start fresh in a place where nobody knew me outweighed everything. I was certain people would like me right away in my new school. No one would talk or snicker at me behind my back but within earshot. I was still me, though, and whatever that meant triggered the same response at my new middle school. It was rough, but it ended pretty quickly, and Summer came.

I had my first girlfriend that Summer. She was a nice girl from church, and it was fun to do things together, to be friends who held hands. Technically, I couldn't date until I was 16, but having a special friend with whom I liked to hang out was ok as long as we never hung out alone. That was fine with me. I liked being with her, and I enjoyed holding hands, but that was where my impulses ended. As Summer came to a close, she broke up with me. I found out later that she had wanted me to kiss her, but since I never tried, she thought it best to break up. All I had to do was kiss her, and we could have stayed together. But, the thought never even crossed my mind.

The O'Fallon Township High School marching band boot camp started a few weeks before the school year began. I was excited to start because Todd was in the band, too. He was an accomplished percussionist in the drum corp. Having Todd there made me feel safe and confident because we were brothers. Our bond was solid. To say that marching band was a big deal in O'Fallon, Illinois was a serious understatement. Marching band was everything. The stands at football games diminished by at least half after the halftime presentation. Our band travelled all over the state competing with other high school bands. We had a solid and well-deserved reputation thanks to the tireless efforts of our band director, Mr. Cosmano.

Marching band boot camp was exhausting. We spent all day every day in the late Summer sun learning music, perfecting our marching skills, and learning the halftime routine. Despite the grueling schedule, I was in heaven. This was stuff that I could do, and I was surrounded by people who enjoyed it as much as I did. We not only enjoyed it, we took pride in it. I focused my attention on becoming the best marcher and player I could be. As a matter of fact, one morning as we marched out to the practice field in formation, I was concentrating so hard on staring ahead through my trombone which I was holding parallel to my body, while at the same time staying perfectly in line with the people beside me and in front of me, that I walked right into a telephone pole that everyone else had walked around. I bent my trombone bell, which wasn't a good thing, and I got a good ribbing from the upperclassmen, but I laughed it off and moved on.

When school started, it wasn't only band that kept me occupied. I joined the choir, the swing choir, the speech and debate team, the madrigal brass, and the math club. I made it into the Fall play and the Spring musical. My extracurricular activities were so numerous that I rarely got home before bedtime, then I would have to do homework. I was not old enough to drive, yet, and we lived 20 minutes outside of O'Fallon in the middle of farms and woods, so I was dependent on Tony, Todd, Mom, and Dad to pick me up at the end of my day. Oftentimes, they were coming home from other activities and went out of their way to swing by the high school where I would be sitting on the curb in the dark under a street light doing homework, but sometimes it meant a trip specifically into town to pick me up. They were all generous with their time. No one ever complained, at least not to me.

One of the nice things about having to drive everywhere was that we were able to talk to each other. Tony, Todd, and I spent a lot of time in the cab of our brown pickup truck (which had belonged to our Grandpa Sutton's contracting business) driving the back country roads of Southern Illinois. We got to know each other better. The radio didn't work, so when we ran out of things to talk about, we'd sing. My dad was a big fan of The Four Freshmen, the Lettermen, and other male trios and quartets from the 60s. He'd sung in similar groups during high school and college and really loved the camaraderie that was born when singing tight harmonies. He wanted to create and nurture that kind of relationship with us, so we started singing together early, beginning with hymns. As our voices changed and we could actually swing tenor, baritone, and bass lines, we delved into barbershop quartets and all kinds of choral and group music. That tradition of standing around the piano with whomever happened to be home one or two nights a week for an hour or so singing together carried over into our driving time. Dad was right, singing did bring us together. It was a camaraderie that we felt even with our youngest siblings who joined in as soon as they could and Thad, who couldn't sing with us, but who was always in the room sitting in his chair enjoying it all.

Apparently, God wanted us to have another soprano. On May 12, 1982, several months before my mom's 40th birthday, Lesa Carol was born, another bright redhead with cheerful, blue eyes and a lovely, buoyant personality. We couldn't have been happier. Lesa fit right into our life. Thad was happy to have another floormate. Lara was walking and talking. Travis was toddling and finding new words every day. It was fascinating to us to see the nonplussed beauty of the relationship Thad had with the youngest three. Thad was a part of their lives from the very beginning. As an adult, Lesa observed, "I thought everybody had a Thad!"

Lesa was born just a month before Tony graduated from high school. We spent the Summer together, then he left for college at Brigham Young University. Our family began to dwindle just moments after becoming complete.

As Tony was leaving, Todd and I were throwing ourselves into band camp again. I liked high school because it was a different experience from junior high. I was maturing, and I was involved in activities that boosted and supported my confidence. Even so, life outside the music building, within the general population, hadn't changed much. I put up with my share of name calling, whispers behind my back just loud enough for me to hear, disparaging notes in my locker, aggressive attacks and coarse, derisive language—all the while trying to be outgoing, happy, friendly, and normal.

My sophomore year started out as the roughest year in my whole twelve years of school. The bullies seemed to have multiplied, and I couldn't get away from them. I wasn't a small kid, but I felt small. I wasn't a weak kid, but I felt weak. However horrible they thought I was, I felt even more horrible about myself. I was incapable of standing up for myself because I thought they were right and that in some way I deserved the abuse I was getting.

One day in the Fall during gym class, we were playing soccer. I was excited about this activity because I was a good runner. I felt like I could keep up with everyone else and that I might even have been able to excel. I was playing a defensive position back near the goal, trying my best to be a vital and successful part of the game. I noticed that I was getting kicked a lot when everyone was near our goal. I thought, *It's a kicking game, Tim. You're going to get kicked.*

There were two games going that day. Things changed when the gym teacher went to the other field to watch. Then, it didn't matter where the ball was on the field, players from both teams would run by and kick me—one after another after another. I finally broke. When the gym teacher came back to our field, I walked over to him, opened my mouth to tell him what was happening, but sobs were the only thing that came out, which didn't help my cause in his eyes. Unable to explain myself through the tears, I left, and I went straight to the guidance counselor to drop out of gym class for good, even if it meant that I would never graduate from high school.

I explained to the counselor what had happened not only that day but all days. I wish that I remembered her name because her visceral, honest indignation at what I was saying surprised me. She said that I could transfer out of P.E., but only after she had a chance to talk to the boys that were perpetrating and perpetuating the bullying. She was furious. I don't know what she said to them. I did not transfer out of P.E., but no one—I mean, *no one*—ever bothered me the rest of that whole year. Not everyone develops at the same rate. Very few teen-agers are ready to stand up for themselves when they feel isolated and threatened. Most adults are ill-equipped to stand up for themselves under those circumstances. The only way I could stand up for myself at that time in my life was to put my trust in a guidance counselor, and I will be forever grateful that she stood up for me.

Every time we moved, the new location was hard on some of us and just perfect for others. We moved so often that it balanced out over the years. Each one of us got a few places that seemed to be custom-designed for what we needed at the time. Illinois was one for those places for Thad. He got accepted into a program at the Mamie O. Stookey School in Belleville, Illinois which was about a 30 to 40 minute drive from where we lived. A small school bus would come and pick Thad up every day and deliver him home again at the end of the day, much to the chagrin of our neighbors who were persnickety about the movement of the rocks on their portion of our shared gravel driveway.

The Mamie O. Stookey School specialized in education for children with developmental delays and multiple handicaps. It was a non-sectarian school and kept its enrollment low in order to maintain a small class size so that they could give each child the attention they needed. Each class was led by a special education teacher, but there was a team of interdisciplinary therapists to help create and meet realistic goals for each child. Mom wrote, "His school is so great for him. It is fun just to go up there and meet his teachers and friends... [T]hey do such fun things for him, it just thrills me that he has such good teachers. We are being so blest!"

Another wonderful thing about the Mamie O.

Stookey School is that Mom could go in and volunteer during the classes. It gave her first-hand experience in this new part of the education process for Thad. Because it was a school, the scope of the activities was different from what she had experienced at the West Texas Rehabilitation Center, where physical and occupational therapies were the main focus. Mom could understand why Thad liked it so much since it complemented his social nature, and it wasn't uncomfortable the way physical therapy could sometimes be. In this environment, education and physical/occupational therapy became two sides of the same imminently beneficial coin. Mom would often bring Lara, Travis, and Lesa with her. They loved it because there were so many wonderful things to play with. Mom has shared this experience:

> Thad's teacher was a nun, but she didn't wear a habit...There were six kids [in Thad's class] that were severely handicapped...One girl was about six and she was working so hard to get her hands to work. I was so touched by her spirit that I finished helping her and I ran into the hall and started to cry. This little girl is so beautiful and she's trapped inside this body. The teacher came out and put her arms around me. "I'm sorry," I said, "I was touched with this girl." "You know, Laraine, I do that too. It's because their spirit is so sweet and their courage is so strong it will touch your heart. It's normal to be touched by these strong, courageous spirits."

The teachers, therapists, and administrators at the Stookey School were determined that the kids in their care had a place in The Special Olympics, but the normal events were not feasible due to the nature of the children's disabilities. I'm not sure if this was their brainchild or if they were part of a coalition, but they developed a series of events for severely handicapped children and teens and called it "The Very Special Olympics." They had their own tent by the stadium where The Special Olympics were being held, where dowel-holding and crawling competitions, among others, took place. There was so much positive energy and genuine enthusiasm in that tent from teachers, students, family members, and complete strangers. Cheers filled the air as children whose hands tended not to listen to their brains made enormous efforts to keep a 1-inch dowel from falling out of their hand. It was thrilling and supportive and inspiring.

Thad was a really good crawler. If you shook his favorite toy, he would practically run (in a crawling way) across the room to get it. He was favored to win his crawling event. We were all there standing under the tent to cheer him on. Thad sat in his stroller as we waited for the event to start, shaking his rattle toy and laughing. Then, without warning, right as they called his event, Thad went into a Grand Mal seizure. It only lasted a couple of minutes, and everyone in the tent was familiar with the situation, so we waited. When he stopped shaking and appeared to be lucid and present, we gave him a pep talk and everyone cheered as Thad was placed among the other contestants in the center of the big mat that had a large white circle taped a few feet from the edge marking the finish line. *On your mark. Get set. Go!* All of the contestants scattered away from the center toward whichever familiar person was calling to them on the other side of the line— except for Thad, who fell asleep on the mat before the gun went off. Darn seizures!

The Stookey School was supported by the local school districts but relied on grants from The United Way and private donations. During the two years that Thad was a student there, there were quite a few fund-raising activities, including a campaign that involved Mom and a few of the other mothers standing outside of grocery stores in the area asking for donations. They were pleasantly surprised at how generous people were. The Mamie O. Stookey School set the standard for every other program that Thad was involved in from that point on; although, sadly, it has since closed.

We left Illinois in the Summer of 1983 for our first overseas assignment since the late 1960s, when my parents were stationed in Alaska where Todd and I were born. Alaska was considered an overseas assignment. This time, we were actually heading overseas, the Pacific Ocean to be specific, to Clark Air Force Base on the island of Luzon in the Philippine Islands, about an hour and a half north of Manila. Thad's medical needs limited the opportunities for my dad to be stationed overseas, but the hospital at Clark was the best hospital in the region, so the powers-that-be felt that it would be more than sufficient. Dad looked into it, consulted with Mom, and they came to the same conclusion. It was a great opportunity for Dad's career as he would be the Director of Operations for the division of the Military Airlift Command stationed there.

This was probably the most difficult move for me of my whole life. We had been in Illinois for about two years, and it had taken me that long to feel like I had the potential for having a solid group of friends and a high school future with exciting possibilities. I was feeling a lot of success in both the band program and the theatre program. I felt confident and safe, like I had finally hit my stride. When Dad came home and announced that we were moving, I resisted. I tried to find ways to stay in Illinois while my family moved on. As the day to leave got closer, I became more and more distraught.

One afternoon, something happened which started an argument between me and my mom. She probably asked me to do something, and I refused. That was how it usually started. The problem with that scenario was that Mom and I had similar personalities and I, for whatever reason, knew exactly what to say to her that would be the most hurtful. In this case, hopped up on the desperate feelings of being held captive by my dad's career, I let her have it before storming out of the house and realizing I had nowhere to go. The cars were being used. I trembled with rage as I walked down the hill beyond the barn and hid among the tall cornstalks in our garden.

I crouched there for an hour or two before my dad got home with the Toyota. Once he was inside, I took the car and drove and cried and drove and cried and drove some more. I wasn't going anywhere. I was just driving, trying to quell the hurricane of hurt and powerlessness I felt. I also knew deep down that I had crossed the line in my altercation with Mom, and I felt terrible. It took hours before I felt calm enough to go home. I arrived at our house way past midnight and all the lights were out on the first floor. I couldn't see if the lights were on or off in my parents' room on the second floor. I tip-toed into the house and down to the basement where we four oldest slept. I quietly slid into bed hoping that when I woke up in the morning all would be forgotten.

Before I could even close my eyes, Dad was standing over me. "We need to talk. Now." It was a command. I followed him up to the kitchen preparing myself for a long discussion about the motivations behind my actions, trying to figure out what I could say that would capture the distress I was feeling about moving away from a place where I finally felt accepted. I sat at the picnic-style table he'd made years ago when we lived in Alabama. It was clear that Dad was furious. He began talking, but there weren't any questions. He didn't raise his voice, but his tone was sharp and cutting. He glared at me, accused me of stealing his car, told me I was the most selfish person he'd ever met in his life, and that if I ever hurt Mom the way I did that day, I would not have a place in the family. He would always choose her over me. Period. End of discussion.

His reaction felt excessive to me. Yet, his words were neither explosive nor random. He knew exactly what he was saying. The intensity of the diatribe may have added to the weight of the message, but he wouldn't have said any of it if he didn't believe it. Dad was too methodically conscious of his thoughts and how they might affect the person with whom he was speaking to allow hyperbole to muddy the waters. He would often choose not to say something he was thinking if he felt that it would hurt the person he was talking to or make the conversation less productive. This was not one of those times. This was not a conversation. In my dad's eyes, I was selfish and expendable. That is what I walked away with. I wish that he had hit me that day because bruises heal much faster than a wounded soul. He got what he wanted. I fell in line—no longer resisting the move. Nothing was ever spoken again about that night. I didn't believe I was the most selfish person he'd ever met, but I spent the next 15 years trying to prove to myself, to my dad, and to the world that he was wrong about me.

Tony came home from BYU while we were starting to pack up everything in the house. He was home for a month before leaving to serve his LDS mission in and around Spokane, Washington. Milestones were happening. Life was moving forward, and nothing could stop it.

This move was not like any other move we had experienced. My parents had to figure out the best way to move nine children halfway around the world. They had the physical part of moving down to a science. They knew what to get rid of, what to put in storage, and what to put on the slow boat to the P.I. (That's what people in the know called the Philippines.) Mom's biggest concern was keeping all of us corralled and entertained on the flight. Her plan involved having us all wear bright red t-shirts so it would be easy to pick us out of a crowd and assigning us a buddy that we had to stick close to throughout the trip, so no one would get lost. Her strategy succeeded. We made it through the flight without any casualties or disappearances, though I did have a terrifying start when the gaunt, pale, 60-year-old flight attendant with bleach blonde shoulder-length hair and bright red lipstick shook me awake with her face very close to mine in order to ask me if I wanted breakfast.

The first thing we wanted to do once we arrived at Clark Air Force Base and settled into the motel-like operation that served as our temporary housing for the first few days was go to see our house in the center of the base. It was a big pre-war house facing the parade ground built on stilts with a screened in porch around three sides and a slanted aluminum sheet roof. As we walked along the main road toward the parade ground, Joyce Lemmon, a soon-to-be friend from the Mormon congregation on the base, pulled up in her car and asked if we were the Suttons. Word was out that a Mormon family with ten children was moving to the base. I don't know how she knew it was us, except that we were a bunch of cookie cutter children walking in a single file line down the street wearing bright red t-shirts. We became fast friends with a lot of people and families in the P.I. This was a unique location because there was something positive here for every single member of our family. I think we all look back on our time in the Philippines as some of the best and fullest years of our family life together. My yearnings for Illinois and the life I left behind disappeared almost immediately. The Philippines was beautiful and bursting with possibility.

When we got settled into our new home on the base, we found out, with regards to Thad, that being a Director of Operations had some perks. Mom tells the story this way:

> When we got to the Philippines, they didn't have anything on the military base for Thad. We went to the school, and they said, "What is that kid doing here? Handicapped kids aren't allowed overseas." By law, they were required to develop a program for him, so the school created a learning center called the MacArthur Developmental Center. Thad was the only one in it, but within two weeks there were eight children there whose parents hadn't sent them to school. Thad opened the door for kids who

weren't getting an education because their parents didn't know how to push buttons or that they even could push buttons. Then, the school got a wonderful program going.

Thad really liked going to school. His overall energy improved. He slept better, often as soon as he got home he'd take a nap. His occupational therapist, Fran Murawsky, OTR wrote down this progress report on October 28, 1983:

> We're playing with a purpose. Here are some special things I [Thad] am working on: I have been going to occupational therapy every day where I have gotten to know the therapist very well. We have learned our own ways to communicate with each other. She says she likes the hugs the best. I work on my objectives i.e.: swinging in the net to improve my eye control, verbalization, balance and reflex development. Fran also puts me on a large ball where I stretch my arms and do other exercises. I tried standing in the standing box but I really didn't like it. Maybe I'll try it again later. I did like coming down the slide. My therapist says I'm a "ray of sunshine."

It was during our two years in the Philippines that Thad became less and less able to stand. It wasn't a sudden change, but so gradual that it was almost imperceptible. Standing seemed to have become uncomfortable for him, and his endurance waned, as did his ability to carry his weight, even in the supportive structure of a standing apparatus. My parents also noticed that when he crawled Thad was more likely to move his hands forward one at a time, then pull his knees forward simultaneously. This was a subtle difference, but one that caused concern. We don't know exactly why this happened. Thad's doctors had explained to my parents early on that their guess was that in light of the progress that he was making, it was more than likely that Thad would develop to a point, then plateau before gradually starting to regress. Signs like these seemed to confirm this line of reasoning. It was hard to consider the possibility that in some ways Thad might have reached the outer edges of his development. The only way to process it was to stay vigilant and to remain hopeful.

Because of my dad's rank and responsibility, a lot was expected of my mom. She was in charge of taking care of the wives of the men under my dad's command. It was a big responsibility because everyone was away from home, and life was at once bigger because they were in another country and more limited because they were in another country. Military wives were basically stuck in a traditional stay-at-home role because they were abroad and unable to work. Many were unhappy with the situation, so it was my mom's responsibility to create activities that would provide socialization and uplift the other military wives. Taking care of Thad was challenging at times, but nothing could have prepared her for this role, which, by the way, she did very well. Fortunately, we were able to find a wonderful Filipino woman, Fely, to work for us. She cooked, cleaned, and helped care for Thad, Lara, Travis, and Lesa. Mom trained her in all the specifics of Thad's care, and she did a great job.

One of the best parts about living in the Philippines was the incredible variety and constant availability of fresh fruit. We were introduced to fresh tropical fruit like mangos, papayas, pineapple, and coconut—which previously only came from cans or frozen bags—as well as fruit we'd never heard of like lanzones (an off-white fruit with a sweet milky-white sectioned flesh that you would suck off of a black seed) and breadfruit (a very large fruit with a light green bumpy skin and a sweet, sort of banana-like textured flesh). Bananas were ubiquitous, though, so we continued to give Thad his seizure medication mixed up in a banana mash. I never ate a Phenobarbital or a Tegretol pill, but I can't imagine that they tasted very good. Thad was 7 now, and apparently he had reached his banana limit. A few months into our stay in the PI, Thad refused to eat bananas ever again. He would spit them out and violently shake his head then bite his hand and make loud grunting noises. His aversion to bananas was kind of funny because of its intensity. I wasn't sure if he was finally asserting his "this medicine tastes awful, so I'm not going to eat it!" prerogative or if he just got sick of the taste and texture of mashed bananas. So, we adapted. We tried many different mashable fruits, but eventually settled on giving him his medication mixed in yogurt or some portion of the food he was already eating. We realized variety was the key, and the stronger the flavor, the more likely it would disguise the medicine flavor.

Wagner High School was a Department of Defense school on the base itself. It was smaller than any school I had attended previously. My graduating class would have 70 kids in it. They had a great concert band program, but no marching band. I played trombone and sang (but not that the same time) in the jazz band. They didn't have a theatre program, so I joined the water polo team. That was the best decision I made. It was fun. It was a team sport. I was good at it. I had never excelled in any team athletic sport, so this was a revelation to me. For whatever reason, I wasn't afraid to get aggressive, to be strong, in the water. This made the team dynamic less intimidating because I did not feel like a weak link.

The kids in school took my personality in stride. I didn't have any experiences like I had at other schools. Whatever they thought, they kept it to themselves, or they didn't care. The first Halloween, I went to school dressed as Dracula, cape and all. I was the only one in costume, but it was a good day. Lots of people smiled. There was no jeering or staring. During my senior year water polo season, I found a huge sombrero at a store off-base, and I wore it to school every time our water polo team had a match. The head cheerleader, who was in many of my same classes, came up to me on one of those sombrero days and said, "You know, Tim, you are the only person in school who could get away with wearing that hat." I took it as the compliment I think she meant. It made me smile.

One day, I was walking home from a friend's house on a sidewalk across a large field. There was a guy my age walking the other way. I recognized him from school, but we'd never really talked before. He was athletic with a very well-defined physique. He was a jock. I was not. We stopped and started talking. At the end of the conversation, he said, almost as a side note, "You know, Tim, if you did 100 sit-ups and 100 push-ups every night, you would build up quickly. Think about it. It's easy to do." I was touched that he would think to give me advice. Jocks, in my experience, tended to be dismissive, threatening, and/or condescending, so I steered clear of them. I thanked him, and we went our separate ways. I wish I could say that I started doing push-ups that night, but I didn't. Still, I remembered that conversation as a real kindness. It was something I often recalled when I found myself making presumptions about how someone should or would behave based on who I thought they were.

Todd graduated high school in 1984, went to Brigham Young University, like Tony, for a few semesters, then on to serve a mission in and around Kyoto, Japan. Tony was finishing up his mission in Northern Idaho/Eastern Washington. I followed in their footsteps, graduating high school in 1985 and starting the summer term at BYU before the ink was dry on my diploma. I didn't wait for the Fall semester to begin because I desperately wanted to audition for The Young Ambassadors. I had not forgotten that moment in Abilene the first time I saw them perform when I thought, "I want to be one of them!" They were talented and fun and Mormon all rolled up into a fantastic blue and white package.

I'm not sure if it was because we had a large family,

or because we moved so much, or simply how our parents raised us, but we were all pretty independent, and leaving home was not a traumatic experience. It didn't matter if we were living at home or a thousand miles away, the family ties were strong. We knew that, unless something dramatic happened, we would always be there, irrespective of distance—except for, possibly, Thad. Thad was 10 years old, now. He'd beaten the odds, but still, his life was tenuous. We never knew if each morning would be the morning we'd wake up without him. It's not something I dwelled on day-to-day, but whenever I left home for any length of time, I'd feel a sharp pang deep in my heart that this might be the last time I would see Thad alive. It didn't keep me from leaving, but in the days and weeks leading up to my departure, I'd make sure to spend time holding Thad, talking to him, or reading to him.

OH, LORD, PLEASE HELP ME

Growing up in The Church of Jesus Christ of Latter-day Saints is not a half-hearted affair. Mormonism is a way of life that requires commitment and conviction. That was especially true for us because we grew up in the "mission field," which in Mormon lingo means anywhere outside of Mormon population centers like Utah and parts Arizona and California. We weren't surrounded by Mormons in the places we lived. There wasn't a Mormon chapel on every block, or on every other block, or, even, every few towns. More often than not, we were the only Mormon kids in our school.

In addition to that, for most of my childhood, we lived in the Bible Belt, that wonderful swath of southern and southern-central states dominated by Fundamentalist and Evangelical churches, none of which looked too kindly on Mormonism. It was impossible for us to blend in. The size of our family alone triggered "Catholic or Mormon?" inquiries from any God-fearing Christian we came into contact with. So, as kids, and especially as teens, we had two options: we could rebel, or we could own our Faith well enough to be a good example of Mormonism in the face of skepticism and ridicule.

We didn't rebel. We participated in church activities on Sunday and during the week. We belonged to the Boy Scouts of America, all of us boys attaining the rank of Eagle Scout. We accepted responsibilities within the Church when asked. We had Family Home Evening on Monday nights, for which we got together as a family to play games, sing songs, watch home movies, eat fun food, and have a spiritual lesson alternately prepared by someone in the family, regardless of age. We woke up early and read scriptures together before school—the Bible, *The Book of Mormon, The Doctrine and Covenants,* and *The Pearl of Great Price.* This didn't take a lot of time because it consisted of reading out loud one chapter in whichever tome we were reading, verse by verse, from one person to the next, then talking briefly about what we had read. It started the day off on a spiritual note and made us all good, out-loud readers at a very young age. We had family prayer in the morning and evening, as well as individual prayers before bed and whenever else we felt like it. We didn't drink alcohol, coffee, tea, or even caffeinated sodas. We didn't smoke tobacco or any other smokeable herb. And, we refrained from using harsh language.

If there were a black sheep in the family, it was me. I didn't rebel too much nor too egregiously, so I guess I was really just a beige sheep. I was the only one in the family who was resistant to any of these activities, especially Family Home Evening and early morning scripture study, mainly because I preferred to watch TV or to stay asleep, respectively. One morning, in Alabama, when I was in the sixth grade, it was my turn to say the family prayer after scripture study. I went silent after saying "Dear Heavenly Father." My family waited and waited, assuming that I was thinking deeply about what to say next. Finally, someone started giggling, then someone else, then someone else, until Dad gently nudged my shoulder to wake me up, saying, "In the name of Jesus Christ, Amen." I guess that is more an example of exhaustion than rebellion, but it gave us all something to laugh about for years to come.

Rituals and routines may form a structure upon which to shape a life, but they do not breathe vitality into that life; nor can they stand on their own in the face of doubt or antagonism. One of the strengths of the Mormon faith as I experienced it was that even if one was born into the faith, as I had been, everyone was encouraged, no, admonished to seek their own answers. One's commitment to the faith must come out of one's own personal quest for truth. Through obedience, study, experience, and, most importantly, prayer, one could acquire a personal testimony of the truthfulness of the restored gospel of the Jesus Christ; and, consequently, of The Church of Jesus Christ of Latter-day Saints, itself.

I felt a connection to the Mormon faith from an early age through my parents, and especially through our experience with Thad. As I moved into my teens, though, I began my own quest for a personal testimony—a conviction that could sustain me over time. The Church has a program for high school students called Seminary, which facilitates a more in-depth study of the scriptures. They devote each school year to one theme: The Old Testament, The New Testament, *The Book of Mormon*, and the History of the Church (which includes *Doctrine and Covenants* as well as *The Pearl of Great Price*). In areas where there is a large population of Mormons, like Utah, Seminary classes are incorporated into a normal school day (in a separate building, of course). In O'Fallon, Illinois ("the mission field") we were stuck with Early Morning Seminary, which meant we had class before school started. An adult from the ward was called to be a Seminary teacher, and we would meet every morning during the week at a home near our high school because the church building was too far away.

As has been established, I was not a morning person. It certainly helped that Tony, Todd, and I would drive in together. The theme for our first year in Illinois, my freshman year, was Church History. Essentially, what sets Mormonism apart from every other Christian religion is their belief in modern-day revelation. From the First Vision, when God and Jesus Christ appeared to 14-year-old Joseph Smith in 1820 in a grove of trees near his home in Palmyra, New York, telling him not to join any of the current denominations because Christianity in general had fallen away from its original form and intent, through the many revelations and visitations that in subsequent years would restore that form and intent in the often violent and formidable backdrop of the American frontier, God's direct interest and involvement was unmistakable. In that early morning hour before we moved on to Literature, Algebra, PhysEd, Music, and Chemistry, our tiny band of Mormon teenagers studied the beginnings of the Church in upstate New York, the discovery and translation through divine intervention of *The Book of Mormon*, and the migration of the early Saints in the face of growing persecution to Pennsylvania and Ohio, then on to Missouri and Illinois where Joseph Smith was murdered, leading to the trek West where the Saints, led by Brigham Young, finally settled in the Salt Lake Valley. We studied the restored gospel as it was being revealed, and the circumstances surrounding the visions and revelations that Joseph Smith recorded in *Doctrine and Covenants*.

I remembered visiting many of the places we were reading about on our 1975 family trip through the Midwest to Upstate New York, making these stories and scriptures resonate more completely. They didn't happen in some distant part of the world a thousand or more years ago. I had walked in the home where Joseph Smith lived as a boy. I had touched the trees that filled the grove where Joseph Smith had gone to pray in search of answers. I had walked along the banks of the Susquehanna River where Peter, James, and John, of Biblical fame, returned to confer upon the prophet what would be known as the Melchizedek Priesthood—the official authority to act in God's name. I had been inside the Kirtland Temple, in Kirtland, Ohio, built by the Mormon pioneers where Joseph Smith had received some of the vital revelations we were learning about, now.

Living in Southern Illinois meant that we were only a few hours drive away from many Church history sites from the latter part of Joseph Smith's life. We were able to take some weekend field trips to visit Liberty Jail in Liberty, Missouri, where Joseph Smith and five other men were held captive in a basement cell for roughly four months in desperate conditions; Carthage Jail, in Carthage, Illinois, where Joseph Smith was murdered by a mob of angry men with blackened faces; and Nauvoo, Illinois, the town founded by the prophet Joseph on the Mississippi River, where the early Saints settled before being pushed out by violent mobs after Joseph's death. All of this made an impression on me. I knew what it felt like to be marginalized and to be ridiculed. Though I was never the victim of severe violence, I felt a profound kinship with the early Saints. In my prayers and while I read the scriptures and the histories, I felt connected. I soared through their joyful times and wept for their travails. Ok, I didn't actually weep, but I was frequently moved to tears. These were my people. I identified with them. I was inspired by them. I was proud to come from a tribe who had faced the fire of persecution and not only survived, but had the wherewithal and determination to find a place where they could settle, regroup, flourish, and enter the world again with strength and conviction.

Of everything that I read that year, a small verse from *Doctrine and Covenants*, section 121, stayed with me. Section 121 was basically a cry of anguish in prayer form and its subsequent answer recorded by Joseph Smith a few months into his imprisonment in Liberty Jail. The words that touched me were a simple question, "How long can rolling waters remain impure?" In spite of all of the positive, uplifting experiences I was having, I still felt I had reason to feel impure and therefore unable to fully integrate myself into this world. This verse gave me the inspiration to keep moving, to keep trying, to keep reaching for a better life. It gave me my own personal hope. So, by the end of my freshman year in high school, I had a stronger identity and a prevailing sense of hope about my life and its trajectory.

The next year we studied *The Book of Mormon*. This book is an abridged, mostly religious, history of a group of people who left Jerusalem about 600 years before Christ, built a civilization in what would become known a couple thousand years later as the Americas, experienced times of war and times of peace as well as times of devotion to religious principles and times of complete rejection of said principles, and, in the end, approximately 400 years after Christ, warred themselves to near extinction leaving behind remnants who would become some of the ancestors of the Native Americans on the North and South American continents. It was a book written by prophets, spiritual leaders intent on teaching their people of the coming Messiah back in Jerusalem, the land of their ancestors. They prophesied of his coming and they chronicled the time when Jesus himself visited their people for a brief period after his resurrection and taught them essential concepts from his ministry in the Old World, organizing a structure and giving them authority to carry on in his name. These prophets recorded the peace that followed Christ's visit to the Americas, then the gradual decline and ultimate rejection of all that had been given them, leading to their ultimate demise. The last prophet, Moroni, the son of Mormon who had compiled and abridged all of the records, witnessed the final battles that decimated his people. He took the records, which were written on plates of gold, and buried them in a hill for safe keeping, but not before issuing this promise:

> And when ye shall receive these things, I would exhort you that ye would ask God, the Eternal Father, in the name of Christ, if these things are not true; and if ye shall ask with a sincere heart, with real intent, having faith in Christ, he will manifest the truth of it unto you by the power of the Holy Ghost.
>
> And by the power of the Holy Ghost, ye may know the truth of all things.

Essentially, that was our challenge for the year—read, ponder, pray, and find out for ourselves if *The Book of Mormon* were a true book or not. Since Moroni himself came back and showed Joseph Smith where to find the golden plates which Joseph then translated using gifts that God had granted him, *The Book of Mormon* was the indisputable keystone of the whole religion. If this book were true, then it was all true.

I'd grown up reading it with my family and hearing the stories during Family Home Evening and at church, so *The Book of Mormon* was not a new text to me. This time though, it was on me to read it from cover to cover, to think about what I was reading, and to pray for understanding. I was a good reader and a good thinker, but praying had never been my strong suit. Whenever I started a personal prayer, my brain would open the pandemonium door and allow every thought I ever had, every commercial I ever saw on TV, and every lyric or jingle I ever heard to bounce around my head at supersonic speeds. It took an enormous effort to focus on what I was doing. I would often succeed to the point where I could express gratitude and ask for help or guidance, but I could rarely stay present long enough to be in the prayer or to listen; so, my prayers tended to be pretty one-sided, like I was leaving a message on God's answering machine. The task that lay ahead of me was daunting. I wasn't expecting angelic visitations, or waiting for "Yes, Tim, it is true" to pierce the night sky accompanied by harps; but I felt in order to get an answer, I would need to be able to quiet my brain, to open my heart, and to listen with my spiritual ears. The answer would have to come while I was praying.

About halfway through the year, I finished reading *The Book of Mormon*. Then, I started in earnest to ask God if it was true. I knelt by my bed and prayed before going to sleep and again when I awoke in the morning. I would pull over somewhere between home and anywhere if I was alone in the truck and say a little prayer. When it got warm enough, I even went into the woods around our house to pray. I figured it had worked for Joseph Smith, maybe it could work for me. No dramatic or even notable or discernible answers were forthcoming. I was getting better at focusing, though, even if my head still raced while I prayed.

I continued reading the chapters we were studying in Seminary class. I began to notice that while I read, I seemed to be understanding more. It seemed that I could relate what I was reading to my own life in more subtle ways. I felt connected to what I was reading in a similar way that I had felt connected to the stories of the pioneers the year before. It felt familiar. Clearly, it was more familiar to me because I was reading it more specifically and with intention; but what I was feeling was deeper than that. I felt moved on a spiritual level. I felt as though my *heart* was expanding as if a curtain was gradually being taken away revealing that my Spirit actually lived in a very large and spacious greenhouse filled with beauty and light. This expansive feeling brought with it a lot of peace and happiness. I still wanted an answer, though, so I continued to pray. Finally, one morning as I was getting dressed after saying my morning prayers, these words came into my head, "You have your answer, Tim. No need to keep asking."

Those feelings of understanding, recognition, and connection; that sense of expansion and light; the peace and grounded happiness that seemed to underscore my days in spite of the teenage angst that ebbed and flowed—these combined to form the answer I had been seeking. These were the ways that the Holy Ghost communicated with me. What a moment! I felt as though I were meeting a celebrity and he liked me, he really liked me! It was one of those feelings too big to contain because it felt like I was part of something bigger than myself, something that everyone could be a part of, that everybody was already a part of without even knowing it. This experience defined my point of view. It showed me that my worldview aligned with that of my parents. I understood them because I understood their conviction. It felt amazing to feel that I belonged.

It was after that year that we moved to the Philippines. The last two years of Early Morning Seminary, we studied the Old Testament first and then the New Testament. Our teacher was an Air Force Chaplain who happened to be LDS. He was an amazing teacher, and the breadth of his knowledge about the Bible was remarkable. I loved reading the Bible. The Old Testament was challenging, but rewarding. The New Testament was refreshing. I felt the Spirit (Holy Ghost) during these years in the same way I felt it during the previous two years. All of these scriptures related to one another and reinforced one another. It felt remarkable to make these connections. I felt very fortunate to have the opportunity to learn these things. I felt like I was growing in ways that were important to the rest of my life. I felt hopeful about my life and the prospects that lay ahead of me.

When it came time to apply to college, I put all my eggs in one basket. I only applied to Brigham Young University. I had spent my whole life far from the nucleus of Mormon civilization, so the possibility of being surrounded by people who shared my Faith was impossible to pass up. It made me giddy. The day I got accepted I danced around the house waving the letter in the air. I couldn't believe I was finally going to be in Happy Valley! That was the nickname given to Utah Valley where BYU was situated, and it said everything to a Mormon boy ready to set out on his own. I would be in the land of Donny and Marie! It would be a safe place, a cocoon where I could strengthen my testimony, prepare for my mission, and learn everything I would need to know to be successful in the world.

So, in the Summer of 1985, for the first time in my life, I was living away from my family. I arrived at BYU just 10 days after graduating from high school so that I could take my first voice and dance classes, ever. I had made it into the callbacks for the Young Ambassadors based on a video that I sent in from the Philippines. The callbacks would happen toward the end of the Summer semester, so I had time to learn as much as humanly possible. I'd never wanted anything as much as I wanted to be a Young Ambassador. I was having the time of my life as a college student! My high school experience was great, but college felt like the real deal. It fit me like a glove.

I lived in the Deseret Towers dorms, and my Resident Assistant got me a job with a professor from the Nutrition Department who needed help doing some surveys down in Southern Utah for a weekend. I jumped at the chance because extra cash was extra cash. There were four of us on the research team—the professor, myself, and two women. At the end of the first day, we settled into the hotel. The women in one room and the professor and myself in the other. In the middle of the night, I awoke to find the professor attempting to put his hand down my shorts. I was terrified and a little intrigued, but terror won out. I did not let him know that I was awake, I just rolled away from him so he didn't have access to me, and he returned to his bed. I didn't sleep for the rest of the night, and I don't think I said a word the rest of the trip. Nothing more happened, but I felt traumatized and guilty. Mostly, it made me think that every doubt that I'd ever had about myself and my sexuality was true. I didn't know what to do. I was reeling.

When we finally made it back to Provo, I tried calling my parents in the Philippines, but they were en route to Japan, and no one I talked to could tell me how to reach them. Because of the nature of the incident and the serious questions I had about my own sexuality, I didn't know who I could talk to without being judged or harshly misunderstood. I was alone—desperately alone. Finally, after a few days, I talked to my Resident Assistant who got me the job. He took me to the BYU campus police who took a statement but were clearly unimpressed with what I had to say. He then confronted the professor, who denied everything. The professor wrote me a letter saying that he was friends with Randy Boothe, the main director of the Young Ambassadors, and if I didn't take back my allegations, he would make sure that I never made it into the group. Such as it was, the inquiry ran its course, and the professor resigned before any action was taken. He quickly got hired at the University of Utah, and that is the last I heard of him.

The professor didn't follow through with his threat, and after the callbacks, and against all odds, I made it into the Young Ambassadors as a freshman. It was truly a dream come true. Especially after the unsettling trip to Southern Utah, I didn't have a whole lot of confidence in myself, though outwardly I was gregarious and enthusiastic. I had learned over years of moving from one place to another that the best way to fit into any situation was to be warm and funny, but more importantly, to be open and genuinely nice. I think that may have been what tipped the scales in my favor enough to get me on the upstage risers singing and moving my arms. I overheard Mark Huffman, the director of my group, talking to someone one day about me, and he said, "I chose him because he moves like a man." That was fantastic and surprising news to me!

Before the Fall semester started, we had the Young Ambassador intensive. It was like Marching Band camp in that we lived and breathed Young Ambassadors for a couple of weeks before classes started. I couldn't think of a better, more enjoyable way to spend my days than dancing and singing and being creative. I felt like I had found my calling. Rehearsal was the bomb! We got to know each other, learned music, had dance classes, learned choreography, and by the end, they decided who was going into each group. That year there were two groups. One was touring India and the other China and Japan. I landed in the India group.

Once they knew who was in each group, they took time to divvy out the solos. I was very excited. Some people were returning YAs and they were given material without auditioning because they already knew much of the show, and the directors already knew them. We all had a shot with the other solos. One afternoon, the guys in my group went into a rehearsal room with our assistant director, Nolan Goodwin. We were working on the beginning of the Broadway section of the show and needed someone to sing the George Benson hit "On Broadway." I was ready! The trouble was, I didn't know the George Benson version or The Drifters version. I knew the song from an episode of the sitcom *Gimme a Break!* in which the short, stout, sassy, African-American lead, Nell Carter (a bona fide Broadway star herself), visited New York City and sang this song as she strolled around midtown Manhattan.

When it was my turn to audition, I sang my heart out doing the best Nell Carter impression I could muster. I may have even thrown in a shimmy or two. When I finished, all the blood had drained out of Nolan's perpetually smiling face. The other guys were dumbstruck. When he could speak, Nolan asked weakly, "Do you want to try that again?" I said, "No, thanks, I'm good," as I walked back to my seat thinking, "I nailed it!" The solo went to Chris Thomson, an amazing dancer with charisma to spare. I didn't end up getting solos—ok I got one solo—but I was thrilled to be part of it all. I had so much fun doing anything they asked me to do.

Making it into the YA's, as we called it, changed my life in many ways. It gave me a shot of much-needed confidence. It gave me a hint that people didn't see me through my eyes, and what they saw had promise. The mission of the Young Ambassadors was two-fold: to entertain and to inspire. It was as much our responsibility to have fun and perform well onstage, as it was to share our testimonies through song and short talks during Firesides, in our daily interactions with people, and by living an exemplary life. This inspired me to continue to nurture the spiritual side of my life, to excel in the academic side and to cultivate the artistic side. I felt like I was coming into my own. I felt good in my own skin, like I could do anything if I set my mind and heart and spirit to it.

We toured Northern California in the Fall, then India, Sri Lanka and Nepal in January of 1986. The most significant event of the India tour for me happened in Calcutta, our first stop. We helped some men loading a truck at the airport, and it turned out to be supplies that Mother Teresa had brought back with her from a trip abroad. She invited us to come to her convent the next day, which we happily did. We arrived in the morning and were escorted into a courtyard. There were four or five floors above us filled with young nuns looking down at us. We were going to sing a few of our Fireside songs, which had a more spiritual sensibility. After the second song and before the best ones, Mother Teresa signaled that we should follow her. So, we went up some stairs, took off our shoes at a doorway and entered a small, nondescript chapel. Light was coming in from outside through many windows. The room was empty except for a small crucifix hanging on the far wall. Natural, non-dyed, woven mats covered the floor. We stood in a semi-circle facing the crucifix with Mother Teresa at the top of the curve. It seemed very quiet though I know there was traffic noise coming from outside. We sang our YA arrangement of "I Am A Child of God" before Mother Teresa offered a brief prayer. The Spirit in that moment was palpable. I'm not sure I had ever felt such a deep connection to spiritual things as I felt in that moment. It was only a moment, though, because Mother Teresa quickly turned and walked out the door and down the hall. She moved surprisingly fast for someone her age. We followed, of course, but our shoes were more cumbersome to put on.

For the next few hours, Mother Teresa took us around to various works that her order, the Missionaries of Charity, was responsible for, including an orphanage and a home for the destitute and dying. I was profoundly moved and impressed. At the orphanage, as we walked through a nursery filled with small cribs and babies, Mother Teresa would stop, hold, console, and care for a baby in distress. Each baby seemed to recognize her; there was familiarity. It was clear that Mother Teresa was a hands-on kind of leader. She didn't just manage her order, she worked with them.

It was at the home for the destitute and dying that I felt truly humbled. Mother Teresa explained that every human being deserved to be cared for with love as they prepared to leave this world. These people, many of whom were handicapped in some way, were brought in from the streets by the Missionaries of Charity and tenderly cared for. I thought of Thad, and how the doctors had initially encouraged my parents to place him in a home so that he would not be a burden to the family. I wondered if any of these people had been discarded by their families because of their disabilities, left to fend for themselves on the streets of Calcutta. Flashes of Thad reminded me of the joy he brought into our lives as we cared for him. Suddenly, singing and dancing my way around India seemed trivial, even silly. Singing "I Am a Child of God" one hundred times a day in perfect harmony probably wasn't going to change the world in any significant way. No, I wanted to stay here, roll up my sleeves, and get to work. This work seemed authentic. This labor seemed real. It was different for me, as most of my efforts toward service, toward kindness, were muddied by the need to prove to my Dad and to the world that I wasn't selfish. What I saw here were lives of service and expressions of goodness that weren't followed by an emphatic, "See?!"

To me, Mother Teresa's efforts perfectly encapsulated the teachings of Jesus Christ in profound and practical ways. I thought, "Wow, if Mother Teresa had been a Mormon, she could not have done a similar work. We're just not set up that way." That was an earth-shattering thought for someone who truly believed that the restored gospel of Jesus Christ, the foundation of Mormon theology, was the ultimate and only religious truth and way of life. Mother Teresa was truly better and more deeply spiritual than anyone I had ever met. What she was doing was more profound than anything I had ever been involved in. This didn't throw me into a whirlwind of doubt. I still felt strongly adhered to my spiritual foundation. But it opened my heart to the possibility that there was a place for everyone in this life, regardless of their religious creed. Perhaps, every one of us had something to offer the world and we were placed in situations that would allow us to fulfill our missions.

Mother Teresa didn't leave us empty-handed. As our day ended, she gave each of us a light blue business card which contained the following words:

The fruit of silence is prayer
The fruit of prayer is faith
The fruit of faith is love
The fruit of love is service
The fruit of service is peace
— Mother Teresa

I didn't stay in India. I couldn't stay, but I took this experience with me. I continue to hold our day with Mother Teresa close to my heart. I think about it often, and I try to find ways to bring those words into my daily life with purpose and action. As I ponder my experience in India, our day with Mother Teresa was a highlight in a trip full of new experiences.

Something else happened during those two months which had a lasting effect on me. When we were told that our tour was going to be in India, they mentioned that it would be a challenging experience because India was full of poverty that we could not even imagine. I thought that I would have an advantage in this case because I had lived in the Philippines. I'd seen what it was like to live in a Third World country. I had witnessed the slums of Manila where people lived in makeshift huts among mountains of garbage that filled in parts of Manila Bay. How could India be worse than that?

I was not prepared for what I saw in India. Perhaps it was a matter of scale. In 1986, there didn't appear to be much of a middle class in India. There were the very wealthy and the very poor, and walking around the cities visiting temples and other touristy things, we weren't hobnobbing with the very wealthy. The thing that struck me the most was that throughout India, I saw people living in abject poverty, and yet they weren't downtrodden. Their eyes were filled with light and life. Deprivation hadn't taken their souls. They appeared to be happy in spite of their situation. Of course, not everybody was like that, but there were enough that I took notice.

I remember thinking about growing up in the Air

Force and moving every couple of years. It was difficult, and not every place was ideal. But I learned that if I could find one or two things that were unique or good about the place we were living, then I could be happy living there. If I focused on where I used to live, or the things that weren't that great in the new town, I would be unhappy, and that would spiral into a bad experience for everyone. I wondered if I could find the good that surrounded me if I were living on the sidewalk with my wife and three children, but that's what I saw. It's not that they were Pollyanna skipping around the streets oblivious to their situation, I'm just saying that within the context of their experience, they had not allowed their soul to be extinguished.

I thought about Thad who spent his whole life confined to a body that didn't work. He couldn't communicate. He couldn't walk. There were a lot of things he couldn't do, and yet he exuded positive, happy energy. The twinkle in his eye was similar to the light I saw in the eyes of these people. I don't know if Thad knew that his experience was limited compared to ours, but maybe he did. I don't know if he made a conscious choice to be happy in spite of his limitations, but maybe he did. I took in these thoughts because they felt important, but I didn't analyze them or ponder how they might apply to my life. I figured that one day, if I needed them, they would be there. I hoped they would be there.

When the Winter Semester ended, I visited my family in Japan for about a month. They were having a wonderful time in this new country. Dad was now a Wing Commander which meant he was in charge of all of the big cargo planes and their crews for the whole Western Pacific Region. It was the apex of his career, and he was incredibly busy. I could tell that he was loving it because he radiated a confident and happy energy. This type of job is what he did best, aside from actual flying. He was an effective problem-solver. He enjoyed working with people and encouraging them. He thrived in the structured environment of the military, though he was not the typical rigid, gruff persona that we tend to associate with military leaders.

Mom was equally busy being a mom and a commander's wife. Her responsibilities toward the military wives seemed to be endless, not to mention the cultural exchange with Japanese women's groups from the area surrounding the base. Like with my dad, I could see that Mom was at her best. Although the volume of work was exhausting, with all the socializing, hosting parties, making sure all the wives were taken care of, attending events both on and off base, and sharing cultural experiences in and around Tokyo, Mom discovered talents she didn't know she had. To her surprise, she also really enjoyed it. It was great to see them both at the top of their game and incredibly confident. Knowing what was in store, my parents had brought a lovely Mormon woman up with them from the Philippines, Fé, to help around the house, so Mom was relieved of many of the domestic responsibilities for the first year they were in Japan.

Thomas, Troy, and Trent were ensconced in jr. high and high school. They were fun to hang out with. We traveled in and out of Tokyo on several occasions together. We explored the Ginza, which is the 5th Avenue of Tokyo, and Shinjuku Central Park in the middle of Tokyo. We played at Disneyland Tokyo, then got on the wrong train back to Yokota, ending up somewhere in the middle of nowhere where none of the signs had Arabic letter equivalents beside the Japanese letters. Lara, Lesa, and Travis were beginning to work as models. Lara had blonde, curly hair, and Lesa and Travis had bright, red hair. The Japanese loved them.

Thad was steady. He was healthy, growing, and all Thad. He continued to surprise us. Dad shared this experience in a letter to my grandparents:

> Today while I was sitting on the couch with Thad, I said, "Thad, give me a big hug." He immediately reached out and hugged my neck

with his good arm. Then, Troy came over and sat down beside us. I told Thad to hug Troy, too, and he did. So, it's interesting to learn that he may understand a lot more than we ever thought he did...Pretty impressive, huh?

I came home to Japan on a Young Ambassador high. I was confident and enthusiastic, looking forward to my mission. I felt like I could do anything. The volume on my internal doubts was turned way down. It was a nice feeling. I felt sort of invincible. I made friends with a young woman from my parent's ward named Diane. She was probably in her mid-twenties. She was married, but her husband rarely came to church. Diane and I hit it off. We had a lot of similar interests, but music sealed the deal. She played the piano really well, and we started to write a few songs together. We discovered that we could actually do it. Maybe she already knew she could, but songwriting was a revelation to me. Our friendship opened a door to a creative expression that provided the possibility to explore my feelings in a way that I hadn't done before. It was a real gift. My thoughts at the time were all wrapped up in getting prepared for my mission, so the two songs we wrote together were Mormon pop-like songs. Because of this experience, I felt a real connection to and friendship with Diane. She was one of those people who crossed my path at just the right moment, bringing light and a new set of glasses that allowed me to see and experience more fully the path I was walking. I sang one of our songs at my mission farewell.

Then, I left to be a missionary in the Seville, Spain Mission, which included the Canary Islands, where I would spend most of my mission. My first stop, though, was two months in the Missionary Training Center in Provo, Utah to learn basic language and missionary skills. While I was there, my mom took Thad to Hawaii for some extensive testing and evaluation. She wrote me a letter from there:

> I am very excited about the evaluations that Thad has been receiving and all the doctors have been very thorough and helpful. Each seems genuinely interested in helping Thad to the best of their abilities. Thad had an in-depth eye exam and it was discovered that he has a severe astigmatism and the doctor prescribed glasses...now the challenge is how can they design glasses to fit.

Throughout Thad's life, we continued to find out things about his physical experience that had been unknown to us. We have no idea how Thad's astigmatism affected him—literally, how he saw the world. We don't know how blurred or distorted his vision was, or if his eye caused him discomfort or headaches. There were times throughout his life when he would clearly be uncomfortable and out of sorts—we could tell by a grating kind of groaning sound he would make and a lack of energy—and nothing we would try would seem to alleviate his discomfort. That was frustrating because we would feel helpless. He couldn't tell us what was wrong, and sometimes, we couldn't figure it out. Maybe, some of those moments were caused by his eye. There is no way of knowing. They didn't end up finding a way to provide glasses for Thad, so whatever his field of vision was, that was what it was going to be.

Mom continued in her letter:

> He also has been fitted for a totally new wheelchair. (I'm not surprised. His is on its last wheels, literally) It will take about three months for it to be ordered and fitted for him so we have to make this trip again in October. His new "wheels" will be great.

When they got home to Japan, they had to go through an approval process with the insurance company which didn't end up approving the new chair, so Thad didn't get a new chair for a few more years. When you look in from the outside, you don't really know how costly disabilities can be. Any specialized equipment for disabled people is super-expensive. It's kind of criminal, actually. And, the only way to get it if you are on any kind of budget is to rely on the "benevolence" of the Insurance or Medicaid system. Sometimes it works in your favor, and sometimes it does not. There is certainly a lot of waiting involved.

The most interesting and personal part of Mom's letter from Hawaii followed:

> Thad and I have had a lot of time together to get re-acquainted and we still love each other. In my observation he is growing up in his emotional nature and has become very vocal in his dislikes and those things which make him feel a little uncomfortable. I've even observed moods—where he just wants to be left alone to do and play with his own things. He also has reached out to me on several occasions indicating that he wants to play. So, even in his limited abilities, he is struggling with growth and special desires.

Thad always had an individual personality that stayed pretty constant, but it was fascinating to observe through the years how he matured. He never became moody, but as Mom observed, there were definitely variations that were associated with his desire to be alone or to be with people. Sometimes, he'd sit in his chair and his left brow, right near the edge of his skull leading to the brain, would crinkle, and his attention would be focused on something. It might have been a seizure, but it might also have been some connection that we have no way knowing. I think there was a lot going on inside of him that we'll just never know.

During my mission in Spain, the only way that I could communicate with my family was through letters. Dad wrote me every week with few exceptions and kept me up to speed with matter-of-fact, newsy letters discussing what was happening on the home front at Yokota Air Force Base. Mom would write every few months. Her letters were more personal and more detailed. Except for the letter from Hawaii, the details about Thad in my parents' letters were sporadic and brief:

> (Mom, Sep 27, 1986) Thad has a great school class and I think he will do very well. He's happy and more active lately.
>
> (Mom, April 6, 1987) Thad is really growing long. I think he's added two inches this year. He's making a little progress in personal development. He's been sick a lot with ear infections and strep throat.
>
> (Mom, April 12, 1987) Thad is doing well and is happy today. He has felt poorly a lot this Winter.
>
> (Mom, April 20, 1987) Thad looked so handsome Sunday! He was in a red, white, and blue pants and sweater outfit with a red bow tie. He looked great! His first tie!
>
> (Mom, May 25, 1987) Thad is doing great. He is now standing up in a "prone stander" with support for about 35 minutes. Such exercise is great for his body and legs. I'm really excited for him.
>
> (Dad, Sep 26, 1987) Thad is eleven now and must be feeling some frustration with his handicaps. He fusses a lot and needs more attention. He doesn't like to be by himself for long and enjoys watching TV and playing with family members. He's been crawling more, feeding himself in a simple way and has been struggling with physical therapy.
>
> (Dad, Feb 21, 1988) Thad had the flu, too, but is feeling much better now. I laid him on my stomach last night and rubbed his back while I watched a TV show with the kids. He snuggled right up and enjoyed it so much he went to sleep.

When I arrived in Spain in August of 1986, I felt like I was coming home. It seemed so familiar to me; I immediately felt like I belonged. My first assignment was in Las Palmas, the capital of Gran Canaria, one of the main islands in the Canary Island archipelago. I loved being a missionary. The confidence that found me as a Young Ambassador and the love I felt for the gospel and the Church blossomed. I couldn't imagine a better place to be or a more fulfilling life experience. Spanish was coming to me pretty easily, but I worked really hard on it. I wrote down every word I didn't know, looked them up in the dictionary when I got home, and added them to the flash cards I carried around with me to study when we were waiting for buses, appointments, meals, whatever. My first companion, Elder Quirce, didn't speak English, so it was a perfect learning environment. After two months with Elder Quirce, when I was transferred to Santa Cruz on the Island of La Palma, I was fluent enough to hold my own.

At the beginning of my fourth month I was transferred to Santa Cruz, the capital of Tenerife, and promoted to the role of senior companion. It should have been daunting, but I felt I was up to the task. I was confident because I had a testimony. I knew in my heart that the teachings I was promoting could help anyone lead a full, caring, and meaningful life. Logistically, though, I didn't know what I didn't know. Mormon missions are proselyting missions. Our goal was to find people who would be receptive to our message, read, ponder, pray, and choose to be baptized into the Church. Since baptisms were the goal, numbers were very important, especially in my mission—how many contacts we made, discussions we taught, commitments we encouraged, and baptisms we performed each week. Numbers were the gauge that measured how successful we were as missionaries. I realized I had been given a wonderful opportunity to be a senior companion so early in my mission. It was a vote of confidence, but the numbers were not happening. My companion and I worked very hard. We logged a lot of hours with very little apparent return.

In our tracting and our street contacting, it seemed that we were meeting several people each day who were already members of the Church because they had been baptized by enthusiastic missionaries, but they had had no real connection to the Church since their baptism. In my mind, that was evidence of the downside of the obsession with numbers. What was the point of baptizing people if they never came back to Church, or if they fell away right after? Perhaps our time would be better spent seeking these people out, encouraging them to remember why they decided to get baptized in the first place, and nurturing them back into the Church. Numbers didn't inspire me, people did.

I expressed my frustration in a letter to President Richardson, my Mission President. I tried to explain what it was like on the ground in Santa Cruz. I questioned the motives of missionaries who previously served in this area. I voiced doubts about a number-driven success model. And I asked if we could focus our attention as much on reactivation as on baptisms because, clearly, something had gone awry in Santa Cruz. President Richardson wrote me a scathing reply and counseled me to change my attitude. Still, no one would tell me how to get better numbers that were authentic. They just told me to get better numbers.

I was a rule follower by nature having grown up in both the Church and the military, but I needed to capitalize on my own talents and find a way to have a successful mission. I was good at talking to people. I would talk to members and non-members alike. I was interested in their lives and their beliefs. I wanted to find out what made them happy and hopeful. It was a slower way to go and not really quantifiable, but by being genuinely interested in them, they became interested, or at least curious, in what I had to say about why I was there. Some people joined the Church, but most did not; some people came back to church if they had been inactive and others did not; some active members felt more connected to the gospel and some felt inspired to invite their friends to listen to our message. I believed that whomever the interaction was with, we each came away from it better off than when we started. I also remembered my experience with Mother Teresa, and I tried to find ways with my companion to be of service to the people in our areas.

I was best with members. We would visit members frequently, often sharing meals with them if they invited us, which happened a few times a week because the Spaniards were very generous in that way. But we wouldn't hang out or just chill. We talked about what we were doing in the area. We asked them what their thoughts were on the best ways to reach their friends and neighbors. I liked spending time with them and finding out about their lives. We'd never leave without sharing a spiritual message. Either my companion or I would let our scriptures fall open, and there was always something there worth sharing, and more often than not, it seemed to be perfectly suited for each member's needs. I don't think we can take credit for that; it just happened.

Thanks to my experience with Diane in Japan, I felt confident enough to write several songs during my mission that I would share in Family Home Evening settings, or missionary meetings. I loved being able to share my thoughts and my testimony in that way. It was very Young Ambassador! I can't say that they were great songs, but people seemed to appreciate them. I felt valued by the members and by the other missionaries. That was a good feeling.

I think songwriting helped me more than anything else, because I felt inspired. It seemed like God was aware of me and that He, or someone up there, was guiding me through the process of bringing each song to life. I wasn't a prodigy, nor did I have the specific training to compose music. I'd studied piano for 10 years. But, when it came to music, I was a reader and a memorizer. I couldn't sit down and improvise. And yet, the few songs that I wrote on my mission would come into my head as a melody and a lyric simultaneously. One phrase would find its way into my thoughts, and I would ruminate on it, savor it, and nurture it until it would grow one word or note or phrase at a time through to the end, a fully realized song in my head.

I didn't have much free time to sit down at a piano and figure out anything musically, but when I could spare a few minutes and I was near a piano, I would sit and write out the melody and lyrics. This happened when we were at a church building in between Sunday meetings, before or after missionary meetings, or while we were waiting for investigators or members. I'd try my hand at creating a basic chord accompaniment, so I could sing it. I didn't know that I knew this stuff, but it came out of me easily enough so that my stolen moments at the piano were fruitful. I'd always been told that if our goals were worthwhile, and we did everything we could do to bring them to pass, the Lord would step in if we somehow fell short and "fill in the gaps" or "take up the slack" so that we could accomplish what we set out to do. In this instance, I felt like that was happening. I felt connected. I felt assisted. I felt like each song was a collaboration between myself and the Spirit.

I am most proud of the Christmas song I wrote because it expressed that, like the shepherds who weren't given the address to the stable where Jesus was born, I had been required to search for Him. When I'd found Him, the enlightened and joyful feelings I encountered compelled me to want to share the news with everyone around me. I wasn't pretending to have a testimony. I really believed.

> So long ago, the angels brought the news
> to humble shepherds in their fields that sacred night.
> With haste they went to Bethlehem
> to find the King and worship him.
> Their joyous search had now begun.

Fear not, for behold I bring good tidings of great joy
unto the world, a message to all people
Unto you is born this day, a savior, Christ the Lord
Born to bring the world the peace it's longing for.

And so they ran, guided by a star
to find themselves before the child that sacred night
With breathless joy they looked at him
They'd found the king and worshipped him
Then off to share, the love found there

Fear not, for behold I bring good tidings of great joy
unto the world, a message to all people
Unto you is born this day, a Savior, Christ the Lord
Born to bring the world the peace it's longing for.

I've felt the peace, the joy fulfilling me
I've felt His love surrounding me each day.
A hope in Christ fills my soul and now I know
the world is waiting for this news and I must share.
Unto you is born this day a Savior, Christ the Lord
Born to bring the world the peace it's longing for.

Fear not, for behold I bring good tidings of great joy
unto the world, a message to all people
Unto you is born this day, a savior, Christ the Lord
Born to bring the world the peace it's longing for.

Through my mission, and especially through songwriting, I was learning in a more profound way that we all had something to offer to the world. It often just required the right set of circumstances and the ideal mix of people to bring it to fruition. My family was in such a situation as Thad started school at Yokota Air Force Base. Just as in The Philippines, Thad was mainstreamed into the elementary school on base. There was a policy in this school that all the special education kids were to eat lunch with the rest of the children. There were only two special ed children in the school, Thad and one other child. Word got back to the school administrators that several of the younger students were afraid to go to school because there was a monster in the school. Thad's teacher responded to the concerns by saying, "Well, that just means we need to do our job and educate." So, she and the school nurse, with the cooperation from all the teachers in the school spent time visiting every classroom.

Mom described the experience to her mother in a letter:

> I'm most excited about Thad and the support he is getting [in school]. His teacher is fantastic with a sincere desire to help him. She is already crazy about him and she has him out and about the school. Because he is so new and because of his handicap she has started a project of helping the other children understand about handicapped children and especially about Thad. The children in the school have lots of questions about him and some were even afraid—so some of the teachers have asked her how they should answer them. She and the nurse have been going class to class talking about the handicap and especially Thad and how their needs are different in some areas and in some areas just like theirs. She explained simply that Thad was born like he is and how she is teaching him many things and

> that he is learning. Also, that he needs love, friends, activities, support, etc., just like they do.
>
> I've attended several presentations and they are really nice—only about 15 minutes long then she lets them ask questions. The response of the children of the school has been fantastic—it gives great emphasis that if we teach our children about those who are different, their natural compassion will show and they can understand even if they are very young. His teacher says, "Thad has a million friends." Everyone says hello at lunch and whenever they see him, many come and talk to him. At an assembly last week, the assistant principal was telling everyone to quiet down and as things were settled down somewhat, Thad let out a loud "da!' and the principal said, "That goes for you too, Thad!" The kids loved it and so did Thad! We've got an exciting year ahead for him. His teacher and the aide in class only have two students so he is being worked, taught, exercised and played with a lot. This is the perkiest I've seen him in a long time.

This inspired teacher created a common ground for the students by saying that some children are good at math and others struggle with math. Some children are good at art while others struggle with art. Everyone has strengths and everyone needs help. She told them that Thad needed help doing things that to them came very easy, and her job was help him learn those things, but he was very happy and loved being around people. From that moment on, Thad never wanted for someone to push him around at school. If Mom happened to drive by the school at recess, Thad was always surrounded by children. She would even have children come up to her in the grocery store and start talking to Thad. They'd say to my mom, "It's alright, we're friends!"

Mom had another experience the next year that is also worth mentioning, at the same school. She wrote this in another letter to her mother:

> Last week at school, Lara was child of the week and she was honored by having a bulletin board up with lots of her pictures on it. I was standing in the hallway looking at all her pictures when three little boys came up and were looking at it also. One little boy pointed to Thad's picture and said, "That's Thad, he's Lara's brother. He's really nice. His head looks like that cause he didn't grow right before he was born." Of course, they didn't know I was her mother. So, I went along with their conversation. The boy then mentioned that they see Thad a lot. I was really touched with the friendliness and knowledge they showed towards him. Like Thad's teacher told me—Everyone knows Thad.
>
> He's the playmate these kids will remember and they'll remember what a sweet happy boy he was, and they'll remember what fun and how good they felt when they helped with him. So, he's influencing many children in school about caring—understanding and helping.

It was inspiring how an inclusive, healthy, positive environment could engender such a powerful and pervasive acceptance of difference. Thad was Thad, and I don't think anyone who spent time with him ever walked away without feeling moved in a positive way—ok, maybe there were a few, but I didn't know them. The difference here was that this experience wasn't just Thad's doing, it was his teacher, the nurse, the other teachers, the principal, the assistant principal and everyone else in that school. It was evidence that love and acceptance doesn't happen in a vacuum.

All the components of life at Yokota Air Force Base seemed to integrate my family into the community more than we'd experienced anywhere else. There was more interaction, and less isolation. When it came to

Thad, not every interaction involved my family educating strangers about Thad's condition. Troy likes to tell a story that happened to Fé one afternoon on a playground where she had taken Thad to get out of the house for a bit.

> Fé was a live-in caretaker we had for a few years. She'd baby-sit, clean house, all that good stuff. The thing about merry-go-rounds is that you have to crane your head to keep looking at something, right? So, there were these kids at the playground, and their eyes weren't coming off of Thad as they were going around and around.
>
> Fé said she noticed a four-year-old girl hop off the merry-go-round and start walking toward her. She said to herself, "Oh no, 20 questions: What's wrong with his eye? What's wrong with his head? Can he talk? Can he run?"
>
> But, no, this little girl walked up to her and as Fé waited for that ever-so-popular question, the little girl asked, "What's his name?"
>
> And Fé said, " Well, this is Thad."
>
> And she asked, "Does Thad like hugs?"
>
> And Fé said, "Well, of course Thad likes hugs!"
>
> So, the little girl walked up and gave Thad a little hug. As she hugged him, she looked at Fé and she asked, "Does Thad like kisses?"
>
> Fé said, "He loves kisses."
>
> So she reached up and kissed him. Thad giggled and she got down and trotted away back to the merry-go-round where her brother waited.

I think this story resonated and humbled my family in a way because it reminded us that each interaction was unique. No matter how familiar the set-up, it was important that we be open. Thad was not ours. We were to share him with the world. And his presence in our lives opened the world to each one of us.

One of the beautiful things about being part of a community—whether a military community, a religious community, or a social community—is that you are given the opportunity to meet people that would not have crossed your path in other ways. While in Japan, my family met another family, the Salisburys, at church. The Salisburys had two daughters, Katie and Shelly, both of whom had a rare muscle degenerative condition that would eventually take their lives at early ages. Katie was the oldest, a few years older than Thad, and she had progressed further in the disease than her younger sister, to the point that she had lost the ability to walk, and her speech was slowing down a bit. She could still move herself around the floor with her arms, though. Katie was a bright, smart, observant little girl whose body was betraying her.

Katie and Thad hit it off right away. Mom would visit their house or they would visit ours, and Katie would spend the whole time with Thad. *Top Gun* was her favorite movie, and they would watch it together again and again. Katie would sit with Thad on the floor and pat his back or stroke his arm saying, "I love you, Thad." Thad's forehead would crinkle, and he'd smile. Whatever that meant, it was clear they had a connection. Mom and Sharon, Katie's mom, would joke that in the afterlife, Thad and Katie were going to be boyfriend and girlfriend. It was a joke, but for two women who were daily confronted with the mortality of their children, it was something beautiful to consider.

Thad was 11, now, and he was beginning to experience some growth spurts. Mom expressed it this way, "As he is growing larger, it is getting more difficult to easily care for him, but fortunately I have the older boys who willingly lift and carry him for me. As for the future, it always works out that what we thought might be a problem, isn't, and we continue on with what needs and should be done."

Maybe this is a Mormon thing, but a rite of passage in my family was getting our first tie. Our Sunday clothes consisted of slacks and button-down shirts until we reached 11, then we'd get our first tie which meant that we were more like the men in the Church than the boys. The expectation was that we would rise to the occasion and behave more responsibly and more reverently at church. To this day, when I put a tie on (and I have very little occasion to wear ties), I feel a mantle of responsibility and seriousness come over me. I probably stand straighter and walk with more purpose. Thad reached this moment in 1987 when he was eleven. In a letter to her parents, Mom shared with them the same notable information she had mentioned in a previously cited letter to me, "Thad looked so cute on Easter. We bought a sweater, shirt, and slacks outfit and he wore a tie with it. (His first tie.) He was very handsome!"

This reflects an important aspect of how my mom approached taking care of Thad. She determined from the very beginning that she would dress Thad in nice, age-appropriate clothing. First impressions matter, and clothing plays a vital role in first impressions. She felt that although sweatpants and t-shirts were imminently easier to put on and to take off, they were not clothes that should be worn every day, especially when going out in public. It was a matter of dignity, Thad's dignity and hers. When people saw Thad, she wanted them to see a 5-year old or a 12-year old who happened to have a disability, not a handicapped kid/adult in a wheelchair wearing schlumpy, formless clothing. So, for Thad, it was always jeans or chinos with polos or button-downs.

Halfway through my father's assignment in Japan, he started thinking about where he wanted his career to go. He didn't think it was likely that he would become a General, so he started looking for opportunities teaching in an ROTC program at a university in the states, preferably BYU. He loved the military, and he loved teaching. It happened that BYU was looking for a new ROTC guy, so my father applied. When it didn't work out, he and my mom started looking at their options.

Dad was going to be 50 soon, and they thought that it would be easier for him to get a job at 49 than to get a job past 50. They still had six children at home, and his retirement benefits from the Air Force, though decent, would not be enough to sustain the family. Dad needed a second career. It was a tough pill to swallow because he'd already had his dream career. Flying was all he ever wanted to do, so anything else paled in comparison. Nevertheless, Dad was a practical, if-it-needs-to-be-done-just-do-it kind of guy, so, they began the retirement process. They'd bought a house in south Provo (Utah) as an investment and as a place for the kids to live while they were going to BYU, but now that they were looking at civilian life and taking into account that Utah had great schools and many wonderful programs for disabled children and their families, my parents opted to move to Utah once my father's Air Force career was officially over.

By this time, I was in my final area, Cádiz, a beautiful town on the Atlantic coast of Spain. I was at the height of my mission experience. I loved the area. I loved the members. I loved the people we were meeting. I loved the missionaries I was working with. It seemed that we were really in tune. The spirit was strong in our meetings and in our discussions. We were able to really listen and find answers. We were meeting people who were open to the gospel, still not in great numbers, but they were solid. They were asking great, even challenging questions, but we were able to help them find their own answers by asking questions of our own and guiding them back to the scriptures and to their own personal prayers. This is what I thought missionary work should be all along. It was thrilling and humbling. I didn't know if I was going to have any baptisms in this area before I left, but it looked like I was going to finish my mission on a real high.

I got word from my family that Diane, my friend in Japan with whom I had felt a real bond from the moment we met, and who made me aware that I could write music if I wanted to, had drifted away from the Church. Dad sent me a copy of the letter that she had written to him explaining that she no longer had a testimony and felt it best to move on with her life by divorcing her husband and starting fresh back in the States without any ties to her former life. I vividly remember the day I read the letter. It was a sunny pre-Spring day, probably early March. There was still an edge of cold in the air, but the promise of warmth was strong and imminent. I was sitting on my bed by the window on our lunch break. Light was streaming in. I couldn't believe what I was reading. It didn't seem possible, and yet it was there, handwritten in blue ballpoint ink on lined white paper. I thought, "If only I had been there, maybe I could have averted this tragedy." I was helping people in Spain by asking questions, by helping them find answers, by encouraging them to pray, and by praying with them. If only I had been with her, maybe I could have helped. I was truly devastated. Bad things were happening at home to people I cared about, and there was nothing I could do. I felt utterly helpless.

After lunch we went out to do some tracting, which included door-to-door proselyting as well as meeting and talking to people on the streets. We started talking to this young guy, José Luis, who was working in a small neighborhood bar. (In Spain, a bar is basically a small restaurant that happens to serve alcohol as well. It's not the same type of business as a "bar" in the U.S.) He was very nice, probably in his late twenties, and he had a big, warm smile when we were talking about what we were doing and why we were in Spain. He asked very good questions. It turned out that he was playing with us a bit. He was part of a family in our ward, and he had served a mission in Valencia. After he returned home, he gradually fell away from the Church. But, he didn't seem to have any negative feelings toward it. It didn't seem logical to me that he was inactive. The ward could really benefit from his wonderful energy and enthusiasm, and I was sure that he would benefit from being an active part of the Church once more. If I couldn't help my friend in Japan, then, by golly, I was going to do everything in my power to help José Luis find his way back into the Church.

José Luis fit right into our very busy teaching and tracting schedule. Over the next few months, we met with José Luis a few times a week, shared meals with him occasionally, had Family Home Evenings with him and his friends from the ward, and encouraged him to attend church. His family was very excited to see that he was taking an interest in the Church again. It all seemed to be going very well. One day, he admitted to me, not to my companion, that the reason he was no longer active in the church was because he was gay. From the tone in his voice, I knew that he expected me to reject him or berate him or something. His revelation didn't phase me at all. I had seen so much good in him from the first moment we met. I just wanted him to be happy, and I knew that being active in the Church again was just the ticket. I told him that that shouldn't be a problem, because everything was overcome-able, and I knew that for a fact because I had struggled with questions of sexuality my whole life, and look where I was! I felt like the Lord was helping me out tremendously and he'd be more than happy to help José Luis. He just needed to have a little more faith. Plus, he had a wonderful support mechanism which included family, friends and us, the missionaries!

Before long, though, I realized that I was falling in love with José Luis. I had a new companion who had just arrived to Spain, and he was sick all the time, so he would fall into a deep sleep whenever and wherever he sat down. This made discussions, the lessons that we teach to people investigating the Church, kind of humorous at times. It also gave me just enough time with José Luis to feel even more connected to him. It was truly sublime, as new love, especially first love, always seems to be. When I was with him, I was giddy. I felt like I was walking on air. I had never experienced this ever before, ever. I believed that anything was possible, that any obstacle could be overcome. I felt free!

Somehow, in the beginning, I was able to compartmentalize all of these feelings in such a way that it didn't interfere with the rest of the work my companion and I were doing. But soon, José Luis and I started crossing lines. I had never kissed anyone before I kissed José Luis, and it felt like gallons of ice cold lemonade at the end of a long, hot, dry excursion through a desert wasteland. It seemed I would never be sated.

Still, my repertoire of intimacy was non-existent. If human sexuality were an ocean, I'd spent my whole life sitting on the beach wearing jeans and a t-shirt. With José Luis, I rolled up my jeans and stood at the edge feeling the cool, refreshing water as it rolled over my feet and back pulling sand from underneath. I even waded in and played in the shallows, but I didn't know how to swim. I wasn't ready to swim. In addition to my inexperience, my companion was always asleep in the living room, so what José Luis and I were able to do was extremely limited. I had not let myself experience anything before. It wasn't long, though, before the reverie dimmed enough for my conscience to kick in. I realized without a doubt that I had strayed from the commitments I had made to God and to myself when I chose to become a missionary. I could no longer compartmentalize anything after that. After a few days of turbulent self-recrimination, which I kept inside as best I could, I knew my only recourse was to call President Richardson and let him know what I had done.

Oddly, phoning my Mission President wasn't a hard call to make, but the ramifications of that call were swift and disastrous. They whisked me out of Cádiz the next morning to Seville where they convened a disciplinary council. It consisted of President Richardson and two other gentlemen. I imagine they were his counselors, or maybe they were just two older male missionaries who were in Spain with their wives. I honestly don't know. The environment was neither antagonistic nor demeaning. All three were actually very kind throughout. I explained everything that happened, and they decided, in their words, that they were afraid if they excommunicated me, I would never return to the Church, so they would disfellowship me and send me home as soon as they could arrange a flight—two weeks before I was supposed to honorably finish my mission and go home anyway. Being disfellowshipped meant that I was still a member of the Church, but I could not participate as a member in good standing, until I proved that I was fully repentant and able to be an "upstanding Mormon young man." I couldn't even offer a public prayer during any church activity.

In the midst of all of this, I wrote my last mission song. The lyrics came to me in Spanish because by the end of my mission I rarely thought in English unless I needed to. These lyrics express most clearly what I was feeling at the time. I've done my best translation:

What's happened to my life?
I don't understand
How I've fallen so far
from where I found myself standing
just a moment ago.
I don't know which way to go
I'm losing my self control
I long for the light that once burned within me

Oh Lord, please help me
I need the strength
to find my way home
Be my guide, and my protector
so I can see
the way for me
I want to give my heart to thee
Oh Lord, please take my hand

At times, the feelings I reach for
Seem so very far from my grasp
Emptiness reigns
There are questions I can't even answer
Thou canst bring the help I need
I have so much to change indeed
A hope fills my soul
Now that thou art with me

Oh Lord, please help me
I need the strength
to find my way home
Be my guide, and my protector
so I can see
the way for me
I want to give my heart to thee
Oh Lord, please take my hand

I didn't have a home to go to, because it didn't make sense to go all the way to Japan only to turn around and go to Utah. So, I went to Utah. Our house in South Provo wasn't ready yet because the previous owners hadn't moved out, so Todd let me stay in his room in off-campus housing. Getting sent home from my mission was rough. Being a missionary is iconic. It's a milestone that sets the stage for a successful and fulfilling Mormon life. There is a significant amount of respect and even reverence afforded missionaries who return home with honor. They are given the opportunity to speak about their mission experience in front of the congregation in a Sacrament Meeting. All the boys and young men as well as many of the girls and young women look up to them and aspire to be them one day. Having been one of those boys, the shame I felt returning home without honor was crushing. I felt like I was walking around with a scarlet "I got sent home early" on my chest.

When my family arrived from Japan and we moved into the house in South Provo, those who knew, which as far as I knew were only Mom, Dad, Tony and Todd and maybe Thomas, rallied around me. I knew that my parents were hurt, maybe even embarrassed, but they were more concerned about me, sensitive to my feelings, and they wanted to help as much as they could. I assumed that they had been told the reason why I was sent home early, but my mission leaders had given them no details. They had their suspicions because they knew me, but they never asked for details. There were no ultimatums, no "You've brought shame on this family," just, "We love you, Tim, and we want you to be happy." Of course, wanting me to be happy meant, "We want you to do whatever you need to do in order to become a member in full fellowship again because this is the only way that you will find true happiness." They were earnest and sincere, but they also knew that whatever my struggle was, I needed to be the one to face it, head-on.

I didn't really feel stigmatized for long because I came home so close to my original return date that everyone who knew me before my mission just assumed that I'd completed my mission with honor. Also, since I didn't go back to the ward I left from in Japan, everything and practically everyone in our lives were brand-new. My priesthood leaders in the new ward all knew my situation, but they were kind and non-judgmental as far as I could tell. They were encouraged that I was enthusiastic to beat this and get back on track.

I couldn't go back to school because as a disfellowshipped member, I was not allowed to attend classes at Brigham Young University. So, I got a few jobs, started psycho-therapy with a BYU-approved psychologist, read every book I could get my hands on, regardless of religious denomination, that promised to cure me of same-sex attraction. I took it all in. I believed. I tried to apply what I was learning. I attended Church meetings faithfully. I felt good. In a way, I was making progress. I was learning a lot about myself and about my relationships with others. I was maturing. In another way, I was carefully putting the spring-bodied clown back into his box and doing my darndest to make sure the lid was secure.

In December of that year, six months after I returned home from Spain, they reinstated me into the Church, and allowed me to go to the Salt Lake City, North Mission for two weeks in order to complete my mission experience with honor. I loved being in the mission field again. It was great to feel connected to the work again. It was satisfying because I felt my efforts were proving successful. My parents were relieved and very happy that all was well in my/our world.

It's hard to explain in a way that makes sense, even to my own ears, how the two irreconcilable sides of my life felt equally organic. I love the Church. I love the theology, the history, the mythology. I feel deeply and spiritually connected to its message. It has brought me, through the years, powerful spiritual experiences, recognition of profound truth, joyous realizations about life and family and love. In truth, Thad was a living icon for me. It was through our experience with Thad and his very existence that I felt the hand of God in our lives, that I felt a glimpse of eternal concepts in action that were beyond my comprehension yet within my grasp. Thad made it all make sense somehow, and I could never fully turn away from it.

At the same time, what many people don't understand about sexuality is that, yes, it's about physical attraction, it is about sex, but that's only a small part of the matrix that makes up our sexual nature. For me, especially, the attraction is about who I feel safe with, who I feel capable of opening up to, of sharing my deepest thoughts, of sharing both the momentous and the mundane. Ultimately, it is about who I am drawn toward in the multi-faceted manifestations of love. Never, in my recollection, was the object of my affection a woman. And for that reason, without being able to verbalize it, I felt different, separate and, because of what I was taught, bad for most of my life. And yet, Thad was different, but so easy to love. I knew that we all loved him deeply, neither in spite of nor because of his differences, his disabilities. We loved him, all of him, period. Thad gave me hope that that was possible for me.

EVERYTHING IS GOING TO BE ALRIGHT

During the Summer of 1988, after coming home from my mission, life on South Idaho Street in Provo was amazing. It was great to spend time laughing, playing, singing, and praying with the family after being away for three years. Grandma and Grandpa Sutton came out for a few weeks in July and August and we all worked together remodeling the house: new roof, two new rooms (a dining room and a TV room on what had been a large, astro-turf-covered porch off the kitchen and above the garage), new paint and carpet everywhere. My youngest siblings were all in elementary school, now. I could get to know them better. The rough part of being an older sibling when there is almost an 18-year gap between the oldest and youngest child in the family is that once you leave, you become a visitor instead of a resident when you return home, so building relationships with younger siblings becomes a challenge. Moving back in with the family after my mission was a real gift. I was able to share in the lives of my younger siblings in a way that would have been difficult otherwise.

Since Dad bought the house on South Idaho Street as an investment, he never intended on bringing the whole family there; so the drawbacks of a split level house never crossed his mind. However, we soon realized the challenge that layout presented with Thad. When you entered the front door, you either had to go up some stairs or down some stairs, and the landing at the front door was not that big, so managing a wheel chair in that tight space was difficult. Thad was also getting bigger, so carrying him up and down the stairs, even though there were only six or seven steps, was taxing, especially on Mom's body, and because of work and school schedules, she got the brunt of that. For this reason and others, Mom was never really comfortable in this house, and after a few years they bought some land near the temple and built a house from the ground up with wide hallways and easy-access to everything on the first floor.

The first day of the new school year came faster than any of us wanted. Lara, Travis, and Lesa went to an elementary school right behind our house. Troy and Trent went to a junior high about a half a mile away.

Mom and Dad enrolled Thad in the Oakridge School, which specialized in special education. Since Oakridge was located right across 900 East from the Brigham Young University campus, the school got wonderful teachers, therapists, assistants, staff, and volunteers—people who believed in special education and the value of each individual regardless of their challenges or disabilities. Thad loved this school. It was a very large school with a lot of action and diversity: physical therapy, play therapy, music time, and lots of activities and field trips. The learning activities in Math, Geography, and other subjects were designed to incorporate all of the senses. Because of the core of BYU student volunteers, each child in the school got a lot of one-on-one attention. They would periodically take the children swimming. Thad wasn't particularly fond of the swimming pool because of the cold water, but he could spend all day in the nearby jacuzzi. Thad would come home from school and fall right to sleep most of the time.

In 1988, Thad's first teachers, Gary Lacock and Lisa Crabtree, chronicled the year they had together in an effervescent construction paper and Polaroid book entitled, "The Memoirs of Thad Sutton, Dev II, 1988-89." On the first page, Thad lies across a large red padded cylinder while his physical therapist, Gayle Hyde, helps him learn to bear weight again on all fours, and he's smiling! In "Home Living Skills" they made Butterscotch Rice Krispie Treats. While in art class Thad played with Peanut Butter Play-doh. Music class was where he excelled since they gave him the jingle bell stick, and if there was one thing Thad could do with gusto, it was shake something that made noise! For the Spring Talent Show, Thad's class performed a parody of *Cyrano de Bergerac* called "Thad De Bergerac," on a stage complete with costumes and scenery. Thad, as the title character, wore a black bowler hat in addition to a blanket cape, and a plastic nose/mustache combo. He was adorable! The enthusiasm that leapt from the pages of this memoir were indicative of Thad's time at Oakridge.

Thad's physical therapist, Gayle, worked diligently to encourage Thad to bear weight on all fours, to remind his body what it used to do in the hope that he could regain some mobility. The physical declines that my parents began to notice in the Philippines had continued. Something wrong was happening. Thad's left hand started to pull up and back which caused his fingers to clench. We would try to massage the forearm and mobilize the hand to loosen it up, but it was clear that it was something bigger than just a tight forearm. Thad's crawling slowly became less coordinated. Eventually, when he started to lose strength and control in his left arm, the crawling stopped altogether. He was probably 10 or 11 by the time this whole process finished.

Since he could only use one arm, sitting up on his own became very difficult, and the balance he'd relied on for so many years was no longer possible. If someone was holding him, he'd throw his head back with his special rhythm and shake it to catch the light the way he used to do on his own sitting or kneeling on the floor. Now, he was relegated to lying down on a blanket on the floor or on a bed or sitting in his wheelchair, being held and walked around or sitting on someone's lap, often in the rocking chair, watching TV, or listening to whatever conversation happened to be transpiring. At this point, though, it was explained to us that it was very possible due to the cerebral nature of his birth defect that he had had several minor strokes along the way that caused the paralysis to set in.

I'm so grateful that he didn't lose the use of his right hand because that gave him the ability to express himself by articulating sound coming out of his mouth. He was able to play with his toys and hold us around the neck while we carried him. He could play with our hair. He didn't have all the freedom he had before, but having one useful hand was a tremendous blessing.

A few years later, in our new home by the temple, when I was working hard to complete my studies at

BYU before moving to New York, one of my friends, Veronique Enos, from acting and directing classes came over to work on a project. She arrived just after Thad got home from school. He was still sitting in the entrance near our front door. I opened the door to let Veronique in, and before I could introduce her to Thad, she threw her hands up in the air and happily screamed, "Tha-a-a-a-d!" Thad started laughing, and she gave him a big hug. She talked with him a bit then explained to me that she was a volunteer in Thad's class at Oakridge.

Veronique worked a lot with Thad during their exercises and activities. She told me that there were a lot of children in Thad's class with a wide range of disabilities including various combinations of physical, mental, and emotional challenges. Some were more extensive than others. Thad's calm, happy energy seemed to ground the room. Veronique continued by saying, "Thad fills whatever room he is in with an 'everything is going to be alright' energy." I had never put it that way nor had I thought of it that way, but as soon as she said that, I thought, "That's exactly right! It's been that way from the very beginning." I think that is one of the reasons why there was never any animosity toward Thad from any member of our family at any time. It's hard to be resentful of someone who makes you feel like everything is going to work out.

Thad had a great time at school. It boosted his energy. It made his day diverse and challenging. It created a social outlet that enhanced what we were able to provide at home. There were benefits for my mom, too, in the sense that it freed her mornings and afternoons up to get work done around the house if she needed to, to go shopping if she needed to, or to pursue activities and experiences that were just her own. She was able to go back to school to get a two-year degree that allowed her to be a substitute teacher and a teacher's aid.

In the beginning, Mom did a lot of substitute teaching in elementary schools in Provo, including Thad's school, Oakridge. Teaching at Oakridge gave her an insider's view of the workings of the school that most parents did not get. She was relieved to see how respectful the teachers and staff were when discussing the students. I think that made the biggest impression on my mom because respect is something you always hope for in this situation, but you never really know what happens behind closed doors. Mom was relieved that in the teacher's lounge at Oakridge, even when discussing the challenging aspects of working with some of the students, it was always done with civility and care.

Mom landed a steady, on-call, resident substitute teaching gig at Rock Canyon Elementary School which was just a few blocks from the North Provo home. It was a nice situation because it was close to home, and it was where Lara, Travis, and Lesa went to school. Lesa told Mom that she could take the position as long as she never had to substitute in one of her classes. Mom chuckles when she talks about this because she did end up substituting in some of Lesa's classes, and the world did not end.

Lara was in 6th grade when Mom began her on-call status at Rock Canyon. The main obstacle in this arrangement was that if Mom got called in, she would have to go into work before Thad's bus came to pick him up to go to Oakridge. On those occasions, she would get him ready for school, then she would ask Lara if she could stay and make sure Thad got onto his bus before walking to school. So that's what Lara would do. Sometimes, if Thad's bus were running late, it would mean that Lara would arrive to school a few minutes late. Lara's teacher pulled her aside one morning after she arrived late, and told her that her tardiness was unacceptable and that she should be more responsible. Lara, who was born responsible, started crying and told her teacher that she had a handicapped brother and sometimes she needed to stay home to make sure that he got on his bus, but that sometimes the bus was late and prevented her from getting to school on time. Lara's teacher was touched by her sincerity and told her not to worry, that she could be late whenever she needed to be late. In the phone conversation I had with Mom about this, she laughed and said, "Hindsight is a wonderful thing if you want to beat yourself up! I was working at the same school. We should have told Lara's teacher up front what was going on, but we were still figuring out this new arrangement. We didn't think that Thad's bus would be late, especially on consecutive days."

Mom started out substitute teaching, then she was offered a position as a teaching assistant in the Resource Program at Rock Canyon Elementary School. So, for ten years she helped children catch up to their grade levels in Reading and Math. It was a perfect job for Mom because she excelled in the one-on-one interaction required of her, and the progress for many of the kids, though varied, was trackable, and that was very satisfying. In addition, she would finish work around the same time that Thad was coming home from school, so scheduling was easy.

Just after they moved into the new house, Mom expressed some concern to her parents about how things were going. Physical realities appeared to be catching up to them. Mom was not a complainer by nature, but she was beginning to feel shooting pain periodically from her back going into her legs and feet. It was worrisome, but she kept a lid on it. As far as she was concerned, it was just a sign that she was getting older. She had been a runner when she was younger. She carried ten children, during their pregnancies and after. She had led an active life. And part of that included lifting Thad several times a day for 15 years. She told her parents:

> Thad is doing well. He is growing again—it is incredible how heavy he is getting. Tom is even challenged with lifting him. It's kind of scary—I'm getting weaker with my back and he's getting bigger. I sure wonder about the future. I'm sure things will be fine, they always work out.

That's how my parents approached everything with Thad. Just move forward and hope for the best. They had a troubling experience right before Thad's 16th birthday. We had grown accustomed to a fluctuation in the firmness of Thad's brain. Sometimes it was softer and sometimes it was firmer, but it always held it's shape. One day, Mom noticed that Thad's head was getting droopy. She gave him more water throughout the day because that always seemed to firm up his head in the past, but it continued to deflate. Soon there was an indention at the top of his head. She took him to the emergency room where they did an MRI and a CAT scan. It appeared that his cerebral spinal fluid was draining into his spine and out somehow. There wasn't anything they could really do, so they put him in an observation room and watched him closely. After about two hours, he seemed to stabilize and his head firmed up again. Mom said, "It was real interesting."

The nice thing about living in Utah was that it was sort of a crossroad for anyone who professed the Mormon faith. Over the years, my parents were able to reconnect with many of their friends from their Air Force years who had retired to Utah like my dad or who were passing through to see their kids at BYU, or to attend General Conference or other church activity, or just on their way from East to West or vice versa.

One such encounter happened within the first few years after my family moved to Utah. Mom was looking for a Family Practice doctor who could serve as the primary care physician for our family, especially for Thad. She realized that Dr. Darrell Stacey had a practice in the Provo/ Orem area. As a resident at Scott Air Force Base in Illinois, Dr. Stacey had delivered Lesa. He knew our family, and he was a remarkable Family Practice Physician. He was more than capable of handling the day-to-day concerns in Thad's care. If there were a problem that required a specialist, Primary Children's Hospital was just an hour away. Dr. Stacey became the center of Thad's support network.

Another Air Force reconnection happened when the Salisbury family, from their time at Yokota Air Force Base, settled in Logan, Utah, which was a few hours from where my parents lived in Provo. Katie, Thad's friend, was not doing well. She was confined to a wheelchair at this point and had mostly lost her ability to speak. Mom brought Thad up to visit a few times before Katie passed away when she was 16-years old.

On the day of Katie's funeral, everyone in my family who was living in Utah at the time traveled up to Logan. It was a long drive, and the whole way up, Thad was irritated and grumpy. He had a sound that he would make in this kind of situation that was particularly grating to the ears. By the time they arrived at the chapel where the funeral was going to take place, Trent was beside himself. He was concerned that Thad would continue to make that irritating noise through the service, so someone would have to take him out and miss it. Before they went into the chapel, Trent knelt down in front of Thad so their eyes were at the same level. He explained to Thad what was happening, that Katie had passed away and that they needed to all be quiet and reverent in order to honor her and remember all the beauty and hope she had brought into people's lives. Thad listened, and he quieted down. When they got into the chapel, Trent took Thad out of his wheelchair and sat him on his lap. Thad was quiet, even contemplative, throughout the service.

Lara wrote this to me,

> My most poignant memory of [Katie] was at her funeral. They played a recording of her bearing her testimony at her baptism, I believe. She said that she was not afraid to die because she would finally be able to kick a ball again. That has stuck with me my entire life and still brings tears to my eyes. How often do we take such pleasure in the little things that we are capable of and blessed to be able to do. Her sweet little voice on that recording still haunts my thoughts when I start to take my life for granted.

I wasn't in Utah for Katie's funeral. In 1991, I moved to New York. I had a job offer from McCorkle Casting, Ltd., an office I interned at the Summer before. I was strapped for cash. I couldn't find a job in Utah that paid more than minimum wage. And I couldn't secure a student loan or any financial aid. So, I left BYU with a little more than one semester remaining before I finished my degree. It felt like the right thing to do. Once in New York, I loved my job. Pat McCorkle and Rich Cole, the casting directors, were amazing. I felt like I had a New York family right away. The job didn't pay very well, so I ended up juggling a handful of jobs—ice cream scooper at Ben & Jerry's on the Upper West Side of Manhattan from 6:30 p.m. 'til 2 a.m., five nights a week, weekends at a children's bookstore in Chelsea, and a brief stint as a graveyard shift legal proofreader—in addition to the casting gig, just to make ends occasionally meet. It wasn't an easy life, but I was living it, and it felt great!

Living in New York City opened a world of possibilities. It was filled with people from every part of the world and from all walks of life. I could almost be certain that practically everyone I passed on the street looked at life in a completely different way than I did. That fact alone sealed my connection to the city. I'd lived a pretty homogenous life up to that point, and to be surrounded by diversity of thought and action was invigorating and humbling. The only expectations I had to live up to were sidewalk related—quicken my pace or get out of the way.

I liked going to church in New York. It brought the comfort of familiarity and a connection to spiritual activity, but there was an added sense of progressive thought. I don't mean to imply that the meetings were riddled with heresy, rather there was understanding where there could have been fear. It felt like the people I was meeting had chosen to see the world without being threatened by it, while at the same time cultivating and nurturing their testimony of the Church and its principles.

My ward was a singles ward, which was the Church's way of putting all the unmarried people in the area in the same place so that we could interact, find support, and hopefully, find a mate. The mate search fell outside the scope of my radar, but I enjoyed being around all the people my age as we were experiencing New York for the first time—some of us working, some doing internships, some studying. Sunday was a refreshing break from the stresses of New York life. I knew that these people understood the part of me that my colleagues at work did not. I valued the caring, thoughtful person I was capable of being most of the time and growing up in the Church is what laid the foundation for my character, in spite of the internal conflicts throughout my late childhood and adolescence, or maybe because of them.

Day-to-day life in New York City was exciting, especially working in a casting office. I met all kinds of interesting and talented people. I did my best to stay open to the world I was living in without judgment, while maintaining a connection to my spiritual life and the values I'd grown up with. Once again, I was living on the shoreline of human sexuality, fully clothed with 50spf sunblock and a wide-brimmed hat. My little wading party at the end of my mission hadn't turned out too well, so I was back on dry land. I would tell myself and anyone who asked that I was having fun, that I was completely satisfied, that I'd watch their stuff if they wanted to go play in the water, and that I was perfectly content to stay on land. But, I wasn't. Rich Cole, the associate casting director in the office, would say to me, "You know, you put on a good front, but sometimes I look at you when you don't think that anyone is looking and it seems as though your head will explode from everything you are trying to hold in."

Rich was right. I was holding a lot in, and there were times, many times, when I felt like a 22 gallon soda bottle in the back of a pick-up truck driving 60 miles per hour on a back country road after an erosive rain-laden Summer. What could I do? There was no way to integrate my two worlds. I was stuck choosing one or the other, and neither choice felt whole, or even right. I knew the Mormon experience very well, and, except for the sexuality thing (a big exception), I felt right at home. I loved the theology, the culture, the social interaction, the way it brought a spiritual paradigm into my everyday life. On the other hand, I didn't know enough about the gay experience to know whether it would fulfill me or not, but I yearned for intimacy, for connection, for someone who mattered and to whom I mattered. The Church told me to stay celibate and alone if I wasn't interested in women. My friends in New York told me to find another church. Neither option felt do-able.

My understanding of life as well as a deep connection to spiritual things evolved out of my life with Thad. His birth forced me to contemplate big questions at a young age when I was starting to search for my place in the world. We, as a family, were cradled in the strong arms of the gospel of Jesus Christ as we understood it, and that gave us a sense of peace that was hard to explain to anyone else. I felt like there was a profound rhyme and reason to Thad's life, and I understood that through the gospel. For this reason, I struggled. I knew where I belonged, but I didn't belong.

Over the years I had seen friends and acquaintances leave the Church for various reasons including, but certainly not exclusively, sexuality. Without fail, they appeared to become rudderless. They were strong enough to break the "chains" they felt were holding them back, but they were unprepared to face the world with any sort of restraint. Bad language, cigarettes, drugs, alcohol, coffee, and promiscuity seemed to throw them into a storm of degradation and vice. Some survived relatively unscathed, but others did not. As I walked along the metaphorical beach, inching closer and closer to the water, I knew that wasn't me in my heart. Drugs, alcohol, none of those things interested me in the least. I was looking for love, plain and simple.

I eventually made it into the ocean, but I stayed in the shallows for a long time gradually getting used to the experience as I waded deeper and deeper until after a few years, I learned how to swim more or less effectively. I had a lot to learn because I'd avoided the experience altogether through my teen years. I didn't throw myself headlong into "the lifestyle." I kept myself free and clear from cigarettes and drugs and alcohol, though my language did eventually become more colorful—simply a result of living in New York. I wasn't interested in meeting people at bars or dance clubs or anything like that, so I didn't go there. One-night stand kinds of experiences, although I had them on occasion, were neither satisfying nor desirable. I met people at my different work venues, because I wasn't going to meet them at church, which was my only other social interaction, when I was still going to church.

I don't want to belabor the metaphor, but an ocean is an apt parallel to human sexuality, because it can be wonderful and refreshing and exciting while at the same time currents can pull you far from the shore before you know it, riptides can drag you under and waves can crash and spin you around or drive you into the sand. I learned that many people weren't looking for love. I would get attached very quickly, so more often than not, I found that I was embracing ideas and aspirations more than anything else.

Of course, I didn't share any of this with my parents or any family members. I feared they wouldn't understand, especially since I didn't fully understand, certainly not enough to explain myself. This made my interactions with them incomplete. I could talk about work, about friends, about the writing I was doing, but I couldn't share my whole experience. My parents weren't naive, though. They were very concerned about me and about my life in New York City. Dad wrote, " We enjoyed visiting with you on the phone tonight. I look forward to hearing your voice if for no other reason than to get a sense of your real feelings and your well-being. I, of course, do worry about you and suspect that all is not well, but I wait."

Mom channelled her apprehensions into sending me books or articles that she found spiritually enlightening, or memorabilia from BYU, so that I could remember where I was from. "Tim, do you take the *Ensign*?," she asked. "The last conference was so spiritual and full of needed current spiritual guidance." She wasn't grasping at straws. Mom and I had shared many deep and meaningful conversations over the years about books and other writings. We often talked about what touched us most during a particular General Conference of the Church. She hoped that if she reminded me of those moments we had shared, of all the things that I had felt about the gospel and about life, that I'd find the strength and hope to persevere.

Dad was a diligent letter writer. With very few exceptions, he wrote me a letter every week. He kept me abreast of everything that was happening at home, and he shared his spiritual thoughts as well. Since I had discussed my struggles with him about my identity and my sexuality from the time I was a teenager, always with an eye toward becoming what I was supposed to become, and in light of my mission failure, he was concerned about me being in New York City, away from the family and other positive influences. Because I remained silent about the things of which he was most concerned, he must have felt like a coach who was stuck in a locker room while his team left the official playbook behind and faced their most formidable opponent without him. Parts of his letters were often didactic, and over the course of a year he tried many different approaches to reach me.

Dad was always a leader—at home, at work, and at church. He was the kind of man who didn't wait to be told to do something. If something was needed and was within his power to do it, he did it. He encouraged us to do the same and to take on responsibility whenever we were given the opportunity. He talked to us a lot about the qualities that make the best leaders. His favorite description of leadership, the one that served as his touchstone was found in *Doctrine and Covenants,* Section 121:

> We have learned by sad experience that it is the nature and disposition of almost all men, as soon as they get a little authority, as they suppose, they will immediately begin to exercise unrighteous dominion.
>
> Hence, many are called, but few are chosen.
>
> No power or influence can or ought to be maintained by virtue of the priesthood, only by persuasion, by long-suffering, by gentleness and meekness, and by love unfeigned;
>
> By kindness, and pure knowledge, which shall greatly enlarge the soul without hypocrisy, and without guile—
>
> Reproving betimes with sharpness when moved upon by the Holy Ghost; and then showing afterwards an increase in love toward him whom thou hast reproved, lest he esteem thee to be his enemy;
>
> That he may know that thy faithfulness is stronger than the cords of death.

I'm sure he referred back to these verses many times as he tried to find a way to effectively and successfully convey his feelings to me so that I would make the decisions he felt were the best ones for my future. He was very candid in everything he wrote. I learned a lot about him in the process. In May, 1992, he wrote:

> As a young man, I saw myself as a great political, military or church leader, speaking great truths with hundreds of people recognizing those truths and following zealously. I saw myself as a great writer, producing volumes of best-sellers, each touching hearts and influencing people toward good. I never saw myself as only a father, shaping the lives of great children. Yet, in the end, that has been my single real task in life, and I am thankful for the opportunity the Lord has given me to fulfill such an important role. I have made many mistakes, still do, and will continue to, but I'm trying, and I'm thankful for a forgiving wife and forgiving children.

He told me about his own childhood, about how he felt disconnected. He was a bit of a loner who preferred to stay in his room or roam through the woods surrounding his house and sit high in a tree above the river to just think. He was not adept at sports like his brother, Bob, so he had a hard time fitting in at school.

> I guess I have always related personally to your challenges and have wanted desperately to smooth the way for you...I spent a lot of my teenage years struggling with who I was and with trying to combat the jeers from the stud athletes about my involvement in music and drama...If I had been in elementary school now instead of then, I suppose I would have been labelled gay by some of the studs because I was not athletic, but in those days I was just called an egghead or spastic...

His main point in most of his letters was that being "gay" was possible because modern society made it possible. He never considered himself gay because nobody called him gay. Homosexuality in his mind was a construct of socialization. It was something that was learned: If everyone is telling me that I am gay, then I must be gay. He continued:

> Regardless of the pronouncements of certain psychologists, my hypothesis is that no one is born homosexual, or heterosexual for that matter. We are born with a sex drive and

> our environment teaches us how it is to be expressed. Just like the *Blue Lagoon*, if we were left without environmental teaching, we'd figure it out naturally...
>
> The same sex people can argue all they want that God made them that way, but it isn't true. The characteristic is learned, and if it is learned, it can be unlearned...

Dad was most concerned about my spiritual well-being. If I were to go down this road, I would be turning my back on all that had been given me, shirking my responsibilities as a disciple of Christ. I had a responsibility to myself, to my family and to the world to be an example in the face of a world bent on degradation.

> Whether you like it or not, you are a permanent missionary and your work will bring many to the understanding of the principles pertaining to God's kingdom and you will kindle in them a desire to clean up their lives and become members of God's kingdom on earth...
>
> You have given your sex drive far too much priority in your life. It has a place, but it is well down the list when compared with all the other good and noble things to be doing in this mortal life. You have allowed yourself to dwell on it in your mind and heart and...[to] divert your focus and destroy your control.

I'm sure that it was frustrating to him that I was not responding to his entreaties. I was literally not responding. He didn't know what I was doing or not doing. As I look back through his letters, I can see that he was using every angle he could think of to get a response from me. They were all attempts that would have worked had he been in my shoes. His respect for order and the inherent hierarchy in his worldview would have required him to fall in line if he had been me. But, he wasn't me.

His words weren't falling on deaf ears, though. I heard him loud and clear. I just couldn't tell him it didn't matter without sounding more harsh than it really was. I needed to explore. I needed to discover who I was and what I wanted in the world and from the world. I yearned to know if love was even possible for someone like me.

Finally, in exasperation, Dad wrote:

> Do not lecture God on what is right to see and do, but receive counsel from Him and from his appointed servants. Get this shit behind you and be the talented and gifted and productive man of God he has called you to be.

He didn't stop there, though. He would not end a letter without affirming his love for me and his belief that all would be well.

> In spite of all the difficulties you have faced in your life, I have felt in my heart that you would overcome. I still feel that way. You have too much love, too much talent, too much enthusiasm, to bury them in self-doubt, self-pity and self-deprecation...
>
> I love you, and Mom loves you and your brothers and sisters love you. If we insignificant humans love you, God surely loves you and hears and answers your prayers. You don't feel his caring nor see his answers because you cannot believe that you are worth caring for or answering. Interestingly enough, you're the only one who feels that way about you...
>
> If you get tired of my letters, just tell me. But I won't quit sending them. I'm the Dad! You may not know you, but I do. And I have great faith in your future. But I can't make it happen for you. Only you can do that.

Ultimately, I did get tired of his letters, and for a time, I stopped reading them, at least the parts that had to do with me. I knew that my parents were coming from a place of deep concern. I was not communicating the details of my life, so I was leaving them to their own devices to paint the picture of what my exploratory life might look like. In 1993, the only information they had available to them made it easy to envision their son being "dragged down into the scum of the New York Society." They also had no one to talk to about it because having a gay son was shameful in the Mormon culture that surrounded them. Plus, they had a neighbor whose son came out, contracted AIDS, and came home to die.

Knowing that, though, didn't make it easy enough to talk with them because I knew what their response would be to whatever I said. I wanted them to hear me, but they couldn't. I wanted them to trust me to make wise decisions within this process that I felt I needed to go through, but in their eyes, that decision alone was not a wise one. They had a vision of me that was inspiring, but it came with a set of expectations that I did not feel capable of meeting.

This was where my experience differed from Thad's experience. I connected with Thad from the beginning because he was different, and I felt fundamentally different from the rest of my family. But, Thad did not have the mental ability to make decisions regarding the direction of his life. I, on the other hand, was fully capable of making choices about how I would lead my life. From the point of view of the gospel, it didn't matter if I were born gay or if I learned it through socialization or whatever other means. Every single person was born with some limitations. Free agency was not about making one choice or another, it was about choosing to follow God's plan toward eternal salvation regardless of the obstacles or choosing not to. It was pretty straightforward. Parents had the responsibility to inspire and encourage their children to make right choices so that the family unit could be together throughout eternity.

My father was becoming despondent because he seemed to be failing on more than one front:

> I'm deeply concerned because I am not even saving my own children successfully. Travis [who was 13 years old at this time] says he is beginning to think he must be gay because even people he doesn't know ask him why he is gay...[T]he most important thing is to help him learn who he really is and to help him decide to change the parts of him that he doesn't like, or if he's happy with himself, then he needs to begin to consciously brace himself for a lifetime of insult.

I knew for years that Travis was probably gay, but I couldn't ever broach the subject with him, especially at this young, impressionable age because I did not want to be held responsible for influencing him in any way. Sadly, this was a journey that he had to make on his own, just as I had.

Finally, in the Spring of 1993, I wrote a letter to my parents expressing gratitude for their concern and all the wonderful lessons they had taught me over the years. I thanked them for always being open and willing to listen. I asked them to trust me and to find it in their hearts to cultivate a feeling of unconditional love toward me and toward my journey. I told them that, although I held a deep respect and connection to the Church, it was time for me to step aside and to explore this other side of me that needed to find a healthy expression. I included the sealed letter in a package of gifts from New York.

I got a response from my dad right away, and from my mom a few days later. The anguish in their letters was palpable. They were hard to read, and they still are, but I am including them here because I believe they show above anything else the amazing way in which my parents were able to convey a deep love and concern for me, their son, even while expressing their anger and despair over what I was doing.

(Dad, May 24, 1993)

Dear Tim,

> I bade farewell to my twin sons Troy and Trent and wept as I saw them go off to become men, individuals, and to separate themselves from the ties that have bound them to us for

these past 19 years. Their lives will never be the same. As we returned home from the airport this afternoon, we excitedly opened your package. I was supposed to go to work, but I haven't and won't. I need to respond.

You are right. We have always tried to be parents who are open and understanding, and we are. We will listen to anything our children will confide in us and will support them as they struggle through all their tribulations. We hope that they will always be willing to listen to what we wish to confide in them as well.

Nothing in your letter surprises me. I have known for two years that you were not telling me everything and I suspected the part you weren't sharing. The concerns I tried to make your concerns were apparently only mine. It appears that you are past having concerns. The fact is, while you are too inexperienced to understand, older folks know and understand an awful lot that younger folks don't think they do. Older folks are also a lot smarter than younger folks give them credit for. You'll be surprised someday.

You ask for our unconditional love and trust, and you have it. You know we love you even if you choose to live your life in the sewer. We trust you'll get out. I hope you understand that unconditional love means that one is loved in spite of what he does. It does not mean that the one who loves unconditionally in any way excuses the crimes or sins the one who is loved commits. To put it specifically, we do love you and always will, but our hearts will be continually drawn out in prayer even though they are broken and dispirited by the sins you have chosen to commit and, even more, by the rationalizations you have chosen to believe and support.

Since you have chosen at this time to believe that there is no God, it is merely an intellectual discussion, but God even loves Satan. It was Satan and his angels who chose to rebel against God and Truth. God could not deny truth to save Satan. It was Satan who chose to withdraw from God's presence. He knew the truth—and God and Heaven wept, just as we weep, no, heave in convulsive sobs.

Even from the time you returned from your mission (or before), you chose to withdraw from God and from the influence of the church and its people, choosing instead to subtly ridicule them for their "narrow mindedness," which is another way of saying, "God doesn't agree with me." The symptoms increased in New York until you chose to withdraw yourself completely from the influence of the church. Even though we love you unconditionally and open our hearts to you, there will come a time when you choose to withdraw yourself from your family, unless you decide to change your present course. It will not be our choice, but yours, and we will grieve as King David grieved over the loss of his son, Absolom. We continue to hope that none of this will occur but we know that the joy you are seeking will come via the only course open to you for joy, and that is true recognition of the wrongness of the path you have presently chosen, true sorrow for the time you have lost and the pain you have caused, and true repentance for the wrongs you have committed. Although you will probably assert that Alma didn't know what he was talking about, wickedness still never is happiness.

I love you, but in loving you I cannot accept the premise that homosexuality is an innocent "alternative lifestyle," and that my son is ok in his own sexual orientation. You have deceived yourself as many others have deceived themselves by arguing that homosexuality is a legitimate "alternative lifestyle"...Even if there were no God, the same thing would be true. Families, mom, dad, and kids is where joy is...

I know that if you have read this far, you are saying, "Old fashioned dad just doesn't understand the truth about life and the truth about me." And I say to you, my beloved son, that that is rubbish, just like it is rubbish to rationalize that "wherever (you) end up will be a place (you) will find real joy." There is only one direction you can go and find "Real Joy"...Joy comes from a direct path, a strait and narrow road, not a course that just happens...

As I have said before, I am convinced by the still, small voice in my heart that you will work through this and that you will hear Christ softly knocking at your door which is only latched on your side, and that you will find true joy by letting him in, but I am deathly afraid that you will follow in the footsteps of our neighbor who was foolish enough to choose the road to death by AIDS before the repentance process began. His dad died suffering for his son's errors. I can understand the reasons. We are living on the edge of a very deep chasm. If we fall in, many hearts die, pierced with deep wounds.

I look forward to hearing more from you. I am interested in open communication. I want to hear it from your heart.

I love you,

Dad

P.S. After I had written and stamped this I was dismayed to learn that while I was out, Lara, my 14 year old daughter, who was anxious to learn why I was so distracted...found your letter. She, who has been your most ardent admirer, read the letter and went to her mom in a high state of anguish. Now, I have two women in deep depression and two young children who are acutely aware that something is singularly wrong. I'm sorry, but I'm over my head in all of this. I'm a uniquely inadequate father and husband. Good luck. I'm sure that when we understand life like you do we'll all be a lot happier.

(Mom, May 27, 1993)
Dear Tim,

I read your letter. It has taken me several days to work through the disbelief, grief, anger, hurt and sorrow that has passed thru my heart and soul. Only the news of your death could have broken my heart more. An extreme sadness has settled on our home. Travis and Lesa were quite upset seeing how distraught I was and not knowing why, so I explained to them you choosing to cast aside your faith and teachings, however, I did not mention your rationalization of homosexual behavior. I feel that would destroy them. Travis has been unconsolable these last two days. Tears come easily. Unfortunately, Lara...found your letter and read it. Her blue eyes well up with tears constantly—she is wounded to her soul—as she put it, "This is not Tim, he isn't that way, he couldn't believe that way. When we were in New York, we read scriptures every night. He wouldn't do this!"

These past few days has confirmed to me that the bonds of love in a family have so much depth and feeling that when a family member suffers or chooses to sin as you have, the entire family suffers beyond what we thought we could. "No man is an island" and what you are choosing to do is not your own personal sin, it is a sin that affects us all and we will suffer with you. No matter how you rationalize—none of your friends in New York or wherever love you as intently as your family does. Our feelings stem from years of associations and celestial bonds, none of your friends have that claim on you. You know we love you, we admire you, and we appreciate who you are. We acknowledge that there is good everywhere, you called it "universal good", but we also acknowledge that Satan uses half truths to make something appear good, that really isn't. Family is the base of love and to meet the challenges of the worldliness around us. No one loves you, Tim, like I do, you are part of my body and soul. You have incredible talent and insight given to you for a purpose to be an influence for good on this earth. I have always believed in you and felt your struggles for self-knowledge and self-worth was the refining experience to help you be insightful, compassionate and learn to look beyond ourselves. I know many times how you hurt because you didn't fit in and I hurt with you. However, your success kept piling up, because you wouldn't give up. All the Lord asks us to do is "endure to the end."

I feel your handicap in life has been having to deal with your self-understanding. The blessings of life and forever will be your acceptance of this and how you deal with this handicap. We all have weaknesses, I'm not going to confess mine, but I have many, and life is a constant struggle to stay ahead of them. My weight is an example that sometimes I lose, but my weight isn't going to win the battle.

We've talked about this before of being diligent in trying to stay ahead and win out over our handicaps! Thad hasn't given up—he still does the best he can.

Tim, I feel you have made a serious mistake but I don't feel you are the mistake. I feel you have been caught in a situation that pulled up in a time of weakness and insecurity. I feel that you are above all this and that deep in your heart you know it also. I feel some of your rebelliousness and sympathy for the sinner has set you up for this disaster in our lives. However, no disaster is un-repairable. I am not saying that we should not have sympathy and compassion for the sinner, but we need not embrace their sins.

The Gay community is a powerful lobby these days, especially in New York and in the entertainment industry. However, just because they are loud and powerful doesn't make them right. I woke up crying from a dream Tuesday night and the dream was of you. The message was very strong and I share it with you because it focuses on my despair. I saw you standing somewhat distanced from a group of men, you were sweaty and disheveled and stooped shoulders. The group was laughing at you and making fun of you, but keeping you away from them. The sense was so sorrowful, that it woke me up, and as I pondered this sad occurrence, the understanding came to me, this group of gays are using you for their cause. One more victory for them in members. They don't believe like you, their faith and purposes are different from yours, you are a moment in their lives of many moments. When they have used...you, they will cast you off and laugh at your "innocence." Whether "they" is one relationship at a time, the end result will be the same. They... have not cultivated the same faith and knowledge as you have, therefore your differences will always separate you and after *three* months or so, after the *lust* has worn off, you will leave or be left for another relationship. There is no permanence in their lives. Stability comes in our lives by doing the right thing, making the right choice—or at least trying to.

You are playing with fire and the blaze can consume you if you do not retreat and run. Leave! Do not play with sin in your search for "Who am I?" That you already know—you are a son of God...Don't trivialize that knowledge for it is truth! You have strong roots of love in your life—hang on to us!

Of course I fear that in your homosexual experiences that you have had, the possibility of contracting AIDS is always present. There is no such thing as safe sex—and most people aren't totally honest about their sexuality and experiences. Studies have shown (*US News*) most partners do not share the information of AIDS until well into a relationship or experience. Satisfaction is more important than honesty. AIDS is probably the greatest argument for being *chaste* even if your Faith is weak.

One last thought that I have been mulling over as I have worked through my anger and hurt. A human being is the total sum of our experiences, what we see, feel, think, and do. It is all integrated, we are all blended together. My femaleness behavior affects my total person. Your sexuality affects your total person, it is not separate. It affects how you feel, think and what you do. Our behavior is not separate from our person and who we are. What we think and what we do affects what we are, who we are! I love you Tim, completely. You have been a joy, comfort and a loving son. Your thoughtfulness and caring has blessed the lives of your brothers and sisters and many friends. You are fun to be with and wonderful to talk with and I cherish the blessing of having the privilege of raising you and having you as our son. These love bonds are eternal. We feel your struggles and pray for you constantly. Your choice to have homosexual relationships pains me beyond description. I will always love you, but will never accept this lifestyle. It is wrong and will be destructive to you if you do not cast it aside and rebuild your Faith in you and your Heavenly Father. I do not want to see you destroyed by slick lies and arguments. Hang on to us, your family. We love you and pray for your strength, understanding and success. There are many more things I would like to write, but I understand you don't like long letters. I will probably call. I plead with all my heart, do not continue in your homosexual relationships. Follow the counsel of Bro. Scott. Please Come BACK.

WE LOVE YOU,
Mom

It was hard for me to read these letters because it was clear that my decisions were causing them great amounts of emotional and spiritual pain. There was no way I could explain anything about my experience that could ease their suffering. The only option which could ease the situation for them, would not ease the situation for me. I did not feel like I could make any other choice than the one I was making. I needed to know. I needed to experience. As I had imagined before I "came out," for all intents and purposes, I was on my own. I could not be completely open and share my life with my family. If I were happy, they would be incapable of sharing the joy if it involved a man. If I were sad, they would be unable to fully commiserate if the reason for that pain was the end of a romance with a man.

Back in New York, I wasn't making enough money to fly home to Utah very often even though I was juggling multiple jobs and projects. It wasn't just the money, though, that kept me from venturing West. I was responsible for a lot of suffering on the part of my parents and siblings. It was hard enough reading about it in letters, I didn't think I could bear to be in the same room with it. Not that my family was spending all day weeping and wailing around the house, but even if they were smiling and going about their day, I knew what I knew, and I would be able to see it in their eyes. I had let everyone down. I was a disappointment. When they looked at me, they would be seeing wasted potential.

The warning from Dad's letter, "[T]here will come a time when you choose to withdraw yourself from your family...It will not be our choice, but yours,..." was an accurate one. I was uncomfortable with the idea of spending time with my family. I loved them. I wasn't angry with them. But, somehow, being in their presence would make the pain we were all feeling be that much more real, that much more crushing.

So many of my friends in New York had come from very difficult backgrounds, very challenging, even abusive, family situations. They had been either thrown out by their parents when they came out or they cut their family off until the family decided to accept them for who they were. The prevailing thought was that the beauty of being gay was that you could leave your old life behind and create a new family with people who understood you and would support you.

I wasn't interested in creating a new family in New York. My family meant too much to me to discard them just because we didn't see eye to eye on the direction of my life. Yet, time was going by, and I continued to find reasons to avoid traveling home. Finally, after a very long absence, maybe even counted in years, I arrived from the airport, and Thad was sitting in his wheelchair in the kitchen with Mom. She'd just fed him dinner. I semi-knelt down so that my face was at his level, and I said, "Hi Thad."

He reached up and grabbed the small hairs at the base of my head, pulled me close so that he could look me directly in the eye, and he smiled. In that moment I felt known and loved in a way that I have never experienced before or since.

That moment with Thad in the kitchen was remarkable because I felt a jolt of recognition, and in that recognition I felt peace. I mattered. The simple fact that I was there mattered, and nothing could tarnish that experience. Thad's love was not dependent on words, and I, who am profoundly bound to the limitations of language, was schooled in the limitless gift of true, unfettered love. I had found a sun that would nourish me, because in that moment, I felt like God felt the same way as Thad. He knew me, and I mattered. It was as simple as that.

I also recognized in that moment the love I felt for him and for all my family, the love that resides beyond the reach of any storm. Still waters do run deep, and I felt that stillness in my soul, and it was love. When I saw each member of my family that was residing in Utah on that trip, I could feel that stillness in them as well. The storms weren't gone. I was still supremely aware of how my actions were causing my family emotional pain and worry. It was in their eyes, but beyond that, there was a place in all of us that was unaffected by any tumult, and that is what connected us, what held us bound together. For the second time in my life, Thad brought me back into the family.

This experience was an example of the light that Thad brought with him. You could not be around Thad without feeling loved. That was one of his gifts. He perfected that gift and let it touch whomever crossed his path. We all have gifts, and through my life with Thad, I continued to be reminded that whatever deficiencies I thought I might have, my gifts could still shine if I allowed them to do so.

MILESTONES

My dad aspired to be a writer, someone who could inspire people to live better lives. He wanted to make a difference in the world through his words. As I was growing up, he would help me whenever I was stuck trying to figure out the best way to approach an assignment for school. I enjoyed writing, and Dad encouraged me to continue. Back in 1993, Dad mentioned to me that he was thinking of writing a biography of Thad and, as he put it, "our education at his hand." He continued, "For never having spoken, [Thad] has touched a lot of hearts for good."

I felt compelled to write about Thad, too. His impact on my life had been significant, and I thought that writing about it would help me to understand the breadth and depth of that experience. At this time, I had been working on the weekends at Books of Wonder, a small, independent children's bookstore in Manhattan that had survived the invasion of Barnes and Noble megastores. It was a great place to work because we were required to read 10 picture books and one or two novels a week. Reading is one of the best things a writer can do. It inspired me. It challenged me. I thought I might try my hand at writing a story that could become an illustrated book. I believed that many people could relate to the desire to be accepted no matter how different they were from the mainstream. I took an incident that happened to my brother Todd, and I created a character as an amalgamation of my youngest three siblings, Lara, Travis, and Lesa.

"That's My Big Brother, Thad" told the story of a young girl, Linda, who moved into a new town, and her older handicapped brother was mainstreamed into her school. At first, she was happy that he would be there because it meant that she would not be alone even if they were in different classrooms. On the first day, she began to notice the reactions of the children upon seeing her brother, Thad, and she started to think that they might not like her if they knew she was his sister. She decided the best route for her would be to make friends as quickly as possible, then it wouldn't matter if they found out about Thad because if they liked her, they would like him.

Her plans were thwarted in the lunchroom when

her class arrived and Thad's class was also there. She wanted to go over to Thad because she realized this was all new to him as well, and she wanted to let him know that she was there so he wouldn't feel alone. When she saw the stares and snickering from her new classmates though, she decided to stick with them. Back in the classroom, her classmates were all atwitter with the idea that there was a two-headed monster in their school and that they had all seen him. Then, one of her classmates approached Linda.

"Did you see the kid with two heads?"

Linda froze. Thad's smile from that morning at breakfast flashed through her mind, but so did the snickers and stares from the children at her school. More images began to race through her mind: Thad jabbering alone in the lunchroom, saying good-bye to old friends, feeding Thad, the new house, the old house...a collage of hellos and good-byes mixed with the constant presence of her older brother.

Suddenly, she was torn back into the excited energy of the room when one of the kids touched her shoulder. "Did you see him, Linda?"

"Who?"

"The kid with the weird head."

"Was he in a blue wheelchair?"

"Yes."

"I've seen him." Linda paused for just a moment and looked at her classmates. This was it. She felt her hands shaking, and she was on the verge of tears, but she stood straight up to her full height and said in a voice loud enough for everyone to hear:

"That's my big brother, Thad."

Silence. All the children looked at Linda.

"He doesn't have two heads. It's just a birth defect."

"What happened?" asked a girl close to Linda.

"I don't know. It just happened."

"Can he talk?" asked another classmate.

"No, not really."

"Can he walk?" asked another.

"No, but he crawls."

At that moment, Mrs. Condra returned. Everyone quickly returned to their desks and pulled out their math books. Soon they were all back in the learning routine. Occasionally, on breaks, a classmate would ask a question or two about Thad, and she would answer the best she could. Nobody seemed to reject her because of Thad. In fact, some of the kids who hadn't talked to her all day were talking to her now. They were very curious. Linda felt relieved and excited about the new school year.

I read this story to Michael, my first real boyfriend in New York. We had just arrived at his apartment one night, and we were sitting on his bed. When I finished reading, he touched my face with his hand, smiled and said, "You realize that story is not about your brother, don't you?"

"Of course it's about my brother, what do you mean?"

"Honey, this story is about you and how much you want your family, or someone in your family to accept you and to stand up for you, to tell you and the world that you are ok regardless of the consequences."

That was news to me, but he was right. I did want that, desperately.

Michael was great! The few months we were together were everything I had been looking for. We laughed a lot. I felt safe with him. He was sure of himself, and he knew what he wanted from life. Most importantly, he was kind and he loved me as much as I loved him, probably more. But, I was still fraught with internal turmoil as the war raged on between Mormon and gay identities. At one point, we went to see his therapist together so that we could work through my uncertainty together. It didn't go so well for me. His therapist was condescending to me from the moment I walked into the room. As far as she was concerned, the only solution to our problems was for me stop being stupid. I couldn't stop being stupid, so I broke it off. It was horrible to hurt so deeply and to know that I was hurting another person even more. It seemed that because I would not fully commit to either side of the war inside me, I couldn't make a decision without hurting someone.

I don't know what his process was or how long it took, but, of course, Michael moved on. Like I said, he knew what he wanted from life. He met someone several months later and as far as I know, they are still together. They adopted a child years before it became the thing to do, and created the family he knew was in his future. Michael refused to let the world tell him what was possible for his life. I admired him greatly for that.

My experience with Michael left me feeling discombobulated. I needed to find some kind of perspective, but I really didn't have anyone to talk to. Perhaps seeing a therapist could help, but it had to be a therapist without an agenda. The therapist I saw at BYU after my mission was strictly focused on making me straight. Our sessions consisted mainly of exploring my childhood for the tell-tale experiences that made me desire the company of men, so that I could then create a strategy to circumvent the effects of those experiences in my adult life. Plus, he relied on a long reading list of books from various Christian faiths designed to cure the homosexual. Then, Michael's therapist swung totally the other way dismissing altogether any form of spiritual of religious inclinations or history. I finally found a great therapist, who just happened to be Mormon, so he understood my background. I saw him once a week for about six weeks because that was all I could afford. Our sessions consisted mainly of me expressing what was on my mind and him asking exploratory questions to help me clarify my thoughts. Through the course of those sessions with him, I was able to discuss the weight I felt from expectations that other people, including but not exclusive to my parents, placed on me. I was able to put that into perspective and release the weight I felt.

Through the six weeks with this therapist, I was finally able to put into words that what I wanted most was to be able to just be me, with no exclamation points attached. I didn't want to be a "poster boy" for either side of the conflict that had taken over most of my life. I felt like when I chose the Mormon side, I was the ex-gay guy who proved that it was possible for anyone struggling with same-sex attraction to beat it and to live a *normal*, God-centered life. I didn't want to be the go-to guy on the subject of same-sex attraction, because in my heart I didn't believe it was wrong. If I chose the gay side, I was the ex-Mormon who saw how stupid and oppressive religion was and broke free. Without fail, every time in my adult life when someone found out my background, they would always ask, "Are you still practicing?" with a smug sort of tone that implied, "Or have you seen the light?" Whether or not I was going to church, I was always offended by their superior attitude. The truth is I loved both sides of that conflict. I felt deeply connected to both sides. Though I wasn't blind to the negatives, I saw beauty and goodness in both sides. I felt a profound respect of and responsibility toward the people on both sides of that hellish conflict. The idea that whatever choice I made could be used as a weapon against the other side, paralyzed me. The success of that six weeks lay in the fact that I was able to find words for what had been confounding me for years. There wasn't an easy resolution, but I understood my relationship to the conflict more clearly.

I may have been in a quandary about where I was going to land in the conflict between Mormonism and sexuality, but I did know there was one thing I wanted in my life that was within my grasp, and that was creative expression. It was why I moved to New York. I was taking some writing workshops with Madeleine L'Engel at a convent on the Upper West Side near St. John the Divine Cathedral. She inspired me to listen to the story and to let the story tell itself. I wrote a handful of short stories, and it felt great. She encouraged everyone in the class to write every day no matter what. Her philosophy as I understood it was that writing was the mechanical end of inspiration. By writing every day, we could hone our skills so that when inspiration came, we would be up to the task. She paralleled it with daily prayer, something that I was familiar with but not very good at. She said that by praying every day, even if our words felt like lead balloons, we would prepare ourselves for those moments of transcendence when a connection was made and true communication became possible.

This experience was similar to my experience with Mother Teresa in the sense that I knew that what Madeleine, a devout Episcopalian, was saying was completely true. I felt it touch my soul, and my soul resonated. Her words inspired me to write, but they also illuminated and helped me understand aspects of my own spirituality in ways that I had never imagined. Like Mother Teresa's embodiment of the vital importance of service to anyone in need, Madeleine's conviction that true communion with deity through prayer was not only possible but desirable humbled me. Service and prayer were familiar topics to me. I'd listened to many insightful and inspiring discourses or lessons through the years on the importance of both, but the certainty and the examples of these two women brought those lessons home to me in a profound way.

Among my creative aspirations, I had never included anything visual, but an opportunity came up that allowed me to go to Indiana to visit my grandparents for a week. I hadn't seen them in a while, and this trip was a real opportunity. Grandpa Sutton had been a contractor in Marion, Indiana. He built and remodeled many homes in the area. Somewhere along the line, Grandpa taught himself how to make stained glass so that he could incorporate it into the houses and cabinetry he built. He loved it, and he would spend hours in the workshop behind his house not only working on glass, but teaching classes as well.

Grandpa Charlie's dream for retirement was to travel around the country in a camper van, and when he wasn't traveling, to spend his time making pieces of stained glass art and teaching others the craft. Neither dream became the reality he wished for. Very soon after he retired, he began to lose his eyesight due to a tumor wrapped around his optic nerve combined with macular degeneration. He and Grandma did a little bit of traveling back and forth to Branson, Missouri, while she was still healthy, but that was about it. Grandpa's stained glass studio behind the house stayed dark, collecting dust.

On the first day of my trip out to Indiana, Grandpa and I were having a conversation, and he mentioned stained glass. I'd always wanted to learn and this seemed like a perfect opportunity, so I asked him if he would be interested in teaching me how to do stained glass. His face brightened, and we began that very day. For the rest of my stay we spent most of the day in the studio while he talked me through the process. He taught me how to make and cut a pattern, to score and break the glass effectively, to grind the edges, the two different methods of creating leaded glass which involved either copper foil or strips of lead that were shaped like an H, and to solder. We made two stained glass pieces in our week together, both from Grandpa's own designs.

Making leaded stained glass requires a lot of patience because the work is detailed and precise, even tedious. It is a time-consuming process, but one that allowed us plenty of time to talk. Toward the end of my time there, Grandpa said to me, "You know, Tim, you turned out really good! We're very proud of you. I can't say we didn't worry about you for a long time, but you've done well." I said, "Thank you, Grandpa, that means a lot." I hadn't told him about my life in New York. What would have been the point? But, in that moment, in my mind I thought, as was customary, "If you only knew the real me..." But maybe he did know, and that was his way of telling me that it didn't matter. I'll never be sure whether he knew or not, but it felt great to hear my grandfather say that he was proud of me. I knew he meant it.

Leaving Indiana at the end of my stay with my rental car full of stained glass supplies, I couldn't help but feel enormous gratitude for my father's parents. Grandma Sutton had nurtured me for years with crafts and projects. She surrounded me with kindness. I think she may have understood me from a very young age, and she wanted me to feel good about myself. She seemed to know that for me, creating something beautiful would give me satisfaction and purpose and joy because I believe that was what it gave to her. Now, Grandpa Sutton had given me a new way to express myself. As I arrived home in New York, I began designing and making my own stained glass pieces.

Grandpa was very specific about the rules and about following them to the letter, but I found that as I worked, I could bend those rules to a degree or find ways to work within the construct to fulfill the vision I saw in my head. It was truly the most liberating experience I had ever had. I was reminded of a quote attributed to Pablo Picasso, "Learn the rules like a pro, so you can break them like an artist." I grew up surrounded by rules that confined me. Stained glass taught me that some rules are essential, for example, glass wants to break in a straight line. If you want to break a curved line, the further it gets from a straight line, especially on an inside curve, the more difficult it will become until it is impossible. There were ways to use straight lines as a means to create sharper curves, even circles. I found that some "impossible" inside curves are actually possible with a healthy dose a patience, a lot of little scored lines, a special plier-type tool, and maybe some luck. There was nothing wrong with testing the limits of the rules. If it didn't work, I could always adapt my patterns to accommodate what was possible. The thrilling part was that if I had an idea, I could make it happen! I felt like a true artist. Could it be that my experience with stained glass was suggesting to me that perhaps rules were not meant to dictate or limit my vision, but rather they were to be utilized, maybe even adapted or set aside if necessary, as a means to fulfill that vision?

Through the course of Thad's life, my parents and our family had seen that expectations or certainties were not always realized. Adaptation was often the best course of action. A perfect example of that was Thad's education. If his ability to learn was compromised, why bother educating him at all? What good could activities do if he would not progress through them in the same way that "normal" kids would progress? In April of 1993, Dad shared this experience with me:

> I took Thad to his Oakridge School Play on Thursday. They had a circus with clowns, acrobats, trained dogs (invisible), magicians, lion trainers and lions. Thad was a lion, and a very good one indeed. When the trainer snapped her whip and said "Turn right!", Thad and the other lions, all of whom were in wheel chairs [and most of whom had helpers], turned right. He smiled as well, as all good lions should smile when they perform. The students were extremely enthusiastic in all their parts. The clowns loved to squirt the audience with squirt guns and laugh. It was great. The acrobats did tumbling and walked on the balance beam. They were very proud and responded excitedly to the clapping and cheering of the audience.

Like the experience we had with the Special Olympics in Illinois, it didn't matter that the students were hindered. They were participating. They were excited. They and their families had something to share. Providing opportunities for these children and making adjustments when necessary brought variety and beauty into lives that could otherwise have been monotonous.

We would often have experiences where Thad

would surprise us and make us wonder how much he really knew, how aware he really was. For example, on a trip home from Arizona, the family decided to make a detour to see the Grand Canyon. Most of the family on that trip, including Troy's girlfriend, Thora, had never seen it. "It took four extra hours out of our day," Dad wrote, "but we had a good time detouring to see the great ditch. It was a perfect day, if not a bit windy. Everyone enjoyed it, even Thad. He looked around quite a bit as if he were studying the grand vistas." Moments like that reminded my family that all was not as it seemed on the surface.

And yet, Thad's life was different. He had different milestones than everyone else. In a religious culture that measures life in stages and by accomplishments, it tugs at the heart when a child is not able to meet those Mormon benchmarks: baptism, Aaronic Priesthood ordination, Eagle Scout, Melchizedek Priesthood, mission, temple marriage, children. Those are the signs of a rich and full life for a Mormon young man. "I was moved to bear my testimony in sacrament meeting," Dad wrote to me, "reflecting on Thad and his 18th birthday. I had been thinking about Thad for a few days and about all the key times in one's life that simply went by him. Another lady spoke first and talked about her 12-year old son who was just becoming a deacon and how exciting it was to see these children pass those important benchmarks in their lives. It set me up perfectly for what I was thinking. I reflected on how poignant it had been as each of those pivotal dates had occurred in Thad's life and he could not participate; yet, his life had been a blessing to all who knew him."

What my parents wanted most for me was just the same: to have a rich and full life, one that could bring me joy in this life and the life to come. I'd met some of my benchmarks, messed up others, and some, perhaps the most important ones, were still up in the air. A few months after my experience with Michael, I started going back to church. It felt good. It felt right. Initially, the turbulence in my life subsided. I didn't recognize this as part of a cycle. I was just relieved. My parents were hopeful and excited that I began to sound like the old Tim to them, full of enthusiasm and life. I'm not sure I changed that much, but a weight had been lifted, so life felt easier.

A year or so later, we arranged for Lara, who was 16 years old, to come East for the Summer and to work with me at McCorkle. She and I had spent time in New York together when she was 10, and we had a great time. I knew that she really liked the world of acting, so spending six weeks working in the real world would be a great opportunity for her to see what it was all about. A snafu presented itself, though, because the pendulum had swung again and just after finalizing all of these plans, I started to date a man, a playwright whom I met at work. I had admired him and his work since I saw a film adaptation of one of his plays when I was 19, right before my mission. I couldn't believe he liked me!

I didn't think to tell my parents what was going on. I had always thought of Lara as an old soul. She seemed to take life in at a very profound level. She read *To Kill a Mockingbird* the first Summer we were in New York, and I was amazed at how a 10-year old could process the finer themes in that remarkable book. In my "La-dee-da! I'm in love!" haze, I thought that if anyone could understand and be happy for me, it would be her. She would be able to see that my life was neither base nor degrading, and she could tell my parents. Perhaps she could be my witness. "That's my brother, Tim!" We could work in New York during the week and spend the weekends up in Connecticut at Bill's house going to tag sales, having picnics, maybe even riding horses, something I knew Lara really liked. What could be better than that?

It was a tragic and ill-conceived idea. I had forgotten the disaster that happened when she read my "coming out" letter two years before. Lara's life experience was limited. She was a sweet, simple, pure Mormon teenager who was very excited to spend the Summer with her older brother in New York whom she thought was back on track—a "go get 'em" returned missionary good guy like her other older brothers. I blindsided her, and she didn't take the news well at all. She didn't yell or anything, she just started crying. On my parent's guidance, she refused to meet Bill. I was so lost and befuddled that I didn't make her the priority I should have. Fortunately, Lara had a friend on the East Coast to whom she could escape.

Mom and Dad were justifiably upset. There was one phone call in particular with Dad that sort of changed my life. He was worried about Lara, and furious with me. It was the only heated discussion that he and I ever had about my sexuality. He and mom were upset that I was once again giving up the struggle and that I would put Lara in the middle of it. At the height of the argument, Dad shouted, "Can't you just pretend to be an upstanding Mormon young man while my daughter is staying with you?" I hung up on him.

I was angry. I felt misunderstood. I had not intended to hurt anyone. I just wanted someone in my family to understand me and to feel happy for me. I left my apartment and walked around Brooklyn at 2 in the morning for what seemed like hours, crying and talking through the phone conversation and crying some more. I was infuriated and wrecked. I didn't know what to do, but I knew I could not pretend to be *anything*. Then, out of the blue, a voice came to me that said, "Tim, you are expecting your parents to accept your life and your choices without accepting their lives and their choices. The only way you can hope for anyone to ever accept you is for you to give them the honor and respect you hope to receive, *even if that acceptance is never ultimately returned.* That is the Golden Rule in it's purest form, and it is the only way you will ever be happy." It was one of those rare moments in life of unmitigated clarity, and one that I cannot take responsibility for. Seriously, it was like some very wise and compassionate person were walking beside me telling me what they thought after taking in the breadth and depth of my current situation. In that moment, I knew how I would try to manage my relationships with other people, especially my family.

Bill was deeply offended by the whole experience, and he felt like it would be best if I dealt with my family issues without him in the mix. It's possible that he wasn't that into me and this gave him an easy out, but I don't know that for sure. We salvaged a friendship out of it, and I was back to being single in the city. Lara wrote me a very nice letter in the Fall of that year expressing her gratitude for the time (albeit shortened) she spent in New York with me. Her letter was kind and full of love. Nothing was mentioned of the turbulence I had caused.

I chose to begin to share what was happening in my life with my parents, even if it was uncomfortable to do so. Mom and Dad made enormous efforts to listen and try to understand. I'm sure that even now they would prefer that my life had gone down a more traditional path, because all along their concern for me was based in wanting what was best for me, what would make me the happiest, and for them that meant a more traditional path. You can't fault someone for wanting the best for you, even if it disagrees with what you think might be best.

MUDDY GAP

On October 30, 1994, Dad wrote:

> *I got Thad ready for bed last night and took him to bed with me. We talked and sang songs for a while. He's doing fine. He's in good health and is enjoying school. He watches a lot of TV now. We let him watch the Discovery channel. That way he can get a lot smarter than we are because we only watch sports and ghost shows. He likes football, too. I let him watch it with me.*

Thad was a constant when it came to life at home. He was 18 years old, now, and there was little that surprised my parents. He continued to be full of positive, happy energy. As my mom put it, he remained "this little stick that stirred things in the family with an undercurrent of love." Everyone had their own lives and their own activities, but Thad seemed to be the sun that held our family orbiting in the same universe.

He continued to suffer from respiratory issues like colds, bronchitis, and pneumonia, a few times a year. Sometimes, his pneumonia would require hospitalization, but he always pulled through; so, even that experience, though alarming, became familiar. Ear infections were not uncommon either. We could generally tell that he had an ear infection because he'd become grumpy, pull at his ear and move his jaw around as if he were trying to release pressure in his ear canal. Mom could often tell that Thad had some kind of infection because, for whatever reason, the frequency of his seizures would increase, especially if there were even the slightest fever involved. Instead of having four or five a day, he'd have six to ten, or more. Some of the more subtle seizures would also increase their duration from a few minute to an hour or so. Not surprisingly, he would become listless and lose his appetite. A trip to the doctor and some antibiotics would resolve the infection, and life would continue.

Then, something would happen that would pull the carpet of familiarity out from under us.

> The only real noteworthy thing that happened around our house since I last wrote was that Thad has been vomiting frequently. Last Saturday night, he vomited hard ten times

from 8:30 to midnight, and we got worried and took him to the hospital. We were there until 4:30 a.m. and then went to Primary Children's Sunday morning for another four hours. There seems to be nothing wrong with him that anyone can tell. This leads me to fear that something may be going on in his brain now that is causing the vomiting. The doctors say that pressure on the brain will do it, but he can't have pressure on his brain because he has no skull to contain it. I suppose he could have a tumor, but the CAT scan hasn't shown one.

The biggest challenge with events like this is that there was no way to easily know what was going on. Thad could not communicate what was happening from his perspective, so my parents and the physicians would have to go in blind, taking the symptoms at face value. In this instance, there was serious concern because Thad was not keeping anything down, and that included his seizure medications. The doctors worked continually to maintain a specific level of the three medications he was on, with regular blood tests and liver tests. Any dramatic shift could have troubling ramifications.

It took a few weeks to figure out that Thad was suffering from an inner ear infection that caused him to experience vertigo whenever his head was moved dramatically—like when he was moved from a lying position to an upright position or vice versa. The vertigo was so intense, it would make Thad nauseous to the point that he would continue to vomit for a period of time afterward. Toward the end of May, about six weeks after this started, Thad was back "in good health...and seem[ed] to be gaining back some of the weight he lost." By July, Thad was "doing fine and...enjoying summer school."

Random illnesses like this inner ear infection were to be expected, but more often than not, they were isolated instances that did not recur. Other health concerns came on gradually and became matters of continual vigilance. In September of 1995, Dad mentioned, "Saturday night was one of very little sleep as I was worried about Thad who wasn't having any bowel movements or anything. I gave him an enema...but he did nothing so I worried."

Being sedentary tends to cause a slowing of movement in the large intestine. Mom didn't like for us to talk about Thad's more personal things like bowel activity, but it is important to understand how things were evolving. Since the mid-80s, when we lived in Illinois, my parents began to notice an irregularity in the frequency of Thad's bowel movements. Keeping Thad sufficiently hydrated was a challenge from the beginning. Even though my parents were vigilant, Thad's levels of hydration would fluctuate. Add that to the slowing of activity in his bowel, and we had a perfect storm for impacted bowels, which is a potentially life-threatening situation. Over-the-counter and prescription stool softeners combined with abdominal massage helped a lot but there was still the occasional trip to the emergency room to manually clear out an obstruction. This type of decline required daily vigilance once it started, so my parents added that to their list of worries. Dad summarized their philosophy, "We just have to continue to help him and live with his difficulties."

Some more years passed. Our lives in New York and Utah had hit a steady rhythm. There was forward movement, but nothing really significant was happening. In 1997, Dad wrote, "Thad has begun his last year of school. He will be 22 in April and no longer eligible for state sponsored school. He will stay home for the rest of his life, I guess, but he has benefitted from the school and is a joy in our home." It became a year of contemplation for my parents because they were well aware of how much Thad enjoyed going to school. He loved the activities. He loved the social interaction. Back in 1990, Mom observed, "Thad is bored at home. The days get pretty long for him without school to go to. The kids are good to him and have him with them while they play, but it really isn't the same." It was daunting to reflect on what they could do that would continue to stimulate Thad in the same way, especially considering that within a few years it would be just the three of them at home.

I was in Utah for the last seven months of 1997 as I finished my Bachelor's Degree at BYU while transitioning from one career into another. I enjoyed working at McCorkle Casting, and I learned a lot. I'd progressed from casting assistant, through office manager to casting associate with projects of my own. The problem was that casting wasn't something I had intended to make into a career, so when the time came to choose longevity in casting or something else, I started to look at what my options could be. Nothing in the theatre world panned out. I had lots of interviews with producing and general managing offices, but no offers were made.

Fortunately, after I helped my friend Debra England move from one fifth floor walk-up to another fifth floor walk-up, she gave me a gift certificate for a massage with one of her friends. I had never had a massage before, professional or otherwise, and I walked out of this massage knowing that therapeutic massage was going to be my new career. It was a real epiphany. I enrolled in the full-time evening program at The Swedish Institute, Inc. a couple of months later. This meant that I was working all day in casting, then going to class from 6 to 10 p.m., five nights a week, as well as 4 hours on Saturday. I also had to find time to study and do hands-on practicing in the remaining hours. I didn't get much sleep that year. The classwork was challenging, but it felt like I was being reminded of something I instinctively knew rather than learning it from the ground up. I graduated a year later, in April of 1997, and left McCorkle and New York a few weeks after that.

I had turned 30 years old that January, and it seemed like the perfect time to start fresh. Part of that process involved examining where I was and where I wanted to end up. Of all of the goals I'd set for myself through my twenties, the only two that remained to be completed, that I had some control over, were riding my bike from Illinois to Utah along the Mormon Trail and completing my Bachelor's Degree. My personal life seemed to have hit a plateau with a big crater in the middle. I was still single without any real ability to connect on a deep level with anyone intimately. Aside from the prospects of a wonderful new career, I felt empty and lonely and somewhat lost.

This sort of situation always pushed the pendulum one way or the other, and this time it was toward the Church, again. I had not been to church since I started seeing Bill a few months prior to Lara's visit. I couldn't seem to reconcile the idea that neither option was ever going to make me feel like a full human being. Either way I went, I would always feel a loss. Still, I committed, and in that commitment I had to face my New York friends at a time when I was still trying to convince myself that I was doing the right thing. On April 20, a month before I left New York, I wrote:

> I feel overwhelmed to say the least. I hope I can sleep tonight.
>
> I've had an occasion on the last three nights to try to explain my decisions about my life with regards to sexuality and the Church. I haven't been able to successfully do it. I don't know what the hearers (the ones who asked me the questions) left with, but I felt like I was speaking gibberish, and I began to doubt my conviction and my ability to put my faith in the Lord and trust that a way will open up for me to accomplish what the Lord has commanded me to do.
>
> I don't want to put up barriers. I can't. I must stay open. More importantly, I must stay open to the Spirit.
>
> This is huge. Perhaps I wasn't able to explain this because these are matters of the

> heart and the Spirit, not the mind, and if someone is going to understand, they must be listening with their heart and Spirit (and I must be speaking with them).
>
> It also doesn't help that my eyes are wandering more than ever. I am attracted to practically every man I see. I feel like a walking hormone. The juxtaposition is frustrating. There is a reservoir of doubt about my ability to do this that seems primed to flood and drown my hopes.
>
> I have to go to bed, now. I hope that my mind will rest and that I will be able to sleep.

This was one of the very few periods in my life when I kept a relatively consistent journal. I seemed to be on a quest to feel something—anything—that would assuage the emptiness and the longing I'd felt from the time I was a kid. Yet, my process was more cerebral than either emotional or spiritual even though, at the time, I thought it was just the opposite. I relied more on what I had "learned" or been told than what I truly felt. Even at 30, I lacked a significant emotional and spiritual vocabulary. I tended to repeat things I had heard instead of speaking from my heart or from my experience. In my struggle between what I perceived to be my sexuality and my spirituality, I had failed to fully own any of those experiences on their own merit.

On May 5, Thomas called me at my office. When the intern told me who was on the phone, my heart jumped. My family never called me at work. I immediately thought, "Something has happened to Thad or Grandma Sutton or Grandma Clouse!" Both of my grandmothers had been in poor health for a while. On this day, it was Grandma Sutton. Her battle with stomach and pancreatic cancer, which had lasted for a few years, was over. She passed away that morning. What a loss! My heart reeled as I remembered her gentle smile and her uncomplicated embrace of a complicated grandchild.

Thomas was at medical school in Richmond, Virginia. We decided to meet in DC and drive out to Indiana together. We had a lot of fun on that drive reconnecting—talking, singing, and laughing. The funeral was simple and beautiful, a perfect tribute to a woman whose life embodied those attributes. Afterward, we spent the evening reminiscing, laughing, and playing a rousing game of Liar's Dice at the kitchen table. That was the Sutton way. I'm sure Grandma was leaning on the kitchen counter watching her family play and talk and laugh with a smile on her face. It was apparent that night that she'd done her job well.

When I moved out of my apartment in Brooklyn a few weeks later and drove West, I didn't know what lay ahead. My friends who helped me pack the U-Haul truck suggested that I find lighter hobbies like origami because all of the boxes full of books and stained glass supplies were more than they were ready for. I brought everything with me because I wasn't sure if I would come back to the City. I figured I could do massage anywhere, and maybe I had finished what I needed to do and experience in the Big Apple.

Once I got out to Utah and settled into a room in my parent's basement, I loaded my bicycle into the van, and Mom, Travis, Lesa, and I drove East to Illinois where they dropped me off in Nauvoo before continuing their drive through Indiana to visit with Grandpa Sutton then out to the East Coast where they spent some time getting to know Washington D.C. before caravanning back to Utah with Thomas. I joined a group of 11 cyclists from around the country, organized by The Historic Trails Network, who were set to ride the 1440 miles from Nauvoo, Illinois, to Salt Lake City, Utah in 20 days. This was an important trip for me because I felt a deep need to connect with my own ancestors who walked the Mormon Trail pulling a handcart with whatever belongings they were able to bring with them from Italy. The year 1997 was the Sesquicentennial Celebration of the first Mormon trek West led by Brigham Young. I wasn't as fascinated with the word *sesquicentennial* as I had been with the word *bicentennial*, though it was fun to say. I didn't need to learn to spell it because someone had invented spell-check. My ancestors were not in the first company of Mormon pioneers that traveled West, 150 years before. They came a few years later, and started their trek on the Mormon Trail a bit further West than Nauvoo, but they still walked the majority of the trail.

We were honoring and reflecting on a time when the Church was on the outside of the norm. They were persecuted. Their property was taken. They were beaten, raped, and killed because they were different. Their beliefs challenged what other religions found comfortable and true. Their existence strained a fragile political climate on the geographic fringe of a civilized America. Perhaps in their zeal, the early Saints had stepped on toes and offended the "righteous," but that did not warrant the violence they experienced—violence which was condoned, even encouraged, by the government that should have defended their right to exist and to believe and act in ways that were different from the accepted norms.

Our ride was organized in every detail. We had a van that carried our tents and whatever other supplies we needed. We were given a detailed map for each day's ride. The routes followed the Mormon Trail as closely as humanly possible, and we were allowed to ride at our own pace. The van drove up and down the route making sure everyone was safe throughout the ride. If people needed to get into the van for whatever reason along the ride, they could do that.

We had some racers in the group, and they would try to finish each ride as fast as they could. The rest of us fell in line after that. I averaged about 12-15 miles per hour, so I ended up in the middle by myself most of the time. This was how I liked it, because, for me, long distance cycling provided the time and space for mental rest and meditation. After the first couple of days of riding between 50 and 70 miles out in the middle of nowhere on county highways, the mental loop of sound bites started to vanish, leaving plenty of time for my brain to take in the scenery without analyzing it, to free associate, to ponder what I was reading in books I had brought with me about the Mormon pioneer trek west, as well as random ideas that floated in and sat down for a while before moving on.

Riding the Mormon Trail was a remarkable experience. We left Nauvoo at around 6:45 a.m. on Friday, June 13, and crossed the Mississippi into Iowa. We started our rides early in the morning so we could beat the heat as much as possible, finishing most of our rides between noon and 2 p.m. Iowa was beautiful with farmland as far as the eye could see and lots of rolling hills, which were pretty to look at, but exhausting on a bike. I became adept at coasting down a hill with enough velocity to make it as far up the next hill as possible before I had to start pedaling again. We didn't ride on Sundays, so we made it to the Missouri River and crossed into Nebraska on June 18.

It took us about 10 days to cross Nebraska. Iowa had been challenging physically, but Nebraska was a crucible. I longed for the hills of Iowa because Nebraska was so flat that I never got a break from pedaling. If I stopped pedaling, my bike fell over. As we got closer to the Western edge of Nebraska though, the landscape slowly became more rugged and dynamic as we left the Great Plains and started our gradual ascent toward the Rocky Mountains. On June 25, our eighth day in Nebraska, we left Ogallala at 5 a.m. and rode along a two-lane highway toward Bridgeport, a 90-mile ride. There weren't a lot of trees, so it seemed like I could see forever. The white and grey clouds floated randomly in the dome of the sky which met the horizon in every direction without interruption. I felt small, but not insignificant. I felt like a valid part of the picture if that makes any sense, like I belonged. Suddenly, to my right, an eroded ravine revealed that I was riding on the ridge of a tall butte or mesa. The road was far enough away from the edge that I hadn't seen it because it smoothly blended into the terrain. I stopped riding because the view of the land and lake below was spectacular and surprising. "Wow" was the only word that I could utter, and it sounded like a prayer.

It was a perfect morning. The rain we'd had the night before made the air clean and fresh. The temperature was cool in the morning kind of way, but I knew that as the day wore on, it would get much hotter. Very soon after I started riding again, I noticed a frontier style, one-steeple church far in the distance. There was nothing around that would indicate the need for a church, but there it was, and it got me thinking about the people who settled this part of the country. I'd been reading a lot about the Mormon pioneers, and I was impressed and moved by their dedication and strength in the face of adversity. But they weren't the only ones who left the comfort of civilized life to carve a place for themselves in the frontier. People of many faiths as well as people without a declared faith braved the harsh wilderness in order to forge a life of their own.

Riding a bicycle on a two lane highway with no visual obstructions anywhere meant that what I saw ahead of me began on the horizon and ever so gradually got closer. This gave me plenty of time to ponder what it must have been like to live on this desolate and beautiful frontier. I wondered why someone would do it. Did they choose to be here? Did they follow someone here? Were they forced to strike out on their own into an unforgiving and harsh wilderness? Did they have a family? Did they experience loss? How did they survive? Where did they find the strength to persevere? Was church a way for them to escape the isolation? Did faith in God bolster their resolve and lighten their load?

I'd certainly thought about this before, but seeing this church in the middle of nowhere made it all real somehow. People survive. People even thrive in the face of overwhelming hardship. It was easy for me to deify the early Saints because I'd heard stories about them my whole life. They suffered greatly and made it out to the Salt Lake Valley where they built a paradise out of a desert. It was harder for me to consider that they were people just like me who found the courage and strength and wherewithal to press forward when they really had no other choice: to die in Nauvoo, Illinois or survive in the wilderness as best they could.

I'd heard people say many times through my years in the Church, and I'd expressed the sentiment as well, that they didn't know if they could have done what the pioneers did. They doubted their capacity to survive, to keep the faith, to make it across the Great Plains only to land in a desert valley with a lake of salt water. It was daunting to consider. But do we ever know what we are truly capable of until a day comes when we are confronted with a do-or-die proposition? We may falter. We may struggle, but we lift one foot and place it forward, then we do the same with the other until, before we know it, we are far enough ahead to look back and say, "Wow, I didn't know I had it in me. Thank you, God!"

One of Mom's biggest fears in her life was having a handicapped child, and yet, when faced with the reality of her seventh son, she didn't crumple to the floor in despair. A well of love and strength opened up in her, and she never looked back. It was a joyful, fearful, exhausting, rewarding, challenging, and unforgettable journey. Dad didn't back away either. In his pragmatic way he explained, "I have never been hurt by difficult things that happen. Even when Thad was born, in my experience, it's just, well, it happened. That's a thing that we have to live with and do." As a family, we walked that trail together. There were many beautiful sunny days along the way. But, if there were rivers or ravines, we helped each other across. If storms threatened, we built a shelter together.

I'd wager that my parent's second biggest fear was having a gay son, and yet they consciously took one step and placed it ahead before doing the same with the other, all the while doing their best to convey that in spite of their doubts, fears, and misgivings, I was their son, and that would never change.

All these thoughts percolated along a vacant stretch of Western Nebraska highway. As I got closer to the church, I realized it wasn't a church at all, but rather a broken windmill and a dilapidated cowshed. Distance had combined the two, which were on the same plot of land, but not overly close to each other, and I interpreted the sight to be a one-steeple frontier church. I thought to myself, "It would be silly to continue to think of this as a church, since I know what it really is, now. Still, does the fact that I was looking at a broken windmill and a dilapidated cowshed invalidate the profound experience I had along the way while contemplating the "church" that I saw? How many things in my life have I been certain of only to realize they were something else altogether? Is it more important to commit to what I see and to learn from it even if it changes as I get closer, than to not commit at all?" It seemed to me that it would be foolish to deny the transformation and equally unwise not to honor the experience that got me there.

We crossed into Wyoming on June 27. The inclines were long and gradual with not much respite in the downhill department. Just outside of Fort Laramie, I caught my first glimpse of the mountains looming far in the distance. In Nebraska, there had been a town every ten or fifteen miles, but that wasn't the case in Wyoming. There were long stretches without any indication of human population except for roads, signs and fences. Because I could see what seemed like forever, the progress we were making toward the mountains was incremental at best. Three days after first seeing the mountains on the horizon, we left Casper on a 75-mile ride toward Muddy Gap. Our grueling ascent had begun.

> On July 1, as I woke up I heard the wind start to blow. It was a low howl, and I hoped it would be at our backs. We were not so lucky. Traveling East to West, the wind was rarely at our backs. I left camp at 5:45 a.m., and the wind was in my face from the get go...I rode by myself for a while. Then, about 20 miles or so into it, I joined with Dick and we rode/walked together the rest of the way.
>
> It was a really beautiful ride...Many of the mountains we were passing through looked as though they were slabs broken and pushed up—very diagonal. As we were passing Alcova, it was particularly beautiful how the rock rose diagonally from the river and lake. It looked as though they just disappeared into the water. In Alcova, there was a bar that most everyone stopped at to eat breakfast. The wind was so bad that many people just stayed there and were shuttled to Independence Rock, then to Muddy Gap. Dick (who was in his 60s) and I were determined to keep riding. We would make it to Muddy Gap on our own if we had to crawl.
>
> Coming up out of Alcova, we were climbing through a mountain range onto a high plain. It was a very long climb, and the wind was buffeting us the whole time. The wind blew us off the road a couple of times, so we decided to walk our bikes to the top. We even got blown over when we were walking. We mounted our bikes at the top of that first major incline after Alcova only to dismount at the middle of the subsequent inclines. I figured if my bike was only going three miles per hour I might as well walk since I could walk that fast and it wasn't as trying. Dick and I stayed together. Sid passed us on the first incline past Alcova. Susan and Hugh passed us on the last incline before the high plain.
>
> The wind was so strong that we couldn't go over six miles per hour. Even going downhill

pedaling we couldn't break eight miles per hour. It was really difficult! Dick and I drafted off each other, which meant that one of us rode in front trying to block the wind for the other, then we would switch. Sometimes I really felt a difference when I got up front, others I didn't, but the fact that we were riding together made it better...

Since there weren't any towns along the way, we were going to have lunch provided for us at Independence Rock. We assumed that Independence Rock was around halfway through the trip. We were wrong. It was about 50 miles into the trip. We were famished by the time we got there. We ate a couple of pitas with pasta salad and a three-bean salad, drank some water, and rested for about 45 minutes...before we continued on.

We passed Devil's Gate and entered into Martin's Cove. We spent about an hour in the visitor's center where I fell asleep as soon as I sat down to watch the movie about the Willie and Martin handcart companies. Then we walked out on the trail to see Martin's Cove. We didn't go far because we couldn't figure out where it was, and the sun was beginning its descent toward the horizon so we decided to walk back to our bikes and continue on...

The wind was still blowing, but we could ride about nine miles per hour, and on some downhill slopes we even broke eleven miles per hour, but it was still a lot of work. We made it into Muddy Gap at about 8:30 p.m. We were the last two to arrive... Everyone was out cheering as we came in. The sun was on the horizon, playing on the mountains. It was spectacular.

I was so tired that night in Muddy Gap that I barely had enough energy to eat and set up my tent. I was asleep as soon as I hit the ground. I didn't have the energy to fully contemplate what that day meant to me. It was a terribly grueling day and one that I didn't really have to endure except that I had made a commitment to myself that I would ride every mile of that trip from Nauvoo to Salt Lake City. This experience in no way compared to what the early pioneers went through. They walked the entire distance pulling a handcart behind them on what basically amounted to a path, at best; so, I needed to make it the whole way on my own.

This day reminded me that I wasn't entirely on my own. I might have been able to do it by myself if I hadn't teamed up with Dick, but it would have been so much more difficult. I didn't have spending money, so I relied on the two meals a day provided by the organizers of the ride. I'd been fine the whole trip because we'd finish by midday so I could just relax and drink water until dinnertime. That day, though, Dick shared snacks with me along the way that he was carrying. The energy I got from the snacks, the drafting that Dick and I did along the long stretch of treeless plain, and the encouragement we gave to each other made that day a success. It made that day possible.

This wasn't a new lesson for me, though. In a sense, it is what I learned when Thad was born. There will be days, there will be times, when it is best to pull together, to work as a unit, to share whatever it is that we have to contribute. Perhaps that is why family is important, why friends are important and why community is important. Sometimes we need to draft.

The next morning the wind was gone, which was great because we had an 84-mile ride ahead of us from Muddy Gap to Lander. I left camp at 5:45 a.m. and made it into Lander at 1 p.m. It wasn't an easy day, but there wasn't a headwind and there were some really long downhill slopes, one of which was four miles long, on the way into Lander. I was excited to get into Lander because my family was going to be there. Todd lived in Lander with his wife, Brooke, and their children. As luck would have it, Todd and Brooke had organized a family get-together celebrating the Sesquicentennial on the very day that I was scheduled to come into Lander. Seriously. I didn't know our route nor our schedule until I got to Nauvoo, so I wasn't sure if I would be able to attend the event.

All the other riders set up camp around the Junior High School, and I went to Todd's house. Tony and his wife Tracy were already there with their two daughters. Everyone else showed up gradually throughout the day and into the night. The next day as the riders left Lander to the next stop, my family arose early and went to Rocky Ridge. The plan was to pull four handcarts along the 15 mile or so stretch from Rocky Ridge to Rock Creek Hollow.

This was the scene of the dramatic rescue of the Willie Handcart Company, a group of 500 (when they left Iowa City, Iowa) European immigrants who left late in the season, with limited provisions, lost 30 of their cattle in a stampede, and were caught in an early Wyoming Winter with unforgiving blizzards. There was one other handcart company behind them, the Martin Handcart Company with 665 immigrants, and two smaller wagon companies behind them, all of whom suffered great loss. It is an amazing story of survival and faith and heroism on the part of the members of the companies and of the Saints who were sent by Brigham Young with wagons full of food and supplies to rescue them. The first rescue party left Salt Lake City on Tuesday, October 7 with 16 supply wagons. The first blizzard hit the companies on October 19. "By the end of October, at least 250 rescue teams were on the road. Even so, it would be 63 days before all the surviving immigrants would be safely in Salt Lake City."

The rescuers met the Willie Handcart company just east of Rocky Ridge. There were supply wagons around 15 miles away at what is now called Rock Springs. They crossed this ridge in a furious blizzard. I knew what Wyoming winds could be like, and the thought of that combined with freezing temperatures, lashing snow, malnutrition and insufficient clothing made me shudder. Our trek was a pilgrimage to a place sanctified by the sacrifice of these early Saints. We packed our camping gear and food into four wooden handcarts.

> Dad, Lara, and Lesa pulled the first handcart. Todd and Travis the second, which was the covered handcart where the kids were (Leandra, Tony's oldest, walked most of the way, though, and Beck, Todd's oldest, walked a lot of it) Tony, Troy, and Thora, the third. Trent, Tracy, and I the fourth. Thomas limped along the whole way since he'd just had knee surgery.... He never took a ride in the 4-wheel drive that Brooke drove to bring up the rear. Mom also walked the whole way. [Because this was a laborious outside activity, Mom and Dad had left Thad with a caregiver in Utah.]
>
> I think the hardest part was at the very beginning coming up over Rocky Ridge. It is very aptly named. I think we were pulling [ascending] for about four miles [actually five] before we crested the ridge.
>
> Throughout the 15-mile trek over Rocky Ridge to Rock Springs,...we stopped periodically and Brooke shared with us...journal entries from the members of the Willie Handcart company about the experience. Not all were about the suffering, though none could escape it totally. It was very apparent to all of us that this wasn't just another hike or family outing. We were walking on hallowed ground, and even though we couldn't have asked for a more beautiful day, the significance of what happened here seemed to whisper from every step we made.

This was a meaningful trip, but it wasn't a somber one. We contemplated the stories and their relevance to our lives as hallmarks of our cultural and spiritual heritage. But we also laughed and joked and enjoyed each other's company. It was a true Sutton gathering.

The next morning, I woke up at 6 a.m. There was ice on my tent, and it was July 4th! I got on the road right after breakfast. The rest of the riders were a day ahead of me, so I needed to catch up with them in one day. This meant I would be riding 124 miles through the most desolate part of Wyoming. Mom wouldn't think of letting me do this alone. She got in her car, and we leapfrogged all the way to Kemmerer. She would drive past me and go ahead a few miles where she would pull over and sit on the side of the road reading a book while she waited for me. When I passed her, the process would begin again. I made it to Kemmerer by sundown, but halfway through that day, my right Achilles tendon started to hurt which made pedaling difficult. I was too close to the end to give up though. I bought some ibuprofen at a truck stop and made it through the next three days and 152 miles, arriving in Salt Lake City on the afternoon of July 7. I had successfully pedaled approximately 1440 miles from Nauvoo, Illinois to Salt Lake City, Utah. It was a remarkable experience, but I was glad to be home.

The best part of moving back to Utah was that with my new massage skills, I could begin to help Thad in a very direct way. A few times a week, I massaged his legs and arms to help his circulation. He was not mobile at all anymore, so his circulation and lymphatic movement were hindered. Mom and Dad had become vigilant in looking for the signs of decubitus ulcers, or bedsores.

The doctors had explained to my parents that our skin relies on consistent blood flow to stay healthy. If a person, like Thad, is bed-ridden or wheelchair-bound, pressure between bony prominences like the hip or in Thad's case, his right Greater Trochanter, the top of the leg bone where it turns and goes into the hip, causes a diminished blood flow to the tissues that lie between. Without sufficient blood flow, the tissues begin to die. Thad's physician explained to my parents that what makes decubitus ulcers so bad is that the sores develop from the inside out. By the time you can see the sore, or by the time it breaks the surface, there are dead muscles, connective tissues and skin from the bone to the surface. It can be life-threatening. Maybe it was this way from the beginning, especially because of Thad's propensity toward seizures, but I'm pretty sure this was the time in my parent's life that they solidified a system wherein one of them would get up a few times a night to check on Thad, make sure he was breathing, and reposition him.

One of the reasons Thad's right hip was more vulnerable to bedsores was that he had developed a prominent scoliosis with a pronounced rotation and curve toward the left in his upper back, so lying on his right side was more comfortable. His spine and ribs had adapted to the curve so there was nothing I could do to "fix" it. But I could help to soothe the muscles caught in a permanent state of shortness or length, which often caused pain and discomfort. I'd lie him on his side or hold him and gently massage up and down his spine, mostly with circular strokes then finishing with long smooth strokes along the length of his spine.

I was glad to be there to help, but I have to admit that as school got busier, my ability to do that was hindered. I truly regret not helping more. It's rough when you accept the role of caregiver, even part-time, because when you look back, inevitably, you see a host of things you could have done better or more frequently. The activities that seemed important enough to take you away, in retrospect, disappear and what is left, rightly or wrongly, is a lot of self-recrimination. At this time, there were many of us helping to care for Thad. Mom and Dad were there, I was there. Lara, Travis, and Lesa were there. I think Trent and Troy were around, if not living at home, they were certainly in Provo. Thad wasn't neglected, but I hope I did enough of my part.

The classes that I was taking to finish my degree were all Freshman-level general education classes. I'd focused so much on my major courses that I neglected some of the other required coursework. This just meant that I was a 30-year old with a specific point of view and life experience in classrooms full of enthusiastic 18-year old Mormons. I made a point to sit in the front of every class so that I couldn't see the eyes roll whenever I raised my hand. I wasn't a rabble-rouser, but I wasn't afraid to express a differing opinion or challenge the status quo a little. I was bringing the Church back into my life, but I couldn't pick and choose which parts of my life experience were valid or not valid. I had to allow it all to inform my current experience in some way.

During the semester while I was there, the BYU Art Museum brought in a Rodin exhibit called *The Hands of Rodin* with a lot of fanfare and self-congratulation. And yet, they chose to put four of his works ("The Kiss," "The Prodigal Son," "Saint John the Baptist Preaching," and "Monument to Balzac") in the basement, or wherever, because they were "inappropriate" for the Provo audience. President Bateman claimed the decision was made because the works did not fit the theme of the exhibition, even though three of the four statues had very beautiful and appropriate hands. It seemed more likely that "The Kiss" was nixed because of it's sensual nature; "The Prodigal Son" and "Saint John the Baptist Preaching" because they were male nudes; and "Monument to Balzac" because, well, he didn't have any hands. I was very upset by this decision. I couldn't believe that an educational institution would shirk their responsibility to educate. If they were concerned about the public's ability to appreciate these works of art, then, the reasonable option would have been to put them in a separate room so that only the people who wanted to see them could see them. Then, for everyone else, perhaps offer symposiums on how to view art, the role of nudity in Rodin's work, the difference between pornography and art. The possibilities were endless, but the museum and the University did not even try.

This experience is only relevant because of the overwhelming nature of my response. It was visceral, and it blinded me with emotion. There was a small group of Humanities and Art students combined with students from France who picketed and wrote letters, to no avail, but most of the students on campus couldn't have cared less. This indifference is what hurt the most. My dad even said to me, "Tim, I don't understand why you are so worked up. It's just a few statues. Does it really matter?" I declared emphatically, "Yes, it matters a whole lot!"

I talked a lot about Art and Censorship. I wrote letters to everyone I could think of, but I don't imagine the letters were even opened by the people to whom they were sent. It was a frustrating experience. In a very real way, though, my dad was right. They were just four statues, and although the decision was disappointing and perhaps misguided, it didn't warrant the tidal wave of emotion that I was feeling and expressing. I had to really think about that and examine where the intensity was coming from. I believe the experience had pressed my "I don't fit in" button. If this community could not see and appreciate the beauty in "The Kiss" or "The Prodigal Son," or "Saint John the Baptist Preaching," for heaven's sake, how could I ever hope that they could look at my life and see anything but putrefaction and waste?

I finished the semester, and I took a train back to New York as soon as the semester ended in December, because that was all I could afford. I didn't even stay for Christmas. Utah didn't seem to be the right place for me, and I was anxious to be back in a city where the people could see me and either appreciate me or not appreciate me, but they could see me.

At the end of the school year, Oakridge had a prom, and Thad became royalty. He and another student were crowned Prom King and Queen in a cheer-filled ceremony. Lesa was a freshman in high school then, and she was Thad's date. It was a fun evening. They cleared out the main lobby area by the front office at Oakridge, set up a refreshments table, hung a disco ball, and wired the place for sound. There were 15 to 20 students with their families dancing and having fun. Lesa specifically remembered dancing with one of the non-wheelchair bound students while four or five others formed a conga line behind him so they could all dance together. "I was so proud to be Thad's date," she told me. "We were dancing around his wheelchair, and he was rocking and bouncing to the music with that big smile of his. He was captivated by the moving lights from the disco ball." Lara, who was a senior in high school that year, brought her boyfriend, Rich, to the event. She remembers it this way, "I don't have many details of the logistics of the night ingrained in my memory. What I have are pictures. I guess my heart took pictures that night instead of my mind. I see a dance floor with flashing colored lights, many dancing and laughing kids and parents... and Thad, the center of the event. He had on his brightest smile beneath his shiny crown. He loved all of the music, the laughing, and the dancing. We took pictures before the event in our finest clothes and then we danced the night away." It's true, in all the pictures of that night, Thad was smiling like it was the best night ever. I mean, come on, he was surrounded by people, music, and lights. His three favorite things.

A few years after Thad finished at The Oakridge School, the school district decided it was better for children with special needs to be mainstreamed into normal elementary, middle, and high schools, so they closed down this wonderful facility. I have mixed emotions about that. Through the course of Thad's life in the education system, he attended private special education schools as well as special education programs within normal schools. The truth is, he benefitted from both experiences. The advantage to being in a school that is solely dedicated to the needs of children with multiple disabilities is the opportunity to create a focused environment that seeks out and utilizes all of the tools necessary for the many different manifestations of disability from physical to behavioral to psychological. The whole organization can revolve around these goals.

A classroom or program in a normal school has similar goals and opportunities, and there are many wonderful Special Education teachers, but the programs are a small cog in a bigger machine, so it's possible that the focus may become diluted in a way. Nevertheless, the beauty of being mainstreamed comes from the possibility of interaction and visibility. It can create amazing learning experiences for everyone involved, as in what happened at Yokota, where the teachers made an effort to truly incorporate the special needs children into the school environment by introducing them, by educating the other children about what disabilities are, by normalizing the situation to a degree that the children in the school no longer saw them as separate or scary or different.

OUT ON A LIMB

One of the biggest challenges my parents faced while caring for Thad was the 24-hour nature of it all. Since Thad could not be left alone, it often, especially as Thad got older, limited their ability to go out. When there were kids home, we each did our share of babysitting so Mom could leave to do some shopping, go to meetings, or just get out of the house for a while. Now that Thad was no longer in school, and all of us kids were in college or out on our own, mostly in different states, the situation became that much more isolating. Thankfully, one of the benefits of living in Utah was that there were programs to help families who have disabled children. One such program provided a caregiver who would come over to the house for a block of time a few days a week in order to give the principal caretaker a break to do other things. We were very fortunate over the years to have some wonderful men and women, most of whom were students at Brigham Young University or Utah Valley State College (now Utah Valley University), come into our home and help with Thad's care.

I don't want to ignore the many efforts made by my siblings, especially Trent, Lara, Travis, and Lesa. They lived at home or nearby while they were going to school, even after they were married and beginning families of their own. If Mom needed assistance, she could depend on them to step in and help. Lara, for example, took care of Thad during the day while she was attending BYU from 1998-2000. A challenge for us siblings was that oftentimes, Mom would not ask for help because she was highly sensitive about being a burden on the family, especially to in-laws. From our perspective, that was ridiculous, but she and Dad felt like Thad was their responsibility; so if their were any way to avoid laying his care onto a family member, they tended to opt for it.

Mom told me that there were about 15 caregivers who came into our home over the years to help out with Thad. Two of the caregivers who made an impression on me, mainly because I met them and saw them in action, were Maury and Erika. Maury came across as a guy's guy. I think I remember he had a goatee or something. He would come and pick Thad up, and they'd go driving around in his convertible sports car. I was impressed with how he carried Thad. That may seem like an insignificant thing, but there is a difference between picking someone up like they are a body or picking someone up like they are a person. Even beyond that, there is the affection that comes from knowing and caring about that person. I only saw Maury once, but I remember thinking, "Wow, he carries Thad the way I would carry Thad." Mom told me that Thad would always come home from their outings relaxed and happy.

Erika was a beautiful, thin girl with long, blonde hair, but she was tough. You wouldn't think by looking at her that she could carry Thad, let alone put him in and take him out of a car, but she did. Thad really liked her. He would brighten up when he heard her voice. One of the things that Erika would do was take Thad to the Provo City Library every week for their story time. It was Thad and a bunch of toddlers listening to stories being read aloud. On one occasion, the library had a video team there taking shots of the library for some kind of promotional video. While they were setting up to film the story time, one of the assistant librarians came over to Erika and asked her sweetly if she wouldn't mind taking Thad to another part of the library while they filmed. Erika said, "We're here every week, I most certainly do mind." She was so enraged by the request that she went directly to the head librarian and expressed her displeasure. I don't know if Thad ended up in the video or not, but Mom got a call from the director of the library a few days later apologizing for the insensitivity of the assistant librarian. I admire Erika's strength of character in her defense of Thad's right to be included.

While I was back at BYU, I developed a wonderful friendship with a young woman whom I had known peripherally for a long time because she had been part of Troy and Trent's circle of friends through high school. She was beautiful and funny and talented and smart, and she seemed pretty non-plussed about my sexuality. I didn't talk to many people about it in Utah, for obvious reasons, but Emmie and I could talk about anything. When I got back to New York, I continued to go to church. I was kind of accepting the idea that maybe staying single and spiritual the rest of my life was a doable proposition. As frustrating as my experience had been in Utah, I began to think that perhaps it was time to consider that maybe I actually did relate to the Mormon life more than I was willing to admit.

As time went on, I wondered if it would be possible for me to be a boyfriend, a husband, and a father. Did I have it in me? When I would think about Emmie, the answers to those questions was yes, absolutely. She hadn't recoiled when I told her about my life and my fears. I never felt judged by her, and we laughed a lot about everything. That's more than I'd shared with anybody, ever. I had a true affection for her, and I hoped that it would blossom into desire. On my mission, I felt like I had positive experiences with the idea that if I did everything in my power to accomplish something, and if that something were worthwhile, God would step in and take up the slack making everything possible. Now, if God would help me with something as insignificant as writing a few songs on my mission, it seemed probable that He might help me in this decidedly more significant instance; so, on a trip back to Utah, I took Emmie to Ensign Peak overlooking the Salt Lake Valley, and I asked her to marry me. I couldn't afford a ring, so I gave her a crystal bracelet until we could choose a ring together. To my surprise, she said yes.

The whole experience was overwhelming, and it felt right and good and exciting. We embarked on a long-distance romance as we planned a life together in New York or wherever. Emmie had applied to a Master's Program in acting at the Old Globe in San Diego, so I figured that was where we would end up, initially.

She came to New York to visit over Thanksgiving and Christmas. Those were wonderful and challenging visits. We were playing this like any normal Mormon couple would, which meant no sex before marriage.

That was totally fine with me because I was discombobulated by the shift in emotional intimacy. Being a good friend, even being a best friend in my experience was different from being a fiancé. Emmie didn't demand anything from me, but I felt a shift in me, a desire to be more present and understanding, and for some reason this terrified me because I was in uncharted territory. It looked so easy from the outside, but I was lost and foundering.

I don't know if straight guys feel this way, but everything I did felt like it required enormous effort. Nothing seemed to come naturally to me. The affection I had for Emmie was not developing into desire. I felt awkward and stupid and that frustrated me. I was doing the best I could, and God didn't seem to be helping much in the areas where I fell short. I can't speak for Emmie, but by the end of our Christmas together in New York, I think we both started to realize that our fears about our relationship were beginning to overcome our hopes for our relationship, and I knew it was all my fault. Perhaps this was a road I should have never ventured down for both our sakes. Emmie was stronger than I was, and she called off the engagement a few weeks into January. It was the right thing to do, but I was devastated, and it threw me into a deep depression, one that I had never experienced before, which lasted for months.

Rightly or wrongly, I felt betrayed by God. I had crawled out on a limb, I thought, and rather than help, He cut it off at the base leaving me to fall to the ground. I felt more alone than I had ever felt before, and although I thought about ending it all, those thoughts only motivated me to get back up, dust myself off and check for damage. I remember thinking, *If hope is the last thing we lose, then I've got nothing left to lose.* Yet somehow, this gave me the push I needed to press forward. I had learned that I could not force something that wasn't meant to be.

I also reconnected with the therapist who had helped me years before. I needed someone to listen who wasn't invested in my experience, someone who could help me clarify my thoughts and regroup. I knew from before that he was the right person. Once again, I saw him once a week for a month or so, and was grateful for his expertise and kind attentiveness.

I had moved from my sublet in the East Village to a two-bedroom apartment in Washington Heights with the idea that Emmie and I would live there after we married, until we found out whether we'd be moving to San Diego or not. The act of renting an apartment, thinking as a married man, had felt very adult, very "normal." It was like I was finally crossing a threshold and moving forward into the stable life that had evaded me for so long. We would actually live in an apartment with a guest room/office/eventual nursery, buy real furniture, and do all the things that married couples did. Once the engagement ended, though, I was sucked out of that dream and into a vacant 2-bedroom apartment far away from anyone I knew and anywhere I worked. It took a lot of effort to figure out what to do next. Fortunately, over the year that I lived there, I found 2 consecutive roommates who were nice and laid back.

As my one-year lease was ending on that apartment, I once again faced the proposition of moving out West. It was 2001, and Mom had been suffering from severe back and leg pain for several years. She'd tried to manage it with physical therapy, exercise, and medication because she wanted to avoid surgery. When nothing alleviated the pain, she determined that surgery was the only option. It appeared as though life, arthritis, degenerating discs, and years of lifting Thad had done a number on her lumbar spine. Her physician felt like a fusion of the problematic vertebrae would be the answer. They discussed and were planning on a more innovative approach to the surgery, but when they got into her back during the surgery, they realized a more traditional rod and bone graft technique would be more effective.

It had been three years since I left Utah, and my

massage career was growing. I was teaching at the Swedish Institute, building a private practice, and establishing a solid reputation in the spa world as a massage therapist as well as a spa development specialist by creating spa menus and protocols and helping to launch spa endeavors. It was a very exciting time for me—tiring, but exciting—and yet when Mom told me that she was going to have back surgery, I knew in that instant that I needed to go home and help her through the recovery, which would take at least a year. I felt very strongly that massage came into my life for a reason, and if I couldn't use it to help my family, then what was the point?

Dad was still working at that time and given the condition of her back, Mom could not take care of Thad as she had been doing. This was a time of crisis. There was really no one else in the family to step in and help to the degree that was needed, but not for lack of desire. I was single. I didn't have any children. My skills were easily transferable to other locations, I thought. There was no reason I couldn't make this move. So, once again, I put New York in the rearview mirror. Once again, I thought it was for good. I figured if everything worked out, I could create a life and a career in Utah.

My basic education in anatomy and physiology and experience teaching it to newcomers as I had when I taught Musculoskeletal Palpation in conjunction with first semester Anatomy/Physiology at the Swedish Institute meant that I could interpret what the surgeon was telling my mom about what was going to happen before, during and after the surgery. I felt useful and appreciated. Meeting with the surgeon also gave me insight into the ways in which I might be helpful in the course of her recovery. It was a lot to take on, but the challenge was exhilarating.

The surgery went really well. I knew from my training that oftentimes in injuries or surgeries, the current prevailing thought was that the best healing happened within the context of movement whenever possible. That made sense to me, since complete immobilization creates an environment where scar tissue can develop that could ultimately impede movement or cause other problems. Still, I was surprised to show up the morning after Mom's surgery to find out that they were having her get up and walk around the floor. They'd have her walk as many steps as she could, then they would try for more later. She was a real trooper. It helped that the pain she was feeling now was surgery-related, and the pain that she had been feeling for the previous few years was completely gone. That was hopeful and encouraging. It also helped initially that she had a morphine button that she took along with her on walks around the nurse's station.

When she got home, we'd do the same thing, without the morphine. We'd walk around the house, then back and forth along my parent's cul-de-sac as the snow melted and Spring arrived. Eventually, we advanced to walking around the block which included inclines and declines since my parents live at the lower end of a mountain, then around the temple with a much longer incline and decline. I didn't start doing any hands-on massage work, except on her feet and legs, until the surgeon and the physical therapist gave me the go-ahead which was about six to eight weeks into the recuperation. I really considered myself a part of the process. It felt nice.

I was there to help Mom through her recovery, but my main day-to-day focus was caring for Thad. That meant waking him up, bathing or showering him (which Dad would often do as he was preparing for work), dressing him, feeding him meals, making sure he got his medicine on time, moving him from his bed to his chair and back a few times a day, interacting with him, and putting him to bed in the evening. It was a lot of work. I gained a true appreciation for what my parents, especially my mom, had managed for 24 years. Mom insisted on being involved in the tasks that didn't involve bending, turning, or lifting. We would often prepare meals together, and she would feed Thad and give him his medicine. I would get Thad ready for bed and put him in his bed, then Mom would go in and sit on the edge of his bed and talk to him, hold his hand, tell him a story, and often sing or hum the Carpenters' "Close To You" as a lullaby.

I think my biggest challenge was managing Thad's downtime. After a meal, for example, it would be easy to put Thad in his bed for a nap, then get caught up in some other household project. I'd be aware of him, and I'd check on him, but before I knew it, a few hours would have passed, and he was still lying in bed, playing with his toy or listening to a CD in his CD player. He would quiet down and listen intently whenever Carole King's *Tapestry* album played or the *Now & Then* album by the Carpenters. Thad had his Country favorites, too, and others that he'd picked up over the years. Sundays were Mormon Tabernacle Choir days as they had always been at our home. I hope that when we meet in the hereafter he won't say to me, "Dang, Tim, I enjoyed having you around, and I'm grateful that you came home to help, but seriously, did you have to leave me alone for so long?"

One of my favorite things to do was to sit in the upholstered rocking chair in the living room off the kitchen with Thad on my lap. I loved to hold Thad. His body fit my body perfectly. When he was on my lap, his head would rest, sewn eye side down, comfortably at the top left edge of my chest as I rocked him or read to him or just held him. He'd get really quiet as I read. His eye would flutter back and forth, which seemed to be an indication that he was paying close attention. I didn't know if he was listening to the words or just to my voice as it resonated in my chest. His whole body would relax into mine, and eventually he would fall into a deep sleep, without fail, every time. Then, I would rock him gently as he slept. Over the course of my time at home, which ended up being a little over a year, in those moments before Thad would fall asleep, we read together the whole *Chronicles of Narnia* series, all seven books. I can honestly say that those moments with him asleep on my lap are among the most precious and truly beautiful moments of my life.

Back in 1989, Mom had noticed that Thad would wince when she moved his left hip or leg, and he was uncomfortable sitting in his wheelchair. She took him to the doctor, and the x-rays revealed that he had congenital hip dysplasia in both hips and that the left hip had dislocated. From what I understand, congenital hip dysplasia basically means that the cup in the hip bone (acetabulum) that accepts the ball at the top of the leg bone (head of the femur) is more shallow than normal. This means that it is easier to dislocate the hip since the ball-and-socket joint is not secure.

This is in fact what happened. The tightening of Thad's muscles from the paralysis, specifically the adductors which are the muscles on the inside of the leg, had pulled his left hip into dislocation. The pain could be eased somewhat by gentle stretching, but the only way to fix the dislocation would be some kind of surgery. The first problem with that solution was that general anesthesia presented a higher than normal risk for Thad because of his birth defect. It was very possible that if they sedated him for the surgery that he would never wake back up. The second problem was Thad's seizure disorder. They couldn't risk him having a seizure during the surgery, nor during the six to eight weeks of recovery while his lower body was in a cast. After three years of seeing specialists and trying to balance the levels of his seizure medications in a way that would keep his seizures at bay, he was still having multiple seizures a day. They decided that surgery on Thad's hip was not a possibility, and they would have to manage the situation with physical therapy.

Thad had some really wonderful physical therapists at the Utah Valley Regional Medical Center. My parent's insurance would only pay for periodic series of physical therapy sessions with six to eight months in between. So, Thad would progress, then regress, then progress, then regress. During the fallow, non-PT months, Mom and the various caretakers would stretch Thad and massage his legs, but they could not be as precise nor as effective as the physical therapists. This situation didn't provide a system that helped to maintain any sort of suppleness or flexibility in Thad's legs.

When I arrived home in 2001, I noticed that Thad's legs were very tight, so much so that there was only about 3 inches of space between his knees before major muscular and tissue resistance began. This made changing his diaper and putting his pants on very difficult. The spastic paralysis that had overcome both his legs and his right arm was something I had to learn to work with, especially when I was moving his limbs around in any way. If I moved them too quickly they would seize against the movement and start to shake, especially his arm. I learned that this was typical in cases involving spastic paralysis.

Fortunately, very soon after I arrived in Utah, we were able to get another series of physical therapy sessions set up for Thad. I took him to the appointments and the physical therapist talked me through what he was doing, what his goals were, and how I could help. He explained to me that in order to work effectively with spastic paralysis, I had to work very slowly and for longer periods of time. He explained that not only did we not want to trigger a clonus (shaking) response, but we had to remember that every tissue in the leg was shortened. When I stretched him, I had to keep in mind that I was not only stretching his muscles and the fascia that surrounded them, but the blood vessels and nerves as well. With this new perspective on knowledge that I thought I had, I would sit on the couch with Thad lying perpendicular to my body, and I'd slowly wedge my torso in between his legs up to where his knees were halfway across my torso. Then we'd watch TV, mostly *Law & Order* which was shown four times a day, so there were sufficient opportunities. I'd help Thad and see New York at the same time; it was good for both of us.

Initially, Thad complained. He would shake his head and whine a little bit when I would begin to wrap his legs around my torso. If that happened, I would back off just a little so that I wasn't causing him pain. This, combined with a more comprehensive stretching and massage program that I was trying, we gradually got Thad's legs to find a more comfortable resting place in line with his hips. We were also able to eventually straighten his legs so that they were resting in a lengthened position rather than a bent position.

Through a government program in Utah, we were able to get a hydraulic standing chair for Thad. This was different from the equipment we used earlier in his life when he was trying to stand on his own. That equipment had safety measures like velcro straps to keep him from falling. This chair had straps as well but they were for actual support as well as security. We would securely strap his torso and legs into the chair then slowly pump the chair up which would gradually straighten, bringing Thad closer to a standing position. His arms would rest on a tray where we could place some of his toys. It was important for us to be vigilant about his reactions during the straightening phase. The moment he exhibited any sign of discomfort, like a low grinding sound or a moan in his voice, a pain crinkle in his brow, and/or a shake of his head, we would release some of the pressure so the chair would un-straighten just a bit. That way, we could stay on the safe, comfortable side of the stretch which would allow us to make progress without causing injury. Over the course of a few months, we were able to get Thad very close to fully upright, and he would comfortably stay there for about 15 to 20 minutes. He would perk up when we got him upright. His eye would brighten. He'd interact more. I imagine that since he had spent most of his life in a wheelchair or lying down, this change in perspective, the view from above, made him very happy.

One night, Thomas called home. He was doing his residency in Tacoma, Washington. That week he had experienced something profound at the hospital. Paramedics were called to a home because a woman was in labor. They arrived at the house and assisted in the delivery of a baby girl who was significantly premature at 22 weeks. Because the infant was so premature, there was little possibility that she would survive. Even still, the paramedics rushed her back to the hospital. The parents chose not to accompany her.

Once at the hospital, the emergency room staff determined that there was no hope. Her organs were not developed enough to survive outside the womb, so they wrapped her in a blanket and placed her in a room by herself. Thomas was sent to check on her. When he entered the room, he was struck by the loneliness of it all. Her tiny body was warm, and she was making breathing motions, but it was very unlikely that she was getting any significant amounts of air into her underdeveloped lungs. He picked her up and held her. He sang to her as she slowly slipped out of this life. Thomas felt deeply that no one should have to die alone and discarded in a room regardless of the prognosis. He and Mother Teresa were on the same page.

In our conversation, Mom shared with us for the first time how the doctors who delivered Thad felt like the best course of action was to allow him to die. They didn't believe he had a chance. They hadn't banked on the fact that my parents would not even consider that as an option or that Thad had a healthy set of lungs that he wasn't afraid to use and a fierce will to survive.

In September of that year, 9/11 happened. I was at the gym when I saw reports of the first plane crashing into the World Trade Center, and for the rest of the day, Thad and I were glued to the television. In addition to the feelings of shock and loss and violation that our whole country felt, I felt particularly troubled because bad things were happening at home, and I was not there to help. Fortunately, no one in my direct pool of friends and acquaintances died that day, but within a few degrees of separation, the devastation of that day reverberated.

Try as I might, Utah did not feel like home to me. The people in my parent's neighborhood and ward were very friendly, lovely people, but I was 34, unmarried, and gay. I didn't have a lot in common with anyone, so most of my relationships outside of the family were "salutory" friendships—the people you know, smile at, wave at from across the street and maybe even share an occasional "How's life treatin' ya?" conversation. I was living at home and doing something I loved with people that I loved, but the lack of outside friendship gave the experience a lonely overtone.

Mom healed great, and I was very happy to see that massage was indeed helpful in that process. I felt needed, so I was glad to be there. I'd set up a small massage room in the basement of my parent's home, and I had a small cadre of clients, mostly women, whom I loved and for whom I was very grateful. I couldn't charge even close to what I charged in New York, so it didn't bring in a whole lot of money, but it gave me some spending cash. As Mom healed, she took on more and more of the day-to-day stuff, anything that didn't require lifting, so I started to have a little more time on my hands. I got a job at the Utah College of Massage Therapy for a few months, but I believe I came across to the faculty and administration as a New York know-it-all—my fault, I guess. I didn't last long there. In early 2002, I got a call from a former spa director friend, Kristin Squef. She was working on developing a new La Prairie spa for a brand-new Ritz-Carlton Hotel on Central Park South in Manhattan. She asked me if I would consider moving back to be part of the opening team. I said yes, and a few months later I was back in the Big Apple.

Before leaving Utah, I made a videotape of a stretching routine that anyone could do with Thad to help maintain his flexibility. Lesa jumped on that, and she would stretch him out almost every day. That video got a lot of use in the following years, and they were able to maintain the resting length of Thad's muscles at a more useful and healthy place.

My time in Utah was fruitful. I'd had a lot of time to think while my own concerns took a back seat to the more pressing responsibilities of caring for Thad and Mom. It's true what Mother Teresa said on her business card, "The fruit of Love is Service. The fruit of Service *is* Peace." By the time I got back to New York, I started to put things together. The sting of the lost engagement was gone. I began gaining what promised to be a healthier perspective. I'd long since set aside the anger I felt toward God. That had been an easy way for me to assuage my own feelings of ineptitude and responsibility. The fact is that I tried to force something to happen that was neither organic to me nor to my experience. I couldn't blame that failure on God. I had to own it.

While I was growing up, we talked a lot about weakness and adversity at church. Since I felt supremely weak and different, these discussions felt more relevant to me than any other discussion we had. There was a scripture from *The Book of Mormon* that was often quoted:

> And if men come unto me I will show unto them their weakness. I give unto men weakness that they may be humble; and my grace is sufficient for all men that humble themselves before me; for if they humble themselves before me, and have faith in me, then will I make weak things become strong unto them.

I kept waiting for my weakness to become a strength, so my attention for the bulk of my life focused on that part of me which made me feel unworthy. My sexuality, which distinguished me from my peers and my family in a negative way, became the lens through which I saw my whole life. When I excelled at something, I couldn't fully honor it because my weakness was still a weakness. When I succeeded at something, I couldn't fully celebrate because I knew that if anyone found out about my weakness, any success would wither in the eyes of the world I grew up in.

I was 35 years old when I moved back to New York. At least 25 of those years I had relegated myself to a No-Man's Land of doubt, fear, and self-recrimination because I believed that my sexuality made me less worthy, less lovable, and less valid. My efforts to choose a side always failed because life through a lens of weakness is a life without conviction. I realized that focusing on what I didn't have or what I was incapable of made it impossible to truly see and appreciate the things I *did* have and of which I *was* capable. I remembered the many people I saw in India who had less than nothing, but their eyes burned bright with life, even joy. I thought of my parents who saw the beauty in Thad's life and encouraged us to embrace that. Life is enriched when we accept the parameters of our circumstance and choose to live.

I could only do that by allowing my sexuality to take it's rightful place in the matrix of my experience. I set out to determine what my strengths were. If I spent as much time recognizing and nurturing my strengths as I had trying to make up for my deficiencies, I could possibly begin to own my life and my experience. It was a theory, and one that I was anxious to try.

I learned in Utah that it felt good not to be the center of attention. I'd been single for most of my adult life, so the bulk of my attention was on me most of the time. Until I stepped away from that, even briefly, I didn't realize how tiresome that was. I believed that one of the reasons we are on this earth is to learn how to love. The best way to do that was to love someone, to be a part of their life, to think about them when I'd rather think about myself, to learn how to be a couple and a family. I needed to open myself up to that possibility if I were going to truly capitalize on this life experience. I knew deep down that there was more for me to learn, more joy for me to discover. I could only do that by fully letting go of the "I am less than..." paradigm that I had allowed to rule my life up to this point.

The trajectory of my life changed in fits and starts, but I felt relieved. I had to develop social skills that only came through trial and error, mostly error. That was uncomfortable for me, but I could breathe. The weight I had borne for most of my life was disappearing with each day and with each experience that passed.

A few years later, Mom called me one day in a panic saying, "I think I just outed Travis! What do I do?" I laughed and said, "How do you know the verb 'to out'?" She sighed deliberately, "I do watch *Oprah,* you know." We talked about it for a while and decided to let the process run its course.

Travis was bold. He belonged to a new generation that was less afraid. He met someone within a year of coming out, and they moved in together a mile or so away from my parents. One of my brothers was critical of Travis because he didn't seem to have struggled in the same way that I had, but I was grateful because Travis was not going to lose 20 years of his life to indecision and regret. I think it was good for my parents to be able to witness this process because it normalized the experience even more for them. I'd done everything 2000 miles away and I hadn't been forthcoming with too many details because they weren't ready. I wasn't ready.

Travis and his partner Kylie were a part of my parent's day-to-day life, as were Lesa and her husband, Mike, and Trent, who'd finished law school and was working at a firm in Provo. My parents could rely on them when they needed help with Thad.

Mom's time was divided in these years. Both of her parents were in their 90s and in ill health. They lived at home in a neighborhood that was gradually slipping into decay. A homeless man had even set up camp in their very large fig tree in the backyard. Considering how fragile they were getting, that news was scary, so Mom's brothers pruned the tree so there weren't any branches or leaves hanging down below about six feet from the ground. Her brothers that lived in Arizona and their wives shouldered most of the attention and care, but Mom talked to her parents every day on the phone, and she would periodically go down with Thad and spend a few weeks helping out. Grandma loved having Thad around. He lifted her spirits and she would say, "You just wait, Thad, when I cross over, I'm gonna come back and get you. You'll be able to run and play and do everything you can imagine." And she would kiss his head.

Grandma had slowly slipped into dementia over the last decade or so. Her memory would come and go. When we would talk to her on the phone, or if we visited, she would ask us our names, then tell us that we would have to remind her in a few minutes, all with that perpetual twinkle in her eye. She still loved music, and she would sit by herself in the living room playing the piano when she could remember how to play. Later, it wasn't just our names she needed to be reminded of, but who our parents were. One day, when Mom called, Grandma asked, "Who is this?" Mom said, "It's Laraine, Mom, your youngest daughter." To which grandma replied, "Oh, Laraine, my name is Mary. I am named after Mary, the mother of...(long pause)...what's his name."

Grandpa was solid, but aging. He had his share of physical issues, but his attention was focused on Grandma. He had spent most of his later years making sure that all of his aging neighbors had the care they needed. If they needed a ride to the doctor, he was there. If they needed groceries or whatever, he made sure it happened. By this time, though, my grandparents had pretty much outlived everyone they knew from their generation.

On February 19, 2003, Grandma passed away quietly at home. She was 97 years old. She had a beautiful funeral filled with generations of family. Grandma and Grandpa had been married for over 75 years, they had over one hundred grandchildren, great-grandchildren and great-great-grandchildren. True to her character, Grandma's funeral was filled with music. There was no better way to honor her bright and joyful spirit than to sing her on her way, among the eulogies and thoughtful reminisces. A chorus of her granddaughters opened the service singing "Lord, I Would Follow Thee." Mom played "Lincoln's Funeral March" on the piano. A much larger choir of grandchildren of all ages sang "How Great Thou Art." Then, Dad and all my brothers and I sang Grandma's favorite hymn, "I'll Go Where You Want Me To Go." All those years singing around the piano were put to good use that day.

After the funeral, Grandpa insisted on staying in the home that he built by hand even though it was hard for him to get around. He and Grandma had been so close for so long, we worried that Grandpa would pass away very soon after Grandma did, but he persevered. His mind was clear. It was his body that started to give way. He lived until October 6, 2004. He was younger than Grandma, and that extra 18 months meant that he also made it to 97. He actually lived about 10 days longer than Grandma had.

His funeral was also very meaningful. He had dedicated his life to living the gospel and to raising his family according to the principles he held dear. He could be rigid at times, but he had a heart that was full of compassion. He was a man of action. Religion was not something you just talked about, it was something you lived.

In 2006, two important events happened involving Thad's care. First, a friend in Mom's ward told her that she had met a wonderful woman who was looking for work. She felt like this woman would be a perfect fit to help Mom with Thad's care. The meeting between Mom and Claudia was very easy. Claudia was from Colombia. She was beautiful. Not that that matters, but she was. She was probably in her early thirties, and she was divorced with three children of her own. They hit it off from the get-go. Mom hired her to help with Thad and with anything else that came along. They became fast friends and Claudia became devoted to Thad and played a significant role in his life and care from that moment on. She became very much a part of the family.

Mom also got wind of a program called S.T.E.P.S. that was beginning in Orem, Utah. It specialized in working with adults who had multiple disabilities. Karen Yocum, one of the founders, grew up around children and young adults with multiple disabilities because her mother, Elda Lorraine Topham, and father, Norman Topham had founded and run Topham's Tiny Tot's Care Center. It was a residential care center for children and young adults with multiple handicaps. Karen and her sisters realized that after a certain age, there weren't any real services for adults with multiple handicaps, so they developed this idea. They drove the buses themselves to pick up each member of their program. They spent the day with therapeutic activities, music and fun, then they would drive all the members back to their homes.

Knowing how much Thad had benefitted from being in this type of setting, Mom sought the program out and asked them if Thad would qualify. They welcomed him with open arms, and on his first day in July of 2006, they took a picture of Thad with the biggest smile ever. He was radiating such joy and excitement. Karen, her sisters, and the other ladies that worked with them were brilliant, down-to-earth women who really cared about the adults they were responsible for. Mom remembered one day in 2008 when Thad hadn't been to S.T.E.P.S. for a while because he was battling pneumonia. Mom and Thad were sitting in the kitchen finishing up breakfast, and they heard a loud noise coming from outside. It sounded like Thad's name. Mom rolled Thad to the front door and saw that these amazing ladies had brought everyone in the program in all their buses to come and see Thad since he wasn't able to go there. Michelle, Thad's bus driver, was standing there with a bullhorn calling for Thad to come out and say hi.

As I mentioned earlier, Dad had expressed to me in a 1993 letter that he was interested in writing a biography about Thad's life and how he had influenced people for good. It was now 12 years later, and he had written some ideas down and started a few times, but life, church, and husband/father responsibilities seemed to impede his progress. At this time, Travis was in college studying film, so they put their heads together and decided a documentary about Thad through the eyes of our family would be an interesting project to work on together.

Throughout our lives, Dad and Mom were documenters. Mom was obsessed with taking photographs of the family, while Dad was always behind the movie camera, beginning with super-8 film without sound and evolving into VHS and beyond. We had hours and hours and more hours of film that needed to be digitized and catalogued before they could even think about starting to formulate ideas about the how and wherefore of a documentary. We also had thousands of pictures as well as boxes of audiotapes that we had made for my dad when he was out of town or for our grandparents, since we never lived close to them. It was a daunting process, but Travis and Dad worked together and separately for months creating the raw materials that would serve as the foundation for this documentary. The next thing to do was to get whatever additional equipment they would need besides a camera to make the documentary.

I had a conversation with Dad in 2005. He was moved and saddened by the Terry Schaivo case in Florida. She was the woman who was in a persistent vegetative state for several years when her husband petitioned the circuit court in his county to remove her feeding tube and to allow her to die. Seven years went by as the family battled it out in court, with the courts finally landing on the side of the husband. They took her off life support on March 18, 2005, and she died about two weeks later from the effects of dehydration. Dad disagreed with the husband's decision to end his wife's life, because, as he put it, "those circumstances no longer have anything to do with the stricken person, but everything to do with their caretakers. We are here to learn how to love, and by cutting her life short, they are terminating the amazing opportunity they have to learn more than they could ever learn on their own. I mean, look at all we've experienced having Thad in our family. I wouldn't have missed it for the world." I think that the Schaivo case motivated Dad to press forward with the hours of work that he and Travis had to do to get everything ready for putting the documentary together.

I was living in New York, doing massage still at the La Prairie Spa at the Ritz Carlton as well as building a solid private practice in a private studio I had created with one of my best friends, Elliot Potts. I wasn't dating a whole lot, but I was happy, comfortable, and satisfied with where my life had landed. I felt like I was surrounded by good people. My relationship to and connection with my family was better than ever. Life seemed to be rolling along at a good clip with very few obstacles. Then, one evening, as I checked my phone after finishing with a client in the spa, I saw a text from Travis, "Call home. Family emergency."

EXTRAORDINARY MEASURES

In March of 2006, almost exactly a year after Terry Schaivo died and the very day that Travis got the lavalier microphone he needed in order to start doing the interviews for the documentary, Dad collapsed on BYU campus as he was walking into a building for a Church meeting. He'd had a heart attack. Fortunately, someone right behind him started CPR right away and the paramedics arrived quickly. Even so, my dad's heart didn't start beating on its own for a little over 30 minutes. Just as they were about to call it quits and let my dad leave this world, his heart got the message and started pumping. What I didn't know before this happened was that CPR will keep someone alive, but it does not push enough blood into the brain to keep brain cells from dying. Even though Dad was alive, the general consensus among the doctors was that there would be significant brain damage and that if he woke at all, he probably would not regain most of his faculties. Travis has said since that he was thinking, "Dad, surely there was a less dramatic way to get the family together to do the interviews!"

I caught the first available flight out to Utah. It was scary being in the hospital and seeing Dad in such a vulnerable and precarious state. He was awake, but he wasn't coherent. It seemed like his brain was a pinball machine, and his thoughts were triggered by hundreds of simultaneously bouncing metal balls. His arms and legs moved constantly and erratically.

Initially, while Dad was in the hospital, we took shifts visiting him. Since all of us siblings were home, we all couldn't fit into his room at the same time. Travis set up some lights in the basement of my parent's home and interviewed all of us, one by one, for the documentary about Thad. It was a nice break from the worry and fear we were all feeling. Travis asked us what we remembered about life before Thad, about Thad's birth, and about significant experiences we'd had with Thad among family, friends, and strangers. He also asked us about challenges that life with Thad presented. Each interview lasted about 30 minutes. It was fascinating because he was getting different perspectives from the same series of questions. There were nine because Travis did not interview himself, and Dad was fighting for his life in the hospital.

At the same time, Travis began documenting Dad's hospital stay with all its doubt and bleak prognoses. In the interviews, he asked us a couple of questions about what was happening right now, what our thoughts were on Dad, and the uncertain future. Travis immediately drew a parallel between how the family responded when Thad was born and what was happening to Dad. Our thoughts on Thad were, for the most part, reminiscences, but Dad was in the hospital, right now. We were living it. Travis was unsure if any of this would end up in the documentary, but he felt compelled to record it all. In spite of the trauma that brought us together in this moment, it was reassuring to all be in the same place at the same time. When we were certain that Dad was going to survive, and the prognosis was becoming less dire, those of us who lived out of town had to go back to our lives. It was hard to leave because Dad was still in the hospital and there was a long road ahead which we could only be peripherally a part of.

Although I was worried about Dad, I was most worried about Mom. She automatically went into survival mode, and she was trying to figure out the best way to get two beds into the family room by the kitchen so that if she had to take care of two invalids for the rest of her life, it would be easier. Todd and Brooke wanted to take Thad up to Wyoming with their family for a few weeks, but Mom insisted that he stay in Utah. Having him around gave her strength. The routines around his care gave her continuity and calmed her soul. Besides, Trent, Travis, Lesa, and Mike (Lesa's husband) were there, and they were more than willing to help as much as necessary.

As the days went on, Dad left the hospital and spent some time in a rehabilitation clinic as his brain continued to heal, normalize, and find its way around his new cerebral landscape. The uncontrolled shaking of his limbs eased up and disappeared. Over the following weeks and months, he regained control of his body functions, and soon it was apparent that he would be able to walk and pretty much take care of himself. Gratefully, he would not be an invalid.

The fallout from this event lay mainly in Dad's cognitive abilities. He could think and reason to a point, and he got better and better at finding the right word to express what he was thinking; but, the logical, controlled, and reasoned layer through which he had always connected to the world had been stripped away. He lost large sections of his long-term memory, he experienced many challenges with his short-term memory, and he would get confused easily, especially if he was in a situation with excessive outside stimuli. He was gentle and stubborn at the same time.

Mom was married to someone who didn't know her. That was the hardest part. Their shared experiences disappeared, so they were basically starting from scratch 44 years into their marriage. Dad knew that he was married, that Mom was his wife, but there was very little else that he could grab onto. The doctors' hope was that like many of his abilities that he'd regained, his memory would begin to return as time went on. In the meantime, each day was a new memory together that hopefully would be captured somewhere in his brain and would remain retrievable.

Through all this time, Travis transcribed all our interviews and started putting together the narrative for the documentary. It was a monumental task, and he didn't have any assistants to do the grunt work for him. I was not involved in this part of the process. I would talk to Travis on the phone periodically about what he was doing and how it was going. During one conversation, he said, "You know what? I think I am going to include Dad's story in the documentary. Since I couldn't interview him, and we don't know how well he will recover, he's basically missing from a story where he played a significant role. Not only that, they both have to do with brain injuries."

Travis finished a rough cut of the film, calling it *The*

Coming Years, a title he got from something that Mom had said during her interview. If I'm not mistaken, that cut was about an hour and 15 minutes long. Travis' big concern about the film was legitimate—How do we make this very personal story a universal one? Is this film something we will show at family reunions, or is it something the general public would be interested in seeing?

This is where I came in. Travis sent me a copy of this original cut, and I showed it to about 20 of my friends and acquaintances in New York. I tried to get people from many different backgrounds—Mormon/non-Mormon, married/unmarried, with children/without children, gay/straight, optimistic/cynical. Another criteria was that we needed people who weren't afraid to tell us what they really thought. It took me a few weeks and several different screenings of the film, but we got a lot of great and helpful feedback. Everyone really liked the film overall, and many of them called me weeks later saying that they were still thinking about it. There was some concern that the two stories competed with each other instead of strengthening each other, and it felt a little too long; but, everyone agreed that it was a story worth telling and one that many people could relate to. So, I wrote it all down and conferenced with Travis. I don't know how many drafts we went through, but Travis was a trooper, and he edited and rearranged and edited again, countless times. Taking 15 minutes out of a film while maintaining its integrity and narrative voice is difficult and brutal work.

Once we had a film we were satisfied with, we took a year and sent it out to every film festival that we thought would be interested, somewhere between 20 and 40 submissions. Rejection after rejection came back to us. All of them said, "Wonderful film, but we don't have room for it." There was really no way for us to know if the letters were form letters or if they meant what they were saying. So, we kept going. After the first handful of rejections, Travis did some more edits, and we wondered if we should change the title. We brainstormed, watched the film, wrote down ideas, and brainstormed again. Very early in the film, Mom says, "...they [the doctors] weren't going to do extraordinary measures to save his life..." That became our title—*extraordinary measures*. We decided not to capitalize it in order to give the indication that the extraordinary measures that filled Thad's life, both toward him and from him, happened through small, daily, even insignificant, things.

We kept submitting. And we kept getting rejected. It was frustrating, but we believed in the film. We also understood that film festivals were looking for works that stirred the pot, caused controversy, pushed the envelope, or had some kind of star attached—films that would bring people in to fill the seats. Ours was a hard sell. It was a quiet film. None of us said, "This sucks! I hate my brother!" There was no overt dysfunction. Our film was the story of a family that worked in a positive way. It wasn't really festival material, apparently. Finally, though, the San Francisco Doc-Fest said yes to us. We were thrilled! I found out later that the main guy wasn't too excited about our film, but the girl who supported us really stood her ground in the decision- making process.

The festival was great fun. Travis, Kylie (Travis' partner), Mom, Dad, and I were there. The films were playing in two, kind of rundown art-houses. We played in the big theatre once (our first showing). Then we were put into the smaller theatre, which was great because it felt full even though there weren't a whole lot of people there. During our showtimes, we competed with a film about racing dachshunds and another film about Andy Warhol's lover who committed suicide or disappeared or something like that. People lined up around the block to see those films. Ours was the little film that could.

There were a handful of people whom we knew who lived in and around San Francisco, who came out to support us. My friend Rodnie and his wife Jean flew in from New York to attend. Everyone else who came to the screenings were complete strangers, and we were grateful that they were clearly moved and very complimentary. The Q&As after the screenings were very positive.

Once we realized the festival circuit was done, we still wanted to provide opportunities for people to see our film. I'd always been of the mind that if people aren't going to step forward to help, then we just had to do it ourselves. So, that's what we did. We rented a theatre in New York for a weekend for $3,200 and had 12 screenings of the film. (It was an amazing deal because everywhere else I checked on would have been $10,000 for one screening)

The week of the screening was the week that Grandpa Sutton passed away. I rented a car and drove out to Indiana to pick up Lara and her children on the way through Pennsylvania. Mom and Dad dropped Thad off with Todd and Brooke in Wyoming on their way east to Indiana. In Illinois, they were in a major accident with a semi that totaled their travel van. They spent the night in an emergency room, rented a car, and arrived at the viewing all banged up, wearing bloody clothes because all of their luggage remained in the wreckage, but we were so grateful that they were alive.

The funeral was simple but very nice. I owed a lot to Grandpa Sutton, so honoring him in this way was essential. I would continue to honor him with every piece of stained glass I created. After the funeral, Trent, Travis, and I drove to New York City without stopping. Mom, Liz (Trent's wife), Lara, Jesse (Lara's husband), and their family took a little longer to get there, but they made it. Dad stayed in Indiana because he was still recovering from the brain injury. His father's death and the car accident discombobulated him. Everyone felt it would be best for him to spend some time with his brothers and sister.

Not a lot of people came to the screenings. I learned it was probably better to have fewer screenings so that it felt like an event, but I had thought that with everyone's New York schedule, it would be better to have options. I was wrong. Once again, though, the people who did attend, even people who didn't know me or my family, liked the film. In the end, we were able to raise $3,000 (with some pretty large single donations) for a school in Queens that specialized in working with children with physical and learning disabilities. I didn't take any of the money to cover the expenses. All in all, it was a wonderful experience.

Then, we turned our eyes West and arranged three screenings in Provo. We had hoped to secure a theatre on the BYU campus since Travis studied film there and all nine of us had been students there, but they wouldn't even talk to us about it. That was disappointing. We did find a nice little cinema in Orem, close to the mall, and they actually donated the space to us. The screenings were a success. Tony, Tracy, and their daughters were there as well as Lesa, Mike, and their children. Lesa's high school marching band played in the parking lot before the first screening. We had over a hundred people at each screening, and we raised $2,000 for the S.T.E.P.S. program which had been so helpful to Thad. It was an amazing experience!

When you spend time and effort and money creating something, the hope is that thousands of people will see it and share in the experience. This didn't happen for us, but it was gratifying to see that those people who did venture out to see our little film or those who bought the DVD later, confirmed to us that it was a story worth telling.

Mom and Dad insisted on keeping Thad at home. Neither one could lift him by themselves, so they got really good at working as a team. One of them would lift his torso and the other his feet in order to get him into and out of his chair. Trent got a job at a New York-based law firm and was now living in Rochester, New York. Travis got accepted into Graduate School in Texas, so he and Kylie moved to Dallas. After the economic crash in 2008, Lesa and Mike decided to take a job in Troy's financial planning company, and they moved to Abilene, Texas. For the time being, no one was living close to my parents. Thankfully, Claudia continued to be a constant presence. She would help with anything from preparing meals to cleaning up the house to meticulously and tenderly caring for Thad. If my parents needed to go out of town, Claudia would bring her children over to the house and stay with Thad until my parents returned.

In 2008, Mom decided it was time to get shoulder replacement surgery. She'd been working with physicians and physical therapists for years to try to circumvent the procedure, but her shoulder kept getting worse; the pain at this point was unrelenting. Since she would be out of commission for a few months, Brooke (Todd's wife) convinced her to let Thad stay with them for a while. This was a difficult decision for Mom to make, not because she didn't trust Brooke and Todd to successfully care for Thad, but because she felt Thad was hers and Dad's responsibility, and knowing the amount of work it involved, she was hesitant to lay that on anyone else's shoulders, especially a daughter-in-law. Todd and Brooke cared for Thad for a month or so when Mom and Dad came West for Grandpa Sutton's funeral and the film screening in New York, but this would be longer, and Mom hesitated. Brooke prevailed by asserting that this would be a perfect opportunity to give her children a hands-on experience of what it meant to step outside themselves and truly be of service to someone else. Mom couldn't fight the "Isn't that what Jesus would want?" argument.

Brooke said it was a wonderful experience. Her family pitched in to help care for Thad, even when they weren't asked to, and she felt they benefitted greatly from it. Even their black labrador retriever fell in love with Thad—she would often curl up next to him on the floor and fall asleep. In hearing Brooke talk, it seemed to me as though the three and a half months that Thad spent in Wyoming were almost a perfect microcosm of our experience.

Firstly, caring for Thad was not a burden, but it was a full-time job to be attentive to his signals and his needs—to feed him, reposition him, exercise and massage his body, change his diapers, and interact with him. Brooke said that it wasn't hard to get things done around the house because Thad wasn't demanding in that way, but days would slip by faster than they should have. She didn't get out of the house as often nor as regularly as she had in the past.

Very soon after Thad arrived in Wyoming, Brooke realized that he really enjoyed floating in the bathtub, so every night she would put on her swimsuit and draw a bath. She would get in the tub and rest Thad's head on her upper body, allowing him to float in the hot water face up for about 30 minutes or so. He liked it so much that when 8 o'clock came, Thad would get vocal. "*Aaaeh*!" he would call out, until he heard the water running, then he would chuckle and wait for his 30 minutes of weightless bliss.

Knowing that Thad liked music, Brooke would play CDs during the day. We knew that he liked Country music, but he got a real kick out of a Trace Adkins song called "Honky Tonk Badonkadonk." He would laugh and shake his head to the rhythm. Then, on the same CD there was a ballad about a soldier being buried in Arlington cemetery where his grandfather was also buried. When that song came on, Thad would quiet down and pay attention to the music in almost a reverential mood.

It surprised Brooke early on when she realized that Thad had a specific personality. He had moods. He had a sense of humor; even, as she put it, "a mischievous one." She told me that he would do something or resist something that would inhibit her ability to accomplish a task of some kind. When she would say, "Now, Thad..." he would start laughing and relax into whatever needed to be done. Caring for Thad brought an awareness to her and to her family of his deep humanity. It is one thing to intellectually, even spiritually, understand that the handicap is not the person, but when you have the opportunity to interact with and to serve someone in this way, the profound reality becomes inescapable: the person is the person.

Brooke mentioned that bringing Thad to church affected members of her ward in a good way, similar to every ward we had ever been a part of. Brooke was the Primary President. She took a small mattress and rested Thad on the floor in the front of the room during the opening meeting before the kids went off to their age-related classes. One young girl in the Primary had Asperger Syndrome. She was a big girl and could often be challenging for her parents. She loved Thad. She would talk to him quietly and gently caress his arm or his head.

When Thad arrived in Wyoming, he'd been listless for a while. Thad's doctors and my parents couldn't figure out what was wrong. There was no indication that he was sick. His seizure medication levels were on track. Tests said he was healthy, but he just didn't have any energy. His personality was muted. They wondered if this weren't a progression of some kind, like when he gradually lost the use of his legs. A few weeks into his stay in Wyoming, Brooke noticed a tiny spot of blood in his diaper, and she wondered if he might not have a urinary tract infection. She took him to a doctor whom she knew well, and she explained the situation. There didn't seem to be an easy way to get a urine sample from Thad, so her physician prescribed some antibiotics that would treat a UTI if that were in fact what was happening. Within a few days, Thad's energy and his personality were back in full bloom. Similar to what had happened when Thad was spontaneously vomiting due to an inner ear infection more than a decade before, this had been one of those situations where Thad could not communicate what he was feeling, so treating him was often difficult. It was like a game of Blind Man's Bluff.

In hearing Brooke talk, it seemed to me as though the time that Thad spent in Wyoming was also a perfect microcosm of our experience. Before long, Brooke was feeling the effects of sleep deprivation from getting up during the nights to check on Thad and to adjust his body, if necessary. Interestingly, I remember a phone conversation I had with Mom at the time, when said that she was anxious to have Thad home again, but also feeling more rested than she had in years. When the day came for Thad to go back to Utah, Brooke and Todd and their family said goodbye, but knowing that my parents were getting older, and not knowing how long Thad would be alive, they were fully ready and willing to take Thad in for the rest of his life if it became too difficult for my parents to care for him.

Dad continued to improve physically. Eventually, after a few years, he got the go-ahead from his doctors to be able to lift Thad on his own. His short-term memory wasn't perfect, but it was better than before. His long-term memory never came back. When he looked back, the timeline of his life was an irregular and erratic series of dots and dashes. Gaps as long as 10 years impeded his ability to put anything together fully. So, he started to compile a personal history from all of the letters and journals he'd written over the years. He didn't have a memory, but he could teach himself about his own life.

During the nights when Mom or Dad would check Thad, they began to notice that he had trouble breathing. The doctors diagnosed sleep apnea and started him using a CPAP (continuous positive airway pressure), a treatment that uses mild air pressure to keep the airways open. It worked. Thad appeared more rested, and the worry that my parents were experiencing about him dying during the night was alleviated.

They also noticed that Thad started to choke or cough more frequently when he was eating. The doctors diagnosed dysphagia. Apparently Thad had lost or was losing his swallow reflex. Thad's physician, Dr.

Stacey, was not surprised. Dysphagia is not uncommon in patients who have impaired neurological function. Just as Thad once had been able to use his legs and arms but lost that ability in his teens, he was now losing the ability to swallow. There were options to help him, but they needed to find a specialist who could help.

After consulting with Primary Children's Hospital, Mom set up an appointment with one of the leading gastroenterologists in the Provo area. During their consult, this physician repeatedly referred to Thad as an FLK. "With an FLK, the considerations we need to... blah blah blah." It was an acronym that Mom had never heard before, but he used it so much that she determined to do some research when she got home, since he appeared to be more of a monologuist than a conversationalist. Later that day, Mom called Thomas, who was now a pediatric gastroenterologist living with his family in Maryland. She asked him if he had ever heard the acronym FLK? Thomas asked, "Where did you hear that?" Mom explained about the appointment she had just had. Thomas was silent for a moment, then he said, "Mom, that is a derogatory acronym that some doctors use among themselves, mostly its the interns and residents. It means 'funny looking kid.'" Naturally, they continued their search for an appropriate specialist.

They found a doctor in the same medical practice who called Thomas a few times to get a better understanding about Thad's condition. Through his conversations with Thomas and with Dr. Stacey, this doctor filled in the blanks and was able to determine the various options that could be on the table. In the end, though, he felt that the "FLK" doctor would actually be the best one to perform the procedures. Mom was not one to hold a grudge, so she followed his advice, and they scheduled the next consult.

Their first and easiest option involved inserting a feeding tube into Thad's nose and threading it down into his stomach. But the structure of Thad's skull was so deformed that it crimped the tube and made the procedure ineffective. Next, they attempted to put a feeding tube directly into his stomach through his abdomen, but while preparing for the procedure, they realized that Thad's stomach was too high up under his ribs, making the procedure impossible. The final option was to attempt to put a feeding tube through his back into the stomach, but this was a procedure that was only meant for emergency situations. It was not and could not be a long-term solution. Through much deliberation, they decided the only real option was for my parents to continue to puree Thad's food as smooth as possible and feed him as they always had. It would make its way into his stomach, but it wouldn't be the most comfortable experience for Thad.

These small indications of decline were unsettling, but Thad continued to be the bright, happy, everything-will-work-out person he had always been. Mealtimes were not fun, but at least he was sleeping through the night without too much trouble. My parents were in their sixties, now, and their lives in many ways were inextricable from Thad's. The care and tender attention they afforded him illuminated the profound love they felt for him. Seeing them all together in the daily ritual of care that belied years of thoughtful repetition reminded me of the moment many years before when Mom saw that older cowboy gentleman gently carry his teenage son from their pick-up truck into the West Texas Rehabilitation Center. At the time, impressed by the deep affection she saw in that man, Mom thought, "There go I." And that indeed, became her life.

My story in New York City was moving along, too. In 2007, I left the spa world altogether and focused all my time on maintaining and growing my private practice. I was very fortunate to have a strong and interesting client base. In my personal life, I dated a little. I had a couple of relationships that lasted a few months each, which was a record for me. Both of these relationships were with former Mormons. I thought it would be easier since we shared a common background, but that reasoning didn't pan out so well. Every relationship teaches you what you want and don't want. Both of these men taught me a handful of things I appreciated and a truckload of things that I never want to ever experience again. I can't say it was all their doing (or undoing), because relationships are a two-way street. At 40 years old, I was neither facile nor experienced in the nuances of being a couple, but my expectations were high. I wanted an adult relationship, but I was still surprised by things I would have learned as a teenager if I had allowed myself to date.

On December 31, 2009, I planned to go down to Chelsea to see *Avatar*. I knew it was a long movie, and I wanted something to take me past midnight. The showing started at 10:30 p.m., but since I lived next to Times Square, I got down to Chelsea early to escape the New Year's Eve revelers. There was one bar in Chelsea that I was comfortable going to. It was called the Gym Bar, and I had gone there a couple of times over the years with friends. I still didn't drink, but I needed to be somewhere out of the cold for the hour or two before the movie started. I made my way in, got a Coke and leaned against the wall. The bar was packed with normal guys like me and hot guys and their friends. As I sipped my coke, I looked around the crowd. Suddenly, a tall, vibrant Brazilian guy with a big smile and luminescent eyes was next to me shaking my hand and introducing himself as Julio Cardia. I introduced myself, and we started talking. His English was not that great but he was trying really hard. I was surprised how easy it was to talk to him. When he shook my hand, all my walls fell down. Our conversation was light. It was fun. He told me that he was in the States (Croton-on-the-Hudson, NY to be specific) doing an internship for his graduate degree in Business. He was working at a bed and breakfast. This was his first night in New York City. They had given him the night off, but he had to be back by 6 the next morning to start working again.

Julio was so excited to be in the City. He got off the train from Croton earlier that day and wound his way from Grand Central Station to Chelsea stopping in every bar that had a rainbow flag in the window. By this time, he was pretty drunk, but I couldn't stop talking to him. Since I'd never drunk alcohol, I had always been uncomfortable around drunk people, so my reaction to Julio surprised me. He told me that he was from Brasilia. He told me about his family, and I told him many parts of my story as well. We laughed a lot. I'm not sure I had ever had such an easy time talking to a stranger in a bar (not that I had frequented many bars in my day) or anywhere for that matter.

Finally, I couldn't hold off any longer. The movie was going to start in a few minutes, so I told Julio that I had to leave because I was going to the movie. He said, "OK!" and he followed me out. I was thinking, "I hope there are tickets available!" There were. We got in, we sat down, the previews started, and Julio fell right to sleep. It was so funny. He didn't snore, thankfully.

At the end of the movie, I woke him up, and we left. Julio needed to get to Grand Central Station to catch a train to Croton-on-the-Hudson. I thought, "There is no way, I'm going to let him, in his state, try to find his way back to Grand Central Station at one in the morning on New Year's Eve by himself." So, we walked East on 23rd street toward the subway. Suddenly, he pushed me into a doorway and kissed me. He really kissed me, and I saw fireworks exploding above our heads. It was the most sexy and intimately wonderful thing that had ever happened to me in my life. Then, we continued walking, found the subway, made our way to Grand Central, got him on the correct train which happened to be leaving as soon as he boarded, and that was how my life changed.

Since we both had Blackberry phones, we could text between us without any charges, even when he was back in Brazil. I saw him several more times before he left, whenever he could make it back into the city. We got to know each other gradually and enjoyed each other's company. It was very casual and unpressured because he was going back to Brazil. I expected that when he got back to Brazil, life would go on for both of us and that would be that. But it didn't work out that way. We stayed in contact and continued to get to know each other through texts and emails.

Back in Utah, my parents were concerned about Thad. Dad chronicled some of the significant incidents in his 2010 contribution to the *Sutton Family History Collection*:

> January: This year started with great fear as Thad had been in and out of the hospital since 15 December wrapped in a heat blanket and a temperature of 91 degrees and exhibiting total listlessness. As the doctors worked on him, one asked if we had funeral arrangements set up for Thad. It was a sobering question. By the 8th of January they finally guessed that his thyroid might not be performing well, so he went on thyroid medicine and recovered slowly...On January 27 we departed in our van for Colorado to visit Lara and family...Thad enjoyed the trip in his new van, but he was still fragile.
>
> February: ...Thad continued to have bad health, with bouts of pneumonia and an inability to eat well. Thad hadn't been attending school since December...
>
> March: Thad is sick with pneumonia again. We installed a voyager lift system in Thad's bedroom and bathroom to make it easier to move from bed to bath to chair.
>
> June: We left home on 9 June traveling in our van with Thad sitting comfortably in his new car seat...We were so happy with Thad's comfortable trip... [During our stay,] Thad ended up in the emergency room at the Abilene hospital for about 8 hours but seems to be recovered well...
>
> September: Thad was sick again. We cared for him.

In late September of 2010, I flew down to Brasilia for the first time because Julio was running for a seat on the State Legislature for the Distrito Federal, which is like Washington, D.C. I wanted to be there to help during the last week of the campaign. I met his family and his friends, and we had a wonderful time. His campaign was unique in its use social media; he really tried to garner the support of the younger generation. Although he did not win the election, his showing was impressive, especially considering it was his first time out, and he did it with very little money.

Being part of the campaign was a great experience for me because I was trying to learn Portuguese. Knowing Spanish helped a lot in the sense that I understood many of the basics of the language. In another sense, it didn't help because I was basically speaking Spanish using Portuguese words or words that I made up because I thought they sounded Portuguese. I did a lot of talking at social events during the campaign and with Julio's friends and family, but I'm afraid I wasn't making much sense. During one conversation towards the end of the campaign, the 20-something I was talking to turned to Julio and asked, "Does he understand phrases, or just words?" Julio replied with a smile, "He's trying really hard." I had to laugh because I thought I was doing really well.

After the election, Julio and I went to Salvador, which had been the first capitol of Brazil. It is a beautiful city on the coast. Walking through the colonial section of the town, I felt like I was back in Europe. Cádiz, the last town I served in on my mission, was close to the border between Spain and Portugal. This part of Salvador reminded me of walking through the streets of Old Cádiz. We were having such a good time getting to know each other, without the pressures of daily life.

From there, we went to Rio where we spent a few days at the beach. The apartment that we rented was just a few blocks away from Ipanema beach. We went to see the Cristo Redentor Statue, we froze to death on the Sugar Loaf mountains (I didn't think Rio could get cold, but I was wrong), we danced late into the night at some fun clubs, and we met some very nice people. I began to see that the joie de vivre that first attracted me to Julio was authentic. He loved life. He loved people. He was one of those, "What you see is what you get" kind of people. I could trust him when he said he loved me, and that felt wonderful.

On the second to last day in Rio, we got back from the beach and we were going to take a disco nap before getting ready to go out dancing at an all night outdoor event. I noticed that I had messages on my phone. Troy had called, saying that Thad was in the hospital in Colorado after some kind of accident. I called him back immediately. He didn't have all the details, but Mom thought we should all get there as soon as possible. I didn't need to change my flight because I was leaving the next day. I jumped online and found a flight to Denver upon my return to New York.

I was overwhelmed and worried. Would Thad pull through, or was this the day that had loomed for 34 years, just beyond the edge of hope? Once I arrived back in the U.S., I found out what had happened. Mom and Dad were in Aurora, Colorado, visiting Lara and her family. After dinner and Family Home Evening, Dad decided to take Thad (in his wheelchair) out to the camper van so they could go to sleep. In order to get Thad down the porch steps effectively, Dad had to go down them backwards. Because ramps aren't a common feature, this was an activity that was very familiar. This time, though, Dad missed a step on the way down, and both he and Thad fell off the porch. The impact sent Thad into a serious grand mal seizure.

The paramedics arrived within minutes, but they were startled by what they found; they had never dealt with someone with Thad's disability, especially in a full blown grand mal seizure. They called the hospital to get some instruction. Mom told them what medications Thad was on and explained that they could do anything as long as they did not touch Thad's head. She rode in the ambulance with Thad.

Once they made it to The Parker Adventist Hospital in Parker, Colorado, Thad's seizure started to abate. There was blood in Thad's head on the right side and his breathing was ragged. The emergency room team sedated Thad and monitored him. Once they felt he was out of immediate danger, they transferred him from the emergency room to a normal hospital room. Soon, though, they realized Thad was so frail and his breathing was so labored that they decided to transfer him to the Intensive Care Unit.

Todd came down from Wyoming the next morning. That night, Thad started to fail. Fluid was building up in his lungs which made breathing that much more difficult, so they intubated him and put him on a respirator. Mom and Dad stayed in the room with Thad all day and night, except for the times when there was a change of shift and the medical teams cleared the floor of guests so they could transfer information on the patients quickly and efficiently from one team to the next.

Mom spent a lot of time thinking because she couldn't concentrate or focus on any other activity. Thad woke up and was somewhat responsive. Mom talked to him and held his hand. The fact that he was awake and responsive gave Mom hope. It seemed to her like he was stabilizing. Mom asked one of the physicians how soon he might be able to go home. His reply was, "Thad is not stable. He is critically ill. Otherwise he wouldn't be in the ICU." Mom had to laugh because that was the same kind of response she had received when she arrived at Wilford Hall a few days after Thad was born and asked how soon she could bring him home. The truth of the situation was that even though Thad was intermittently awake, his breathing was still compromised, he was having frequent seizures, and there was still bleeding in his head.

The Adventist Hospital was a beautiful place to be, and perfect for my parents. There were murals of Christ at the entrance. Biblical quotes and spiritual thoughts were communicated over the intercom periodically during the day. The doctors and nurses came from a place of medicine as well as faith. Not all of them were Seventh Day Adventists, but they all had some kind of religious foundation that informed their work. Dr. Bratt, one of the neurosurgeons/ neurologists assigned to Thad's case told my parents, "We have never experienced a patient like Thad. We're going to do the best we can, but Thad's life is in God's hands."

Having an environment like this was helpful, and it soothed my mom to a point, but she couldn't shake the growing isolation she felt being so far away from the support system they had cultivated over the years in Utah. She began to doubt the wisdom of bringing Thad on this particular trip instead of leaving him home with Claudia. Because there were very few distractions, Mom started to second guess herself about many things and to spiral into a morass of guilt and self-recrimination.

The next day was Wednesday, and Thad perked up. The respiratory therapist turned off the respirator and let Thad breathe on his own for a few hours. Mom and Dad spent the day talking to Thad, caressing his head, and holding his hands. Lara and Todd came in and out as well, but there was a strict limit on the number of people who could be in the room at one time.

On Thursday, Mom got really sick and had to spend most of the day resting at Lara's house. It was that day, while Mom was away, that Thad's heart stopped beating when they tried to remove his breathing tube. The nurse immediately started CPR, and his heart started beating again. I'm so grateful for that nurse because if Thad had passed away when Mom was not there, I'm not sure she could have recovered from that.

By Friday, October 15, some of Thad's stats were finally back in the normal range. His kidneys were working great. His blood pressure was good. He was awake and responsive, but his lungs were still stiff and soggy. He was suffering from acute bacterial pneumonia as well as congestive heart failure. His doctor commented that Thad's breathing musculature was weak and atrophied. It was not surprising since breathing had been a struggle for a while now. It was something my parents had been trying to mediate and strengthen. Hearing the doctor say that Thad's life hung in the balance wasn't helping the situation. It devastated Mom because it seemed to her that she hadn't done enough to help him, that she had failed him in some way. She kept these feelings close to her vest.

The rest of us made it to Colorado on Saturday, emotionally holding our breath, wondering what the future would hold. The lead physician on Thad's case suggested we all get together with him to discuss what was happening. Tony (and his eldest daughter Leandra), Todd, Me, Thomas (and his wife, Vanessa), Troy (and his wife, Thora), Trent (and his wife, Liz), Lara (and her husband Jesse), Travis, and Lesa all gathered with my parents in a room near the intensive car unit. When the doctor arrived, he explained the nature of Thad's condition. The fall had been traumatic, yes, but it was something he could recover from. I think this was a relief to all of us because of the weight of guilt we imagined Dad was bearing. This was an accident, and it could have happened to any of us.

The doctor clarified that the real challenge was that Thad's respiratory system was incredibly weak. The efforts being made by the medical team and the life support system were keeping Thad alive right now, and hopefully biding time until he would be able to breathe on his own. He advised that there was a difference between improving Thad's life expectancy and simply maintaining his life. If there came a time when any measurable improvements were impossible to discern, we (my parents) would have to decide the best course of action. He encouraged us all to discuss together what the best future for Thad should be. Hopefully, he would pull through, and all would be well, but the physician felt that should he not improve, it would be best to take him off the respirator and allow his body to determine the future, whatever that would be.

When the doctor finished speaking and we were all clear on what he was trying to convey, my mom quietly asked, "If that time arrives, and we take him off of life support, will he suffocate? Because...," she paused to gather the strength to continue. "Because, I don't think I could bear that." The doctor detailed what would happen and how medications would alleviate those sensations for Thad. It didn't make it easier to consider, but it was an answer. I admired Mom for having the clarity of thought to ask exactly what she needed to know.

Dad, then, asked, "If we take him off of life support, are we murdering him?" To the doctor's credit, he understood the moral dilemma my father was facing. He explored with us the moral need to recognize when to hold on and when to let go. He said that they would monitor Thad closely for improvements over the next week, and they would not suggest removal of life support until it was clear that he had plateaued indefinitely or that he started to decline. It was a quality of life issue. Again, taking him off the machines would give Thad's body the right to decide what it would do. That wasn't killing him. It was putting him into the hands of God.

We left the meeting and gathered in the hospital chapel. We talked about what the physician had said. We shared our thoughts and memories about our life with Thad. It was too early to make a definitive decision because Thad was stable. Ultimately, it was a choice that Mom and Dad would have to make, and we would support whatever they decided. The important and most difficult thing from my parents' perspective was that they had to separate their needs and their desires from the equation in order to determine what was best for Thad.

The hospital staff did not enforce the limitations on visitors in the room, but we shuttled in and out so there were never more than four people in the room. There were good signs: The bleeding in his head stopped. The number of seizures decreased to a more normal number, and their intensity also diminished. His eye was open periodically, and he seemed to be aware of his surroundings.

On Sunday, one of the nurses commented to Mom that she could tell that our family loved Thad. It was obvious not only in the way we interacted with him, but Thad's skin was in perfect condition and so clean. She said that in most cases like this where a person was bedridden and fully dependent on care, they have bed sores and other harmful conditions that are separate from the original disorder. It was clear to her that Thad had excellent care. Those were words that Mom needed to hear—her balm of Gilead, so to speak. They comforted her and served as a counterpoint to the internal monologue that plagued her quiet moments.

In spite of the nature of our visit to Colorado, this impromptu family reunion gave us time to reconnect with each other—to have fun sharing stories, playing games and being familial. Whenever we weren't at the hospital, we were hanging out at Lara's house eating, joking, and cherishing the chance to be together.

Monday brought Thad more erratic brain activity. Even when his eye was closed, we could see his eyeball fluttering more than usual. It reminded me of when we stood around Dad's bed after his heart attack, when his hands and feet moved uncontrollably while his brain tried to figure out what had just happened and where it needed to go to reconnect the damaged neural pathways.

Fluids were beginning to pool all over in Thad's body, especially in his hands and feet. He slept quietly all day, but his blood pressure was low, and it seemed that his lungs were not improving. In the evening, right before the shift change, Thad had a huge seizure. His whole body was stiff and arched. It was awful. It took eight shots of Adavan before it stopped.

Despite the Monday setback, Thad seemed to be plateauing. His eye was open, and he appeared to be watching the activity in the room. The respiratory therapist came in to work with him, giving him 5 minutes at a time for him to breathe on his own. He didn't seem to be giving up, and the medical team said that it could go either way, now. They continued to monitor his lungs and the progress of the pneumonia.

Things were not as bleak as we had initially thought, so everyone gradually left for home knowing that they could be called back at any time should Thad's condition worsen. I lived the farthest away, and it was not likely that I would be able to return to Colorado if Thad passed away since I'd then have to go to Utah for the funeral. I was troubled because I needed to go home in order to work. I'd been away from New York for almost 3 weeks, and I needed to earn some money. Being self-employed, I didn't get paid if I didn't work—and the bills wouldn't stop even if my world did. This was a tough decision. I stayed in Colorado as long as I could. The doctors determined that the way Thad was responding, it would be a day-to-day prospect and perhaps they would need at least another week before they could determine which direction he would go.

I decided I would go home to New York and hope for the best. I spent Tuesday afternoon and evening in Thad's room. Thad slept the whole time. Tubes of all sizes traversed his fragile body. The rhythmic sounds of mechanical respiration and the various beeps and tweets of life-support replaced the vocalizations and repetitive sounds that characterized Thad's limited ability to communicate—the sounds that carried deep and familiar meaning to those of us who knew him. I kissed him, told him that I loved him, and said goodbye without saying the word goodbye; then I left to catch a plane back to New York City where all the things that required me to make a living tapped their feet and checked their watches. It was probably the most difficult thing I've ever done. Every time I left home, I left with the fear that it would be the last time I saw Thad, but this time it was more real and more possible than ever, even though the doctors had been almost hopeful.

Thad's breathing improved on Wednesday and the oxygen levels in his blood were good. His kidneys were functioning well and the diuretics were helping to diminish the edema in his hands and feet. These were all good signs, so Mom and Dad decided that Dad should go home to Utah and take care of some pressing business. Lara spent the afternoon and evening with Mom and Thad.

Mom struggled to manage the jumble of feelings she kept hidden beneath her calm, hopeful exterior. She felt fear, panic, anger, hopelessness, sorrow, comfort, guilt, confidence, uncertainty, resignation, acceptance, and loss. She was teetering on the edge of the dark chasm of despair.

Even more progress broke the horizon on Thursday morning when the neurologist informed Mom that Thad's only real problem now was his lungs. To stem the progress of the pneumonia, they decided to try a different, more powerful antibiotic. Their hope and plan was to gradually wean Thad off the ventilator. This good news came moments before the day's spiritual message was announced over the intercom, "May His grace fill us with peace today, especially those facing uncertainty at this time. May they know His love." All day, a refrain from the hymn, "The Lord is my light; then why should I fear" played in Mom's head, soothing her soul and giving her a measure of peace. Dad made it back in the late afternoon.

Friday, Thad had a fever. He seemed to be restless, impatient, and uncomfortable. Lara spent most of the day with my parents and Thad.

Thad's progress was short-lived. On Saturday, his lungs were completely filled with fluid and his body was failing. The diarrhea caused by the new antibiotic was scalding and blistering Thad's skin. The medical team advised my parents that recovery was no longer likely, that they needed to consider making the decision to phase out the life support measures and allow Thad's body to determine his fate.

Mom and Dad talked and prayed together. Dad said to Mom, "I'm not going to be the one to say it. This has to be your decision." Looking at Thad lying in his bed, knowing all that the doctors had said, Mom took Thad's hand in hers. She kissed his head and whispered into his ear, "I don't want you to go, but you can go, but I don't want you to go."

Everyone returned to Colorado who could return, which was all but three of us, and on the afternoon of October 24, 2010, the medical team removed all the tubes. Todd called me so that I could be there on the phone, Trent and Tony were also there on other people's phones. Thomas lifted Thad out of the hospital bed and placed him in my mother's arms. My father knelt beside them with one arm around Mom, and he caressed Thad's head. Troy began singing our favorite Protestant hymn, and others joined in:

Softly and tenderly Jesus is calling
Calling for you and for me
See on the portals he's waiting and watching
Watching for you and for me

Come home, come home
Ye who are weary come home

Thad took a few breaths, then no more.

One room, two realms
Our hymns and tears bid you farewell
From beneath this mortal canopy
Our hands caress your fragile frame
A loving phrase, remembered smiles
On wings of song your spirit soars
Our sorrow held to let you fly

One room, two realms
So many hearts are waiting now
Their hymns and tears to welcome you
Another plane, yet not unknown
Familiar faces, common ground
On wings of song your spirit soars
A life fulfilled, a life begun

One room, two realms
One life moves on.

I have no doubt that on that day, in that moment, Grandma and Grandpa Clouse, Grandma and Grandpa Sutton, Katie Salisbury, and countless others waited on the other side with arms wide open to receive his beautiful, unhindered Soul.

Gifts come in all forms: wrapped boxes full of breakable fun; clothes to outgrow or wear out; a surprise trip to the ice cream store in the middle of Winter; a smile from a stranger on a lugubrious day. For me, the best gifts are the least obvious, the ones that take time to reveal themselves as they become an integral part of your life. I've been fortunate to have many such gifts in the people who have crossed my path, even walked a ways with me before traveling on their own unique journeys. Thad was just such a gift.

Living with the possibility of losing Thad for 34 years didn't prepare me for the devastation I felt when it actually happened. It was one of those experiences for which language falls short, an experience so profound that words like sorrow, misery, desolation, and despair only hint at the enormity of it all—like using a penlight to illuminate a mountain on a moonless night.

Arrangements were made to transport Thad's body from Colorado to Utah, and the funeral was planned for November 1. Julio's student visa had expired, but he moved heaven and earth to secure a tourist visa and flew back up to New York. I figured I could do it alone, but it was a relief to know that I now had someone I could lean on. My cousin Sharon worked for an airline, and she gave us tickets to fly out to Utah. The outpouring of love just didn't stop. I was nervous for my family to meet Julio, especially in such a vulnerable situation, but they couldn't have been more gracious and warm.

The evening before the funeral, we celebrated Halloween with all of our nieces and nephews. We spent the evening talking, reminiscing, and laughing with each other. Though, underneath it all, we were carrying a tremendous sadness because Thad's absence was palpable.

The morning of the funeral arrived as a bright, sunny, gorgeous Autumn day. We had the viewing before the funeral, and I was moved by how many people came, even from very long distances. Many of our relatives from Arizona and Utah were there, Fé and her family, the Salisburys, many friends from our time in the Philippines (who, like us, had settled in Utah), Maury, Erika and Claudia, (even though it had been years since Maury and Erika had cared for Thad), the wonderful ladies from S.T.E.P.S., so many people from my parent's current ward and the one in South Provo—each person bearing the sadness of the day, but sharing in the beauty of Thad's life. I was very touched by that.

The service was full of music, and each one of us had a couple of minutes to share our thoughts about Thad. I was impressed by each of my siblings and my parents as they bore their souls. Dad, in particular, for the moment that he stood at the pulpit and spoke confidently about Thad, sounded once again like the Dad we had known for most of our lives.

When it was my turn to speak, I shared this idea. It was a thought that has stayed with me, and one that has guided me through this process of writing about Thad's life—and my life:

> I thought the other day how Thad quickly became the sun at the center of the Sutton family solar system. He held us together in our individual orbits. I have to be honest and say that there were a few days after he passed where I felt like my planet was hurtling away through space as though slung from an ancient slingshot. I wondered how I would survive this, if my family would survive this.
>
> I'm not worried, now. God is love and love is truly the sun at the center of the Sutton family solar system. Thad's orbit was so close to that sun it was easy to mistake him for that sun. Nevertheless, the amazing light he reflected will travel in our universe forever.
>
> I loved Thad. I love my family. I hope to be able, one day, to love as true and simple and profound as Thad loved.

EPILOGUE

I was away from home from the time just after Thad turned nine years old. There were some exceptions: I spent time at home during college, when I returned to finish my degree, when I came home to help before and after Mom's back surgery, as well as short visits for holidays, reunions, weddings, other events, and "just because" trips. I always looked forward to being home so that I could reconnect with everyone, especially Thad, but my day-to-day life was about 2,200 miles away.

When Julio and I returned to New York after the funeral, the routines of life gradually took over. Julio stayed for a couple of months before going back to Brazil. Having him around was truly a blessing because I was not alone in the times I would have been alone otherwise. We continued our long-distance relationship for four years, spending as much time together as possible, including two super-fun Sutton family reunions which gave everyone time to get to know each other. Finally, on December 31, 2013, the fourth anniversary of when we met, Julio and I were able to legally marry, and start our life together looking forward to a wonderful future.

Of course, the sadness over Thad's passing was present especially in those first years, like a cloak that wrapped around my body, but I got used to the weight of it hanging from my shoulders. Over time, I wasn't aware of it most of the time, until it moved suddenly as if caught by a wind of memory. There were random moments when I would happen to see a special needs child in a supermarket or on the street with a parent or a caretaker and the sense of loss would overwhelm me, and I'd collapse into a lake of tears. I admit to exaggeration or hyperbole, but I would literally be overcome with tears. Once, I even set aside my groceries and left the supermarket because the emotions were so big that I knew I wouldn't make it through the checkout line.

I have had various snapshots of Thad framed and hanging in my home for many years. They kept me connected, and now they represent the impact he had on my life, for which I am grateful. In my massage studio, I have a wonderful portrait of the whole family including spouses and grandchildren that was taken at our family reunion in 2009. Thad was sitting on my lap. It doesn't remind me of Thad's passing, but of his life and how integral he was in our family. This portrait makes me happy.

Thad has been a regular visitor in my dreams. I think about him a lot, especially as I have been working on this book. I wouldn't call them visitations, per se. He doesn't seem to be coming to me with a message from the other side. He is just present in my heart and in my thoughts, so he plays a role in the process my brain goes through of figuring things out as I sleep. Thad never speaks in my dreams though there is some interaction, on occasion. He, more often than not, represents the voice of reason in whatever situation is playing out. Having him there allows the Tim character to make better decisions, to be more kind, more grounded, and to think about family.

As I finished writing this book, Thad's presence in my dreams became less frequent. In the final dream that I've had up to now, I drove a minivan filled with my nieces and nephews and their friends. We arrived at my parent's house and there were a lot of people there, family and non-family alike. When I opened the doors to let everyone out of the minivan, I saw that for a brief moment each one had Thad's face, then their own again. As I lifted out the youngest children from the van, I looked around, and everyone there had a flash of Thad's face. Through the years, Thad has been the touchstone that allowed me to see the beauty within myself, even when I felt loathsome and unworthy of anything good. Perhaps it's time for me to stop looking inward, and to see more clearly the beauty in everyone else.

Living so far away from home, I was not reminded in every moment of Thad's absence. My parents, however, lived in the same home as before. Thad's room was still down the hall. They still awoke several times a night to check on him, only to be reminded that he wasn't there.

Dad focused his attention onto finishing his personal history. He spent many hours compiling journal entries, letters, and finding photos to help tell his story. If there were a period of time that wasn't reflected in any written material, and he didn't have any memory of it, he would ask Mom to help him fill in the blanks. He also sent photos to us, the kids, and asked us to write down what we remembered about the events captured in the photos.

In addition to the work on his personal history, Dad was given a calling to work in the baptistry at the Provo temple once a week. There wasn't a job more suited to Dad than temple work. He loved it from long before his heart attack. Dad was a diligent genealogist through the years in those moments when family, work, church, civic responsibilities, and the like didn't crowd out his calendar too much. In a way, Dad's heart attack provided a space in his life to dedicate time and effort to this pursuit.

Since his heart attack, Dad processed his emotions differently. He had never been stoic, even in the military, but he became more tender-hearted although his outward displays of emotion were infrequent. Even though his memory didn't hold onto many details, he felt Thad's loss deeply and tried to push forward in spite of it all.

At the same time, the vacuum left in the house after Thad's passing held my mom captive. She was devastated. Her grief continued to cause her to second guess many things that she had done or not done, and she got sucked into the vortex of "if only." She was in deep spiritual pain, and there didn't seem to be anything we could do to help her. On the outside she appeared to be coping well, but the grief and the self-recrimination were destroying her.

When she felt particularly bereft, she would sit in Thad's room and talk to him, just to feel a connection, but the truth of her grief was that she felt far removed from him. She confided in me that she had never in her life felt so separate and alone. Thad was gone. He was not even in her dreams. He was nowhere. As time passed, her "if only's" turned into guilt, and she felt like she had let Thad down, that she had somehow shirked the responsibility given her by God.

Time is a healer, they say, but time was not healing the gash in Mom's soul. Each of us, in our way, grieved with her, supported her, encouraged her, held her physically when possible, but mostly in our hearts and in our prayers. She would acknowledge relief and gratitude for our concern. She *knew* that what we were saying about all that she had done for Thad was true, but our words couldn't give her the assurance she needed to carry her through the quiet times, when it was just her and her pain, the moments just before sleep as her conscious mind gave way to the unconscious, the Thad-less dreams, and the prayers for relief that seemed to fall out of her mouth like jagged shards of black obsidian, landing in a pile on the floor.

One afternoon, more than two years after Thad's passing, Mom was finishing up a session in the temple where she had spent some time thinking about Thad and praying for some kind of understanding. As she left the temple, she ran into Dr. Stacey and his wife. He asked how she was doing, and rather than brush it off with a "Just fine" or "I'm hanging in there," Mom told them that she was really struggling. They asked her if she wanted to talk about it, and they sat down together. Mom opened her heart to them. She described the emptiness she felt, the guilt, the desperation, and the pain.

The Staceys were just far enough removed from the situation to give Mom a sense that they had a different perspective, which allowed them to be objective. They talked with her about these feelings of guilt, of how easy it was to get caught up in the aspects of ourselves that we don't believe measure up to the ideal. They pointed out her strengths as a person, as a mother, and as a caregiver. Dr. Stacey told Mom that having been Thad's primary physician for many years, he could honestly attest that Thad lived much longer than he should have lived, given his condition, his seizures, and his frequent bouts with pneumonia. Thad's longevity was due to the care that she and Dad had given him and, more importantly, to the love that they all shared. He encouraged Mom to focus on the loving details of Thad's life and predicted she would realize that the doubts and the guilt she was feeling were fabrications of her grief.

This conversation with the Staceys was a tipping point for Mom. The burden she felt wasn't lifted right away, but gradually she became more able to acknowledge all of the good that flowed through her life with Thad.

I went home for a few days in September, just before the third anniversary of Thad's passing, to do some last minute research for this book. As soon as I arrived, Mom shared an experience with me that happened to her just a few weeks prior to my trip. It was a Sunday morning. Dad had already gone to church because he needed to see some people before the meetings started. Mom was running a little behind, so when she finished dressing, she grabbed her bag and started to run out the door. Suddenly, in her mind, the impression came, *Did you think to pray?* Rather than say, "No, but I'm on my way to Church," Mom thought she should go back to her room and say a prayer. In the prayer she expressed gratitude for many things and for her family, she mentioned each one of us by name and expressed her feelings. Then she said, "Please, let Thad know that I miss him terribly, but that I am so grateful for the time we were able to spend together on this earth." At the conclusion of her prayer, she rushed out to the car, put her seatbelt on, and pushed the ignition button. As the car started, so did the radio:

> Why do birds suddenly appear, every time, you
> are near?
> Just like me, they long to be, close to you...

The light in the car was bright and rarified. Mom

felt a loving embrace as she listened to the Karen Carpenter song that she had sung to Thad innumerable times over the course of his extraordinary life.

COLOPHON

Me and Thad is set in Halis R S Black, a font designed by Ahmet Altun, a contemporary designer from Turkey, and Sentinel Light which is a modern variant of Clarendon, a 19th century British font. The book was designed by Cameron King.

It was originally published as a limited edition volume, and printed and bound by hand by Glen Nelson. The text paper was Mohawk superfine, printed on an Epson Artisan 1430 printer. Published by Mormon Artists Group, it is our 28th project. Mormon Artists Group is unaffiliated with The Church of Jesus Christ of Latter-day Saints except for the fact that its participants are current or former members of the Church.

Six screenprints were tipped into the book as illustrations, and they are reproduced in this edition as black and white images. They were created by Tim Sutton based on family photographs of Thad. The multi-color screenprints were printed by the artist in an edition of 25 at the School of Visual Arts, New York City.

Me and Thad was published in an edition of 25 copies, signed and numbered. Six copies included a slipcase holding a leaded glass panel designed and created by the artist. Each glass panel was based on one of the screen-prints. Two additional leaded glass slipcases were created as artist's and publisher's proofs.

Information about this publication and other projects by Mormon Artists Group can be found on its website.

MORMONARTISTSGROUP.COM

61797845R00082

Made in the USA
Lexington, KY
20 March 2017